VENI·VIDI·VICI

Peter Jones was educated at Cambridge University and taught Classics at Cambridge and at Newcastle University, before retiring in 1997. He has written a regular column, 'Ancient & Modern', in the *Spectator* for many years and is the author of various books on the Classics, including the bestselling *Learn Latin* and *Learn Ancient Greek*, as well as *Vote for Caesar* and *Reading Virgil's* Aeneid *I and II*.

Also by Peter Jones

Vote for Caesar

Classics in Translation

VENI VIDI·VICI

EVERYTHING
you ever
WANTED TO KNOW
about the
ROMANS
but
WERE AFRAID TO ASK

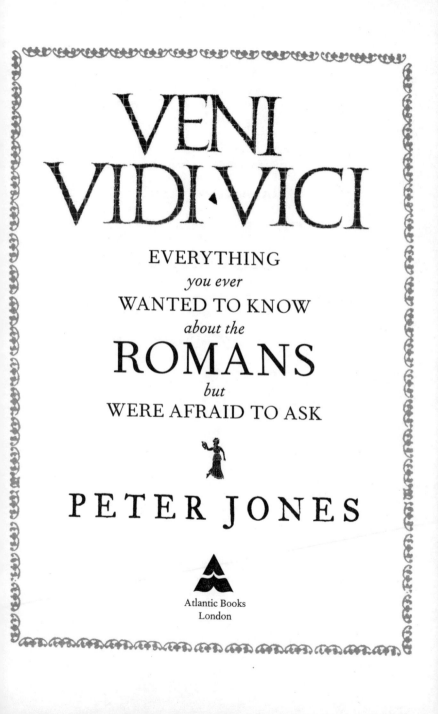

PETER JONES

Atlantic Books
London

First published in hardback in Great Britain in 2013 by Atlantic Books,
an imprint of Atlantic Books Ltd.

This paperback edition published in Great Britain in 2014 by Atlantic Books,
an imprint of Atlantic Books Ltd.

10 9 8

A CIP catalogue record for this book is available from the British Library.

Paperback ISBN: 978-1-78239-390-0
E-book ISBN: 978-1-78239-020-6

Designed by Carrdesignstudio.com
Printed in Great Britain.

Atlantic Books
An Imprint of Atlantic Books Ltd
Ormond House
26–27 Boswell Street
London
WC1N 3JZ
www.atlantic-books.co.uk

CONTENTS

Maps   vii – xi

Introduction   xiii

I

Lost in the Myths of Time
From Aeneas to Romulus, Remus and Rome   1

II   753–509 BC

Not a Roman in Sight, but Rome in Our Sights
The Early Kings   17

III   509–264 BC

What It Meant to be Roman (I)
From Rape to Conquest   39

IV   509–287 BC

What It Meant to be Roman (II)
The Rise of the Republic   63

V   810–146 BC

Their Finest Hour
Carthaginians, Hannibal and Empire   83

VI   146–78 BC
The Problem with No Solution
From the Gracchi to Sulla   113

VII   81–44 BC
The End of a World
Pompey and Caesar   137

VIII   44 BC–AD 14
Rising from the Ashes
The First Emperor – Augustus   183

IX   AD 14–96
Bedding Down Together
Emperor and People   219

X   AD 96–192
Bread and Circuses
Empire without End?   279

XI   AD 193–476
Germans, Huns and the Fall of the Roman West   321

XII   AD 1–430
The Growing Revolution
Church and State   353

Bibliography   378
Index   382

MAPS

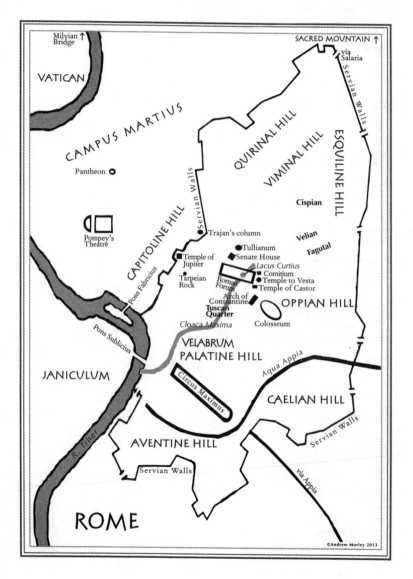

Milyian Bridge ↑

SACRED MOUNTAIN ↑

via Salaria

VATICAN

CAMPUS MARTIUS

Servian Walls

QUIRINAL HILL

VIMINAL HILL

ESQUILINE HILL

Pantheon ◉

Servian Walls

Cispian

Velian

Fagutal

CAPITOLINE HILL

Trajan's column

Pompey's Theatre

● Tullianum

■ Senate House

Temple of Jupiter

Lacus Curtius

Tarpeian Rock

Roman Forum

● Comitium

● Temple to Vesta

■ Temple of Castor

Pons Fabricius

Arch of Constantine

Tuscan Quarter

OPPIAN HILL

Colosseum

Cloaca Maxima

VELABRUM

PALATINE HILL

Pons Sublicius

Aqua Appia

JANICULUM

Circus Maximus

CAELIAN HILL

R. Tiber

AVENTINE HILL

Servian Walls

Servian Walls

via Appia

ROME

©Andrew Morley 2013

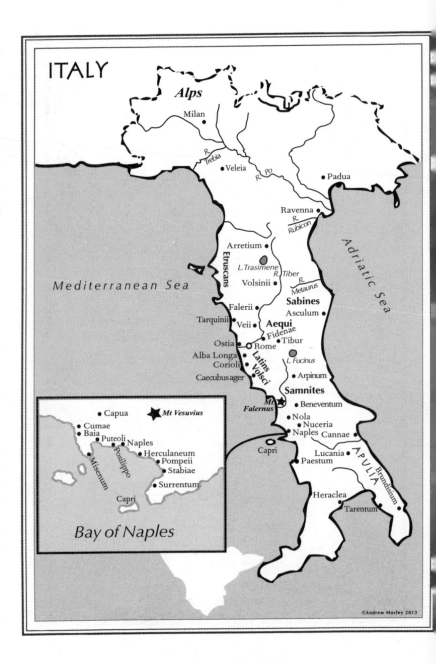

ITALY

Alps

Milan

R. Trebia

Veleia

R. Po

Padua

Ravenna

R. Rubicon

Arretium

Adriatic Sea

Etruscans

L. Trasimene

R. Tiber

Volsinii

R. Metaurus

Sabines

Mediterranean Sea

Falerii

Asculum

Tarquinii

Veii

Aequi

Fidenae

Ostia

Rome

Tibur

Alba Longa

L. Fucinus

Corioli

Latins

Volsci

Caecubus ager

Arpinum

Samnites

Mt Falernus

Beneventum

Nola

Nuceria

Naples

Cannae

Capri

Lucania

APULIA

Paestum

Brundisium

Heraclea

Tarentum

Capua

Mt Vesuvius

Cumae

Baia

Puteoli

Naples

Misenum

Posilippo

Herculaneum

Pompeii

Stabiae

Capri

Surrentum

Bay of Naples

©Andrew Morley 2013

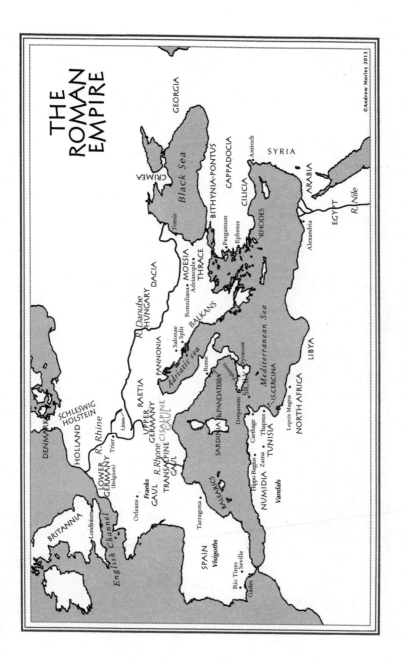

THE ROMAN EMPIRE

©Andrew Morley 2013

BRITAIN
during the
Roman Conquest

Iona

Aberdeen

CALEDONIA

Inchtuthil

R. Tyne   Hadrian's
Vindolanda   Wall
        Stanegate   Arbeia

Hadrian's
Wall
Arbeia

Brigantes

YORKSHIRE

York

Iceni

EAST
ANGLIA
          Colchester

St Albans
Londinium

CANTIUM

via Julia

English Channel

©Andrew Morley 2013

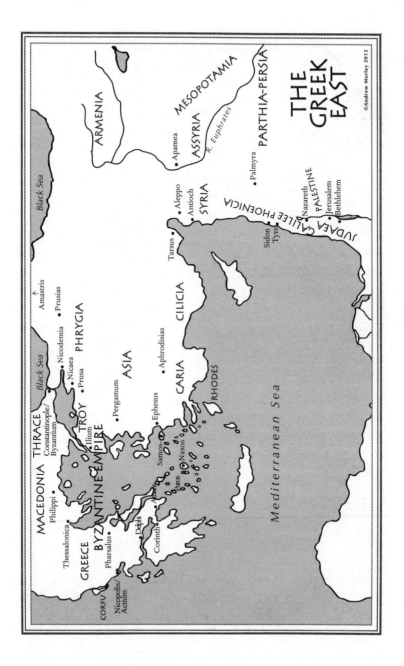

THE GREEK EAST

©Andrew Morley 2013

ARMENIA

MESOPOTAMIA

ASSYRIA

R. Euphrates

PARTHIA-PERSIA

Black Sea

Apamea

Palmyra

Aleppo

Antioch

SYRIA

Nazareth

PALESTINE

GALILEE PHOENICIA

Jerusalem

Bethlehem

JUDAEA

Sidon

Tyre

Tarsus

CILICIA

Amastris

Prusias

PHRYGIA

Black Sea

Nicodemia

Nicaea

Prusa

ASIA

Pergamum

Aphrodisias

Ephesus

CARIA

RHODES

MACEDONIA THRACE

Constantinople/
Byzantium

TROY

Ilium

BYZANTINE EMPIRE

Thessalonica

Philippi

Samos

Naxos

Athens

Paros

Delphi

GREECE

Corinth

Pharsalus

CORFU

Nicopolis/
Actium

Mediterranean Sea

INTRODUCTION

This book is the 1,200-year story of Rome from its earliest foundation in 753 BC to the end of its empire in the West in AD 476. It is a story everyone should know because, like that of Ancient Greece, it has shaped our world and penetrated our imagination: from its language, literature, politics, architecture, philosophy, empire and legal system to the individuals that created its story; from Romulus and Remus to Scipio and Hannibal; from Lucretia to Lesbia and Boudicca; from Pompey and Julius Caesar to Cicero and Augustus; from Pontius Pilate to Constantine; from Nero and Hadrian to Marcus Aurelius and St Augustine; from Catullus to Virgil and Tacitus to St Jerome; from the unknown inhabitant of Pompeii who scratched on a wall: 'I came here, had a shag, then went home' – the last of the great romantics – to the equally unknown person who invented the book or produced concrete that would set under water.

Each chapter begins with a broad summary of the period it covers. The rest of the chapter is taken up with a sequence of 100–500-word 'nuggets'. These reflect the same chronological sequence as the summary, and expand on the topics that the summary raises (this leads occasionally to small repetitions) or explore new, related ones. The nuggets aim to be self-contained, as far as possible; but occasionally there will be a sequence of nuggets on one topic (e.g., gladiators) where a degree of continuity will be observed. The overall purpose is to present sharp, focussed and stimulating information within the developing story of a crucial period of European history.

This is, unashamedly, a book for the general reader. It is designed for someone who wants to see something of the big picture, but also to be alerted to some of the detail that underpins it. Intense argument lies behind many of the assertions made here. Those who wish to find out more about these may care to consult the reading list at the back. A few passages have been adapted from my *Vote for Caesar* (Orion, 2008) and *Classics in Translation* (Bloomsbury, 1998).

The sources I have quoted are adapted from translations that are out of copyright, many of them from the first editions of the *Loeb Classical Library*. The poems have been adapted where necessary. I am most grateful to His Honour Colin Kolbert for permission to quote from his superb *Justinian: The Digest of Roman Law* (Allen Lane, 1979). I am also very grateful to Dr Federico Santangelo at Newcastle University for help with some difficult questions of chronology; and, as ever, to Andrew Morley for the maps.

Peter Jones

Newcastle upon Tyne, November 2012

www.friends-classics.demon.co.uk

NOTE ON
FINANCIAL VALUES

It is impossible to fix the relative value of Roman money to today's prices. Here are some prices expressed in sesterces (*ss*), around AD 1: a 1lb (0.45 kg) loaf of bread, a plate, a lamp and a measure of wine cost less than 0.25 *s*; an unskilled labourer could earn three *ss* a day; it cost 500 *ss* a year to feed a peasant family; a soldier's pay was 900 *ss* a year; an unskilled slave cost 2,000 *ss*; you needed property worth 400,000 *ss* to qualify as among Rome's richest, and one million *ss* to become a senator; Pliny the Younger over a lifetime gave away 5 million *ss* in benefactions.

PAGANISM

When I talk of 'pagans' I do not mean Wicker men and such like. I mean those who engaged in the civic cults and rituals of the pre-Christian Roman world (see p. 359). Paganism in this sense, organized by state-sanctioned colleges of priests, died out in the fifth century AD. That said, Roman literary and political culture in the broadest sense – the sense of the tradition behind the 'grandeur that was Rome' – continued to shape Christian thought for centuries to come.

I

TIMELINE

1150 BC   Mythical Trojan War between Greeks and Trojans

1000 BC   Rome a small collection of hilltop huts in Latium

753 BC   Traditional Roman date for King Romulus' founding of Rome

First record of early form of Latin

700 BC   Homer's account of Trojan War (*Iliad* and *Odyssey*)

400 BC   Greeks reckon Trojan Aeneas founded Rome after Trojan War

LOST IN THE MYTHS OF TIME

From Aeneas to Romulus, Remus and Rome

Romans came up with two stories about how they were founded. One (bewilderingly, we might think) was pure Greek. It was drawn from perhaps the most famous episode in what Greeks thought of as *their* very early, heroic history: the Trojan War, the story of the Greek siege of Troy (in western Turkey) to win back Helen. Ancients thought of it as occurring about 1200 BC.

This formed the subject of the West's first literature: the epic *Iliad*, composed by the Greek poet Homer *c.* 700 BC at a time when many Greeks were emigrating to Sicily and southern Italy. In Homer's story a minor Trojan hero, Aeneas, was fated to survive the war and later establish a dynasty that would rule over a resurrected Troy. But, Homer went on, Troy was burned to the ground by the Greeks and abandoned, and the surviving Trojans fled the country. So where did they and Aeneas go? How could Aeneas 'resurrect' Troy? From as early as the sixth century BC Greeks began to wonder about this too; and some said that Aeneas passed through Italy with other Greek and Trojan heroes of that war. In the late fifth century BC the Greek historian Hellanicus named Aeneas as the founder of Rome – whether prompted by Romans, we do not know.

Romans certainly wanted to make Aeneas' story their own. Why? Because for Romans the Greeks were a 'living legend', and they wanted to be associated with them. So Romans told how, after the fall of Troy and many adventures across the Mediterranean, Aeneas and his followers reached Italian shores and, with the blessing of Jupiter (king of the gods) founded the Roman race (753 BC). Now they could boast that their place in history was on a par with that of the famous Greeks. The history of Britain was reconstructed in the same terms by the twelfth-century AD historian Geoffrey of Monmouth. He claimed its first king was a descendant of Aeneas: Brutus – Britain – Brutain! Everyone wanted to be linked with the Greeks and Romans.

So Aeneas was one legend told by Romans about their foundation. The other story is very different. Numitor, king of the very ancient Italian town of Alba, was deposed by his brother Amulius. But Numitor had a daughter, Rhea Silvia, and Amulius did not want her breeding vengeful successors. So he made her a Vestal Virgin (p. 22). But the war god Mars found her alone one day and did what ancient gods traditionally did: he raped her and Rhea bore twins. Amulius promptly had the twins thrown into the river Tiber, but the basket containing them was stranded ashore (one is reminded of the story of Moses). There they were suckled by a wolf until they were found by a herdsman. He took them home to Alba, where he and his wife raised them. When the twins, named Romulus and Remus, grew up, they discovered the truth about their birth. So they gathered an army, threw out Amulius and restored Numitor to the Alban throne.

They then founded a new city near Alba and started to build its walls. Remus, mocking the size of Romulus' walls, was killed by his furious brother. The new city was thus named *Roma*. Its traditional founding date was 753 BC, and Romulus became the first of the seven kings of Rome.

This Romulus legend was pretty brutal stuff – hardly noble, bold and true. But Romans loved it – they were children of Mars! War was in their blood. Meanwhile, the advantage of the Aeneas legend was that it highlighted another aspect of being Roman: for Aeneas came to be depicted as a man of *pietas*, not exactly 'piety' but rather 'respect for and commitment to family, city and gods'. That's more like it! How could the world not benefit from being dominated (as it would be) by a people whose other founder was such a civilized man? But there was a problem. How could one square the story of Aeneas with that of Romulus? The Romans did so by making Aeneas the founder of the Roman *people* and 300 years later his descendant Romulus the founder of the *city*.

Our main literary source for this early period is the Roman historian Livy (59 BC–AD 17). He was writing his history a thousand years after the beginning of the story he wanted to tell. So where did he get his information from? And how reliable was it? No Romans were writing history at the time of Romulus, let alone of Aeneas.

Even the intensely patriotic Livy doubts the strict accuracy of his account of this early period. But what he does affirm is that, in the case of Rome, it simply has to be accepted: 'it is poetic legend rather than solid historical evidence . . . but if any city *ought* to be allowed to refer its origins to the gods, that surely is Rome. For such is its military glory that when they say that Mars himself was their Father, and the Father of their founder, the tribes of this world may as well accept it as patiently as they do Rome's domination over them.'

That's tough talk. There could be no compromise in Romans' unwavering conviction that their dominion over the world was justified because the gods had decreed it.

Livy relied almost entirely on earlier Greek and Roman historians. The third-century BC Greek historian Timaeus wrote extensively about the Romans. The first Roman historian of Rome was Fabius Pictor (*c.* 200 BC). The Roman Varro (116–27 BC) wrote huge encyclopedias filled with information gathered from all over the place. We have little idea where they got *their* information from either. Oral tradition must have played an important part; but Romans also kept documentary records, some going back a long way – lists of consuls, treaties, citizenship grants, legislation etc.; annual records of events such as famines, wars, triumphs, etc.; and lists of official post-holders.

So Livy selected what he wanted out of these historians and then 'spun' their stories to suit his vision of Rome's history. Since he is one of the greatest ever storytellers, the results are sensational. There is no doubt that it all makes for a wonderful read – but how accurate it is, is quite another question.

Can we check any of Livy's material? The encyclopedist Pliny the Elder (killed by the eruption of Mount Vesuvius in AD 79, p. 267), the historical essayist Plutarch (AD 46–120) and historians of Rome, such as Dionysius from Halicarnassus (writing *c.* 10 BC) and Cassius Dio (*c*. AD 165–230), all offer their 'spin' on these stories. But why trust them any more than Livy? True, we also have archaeology, with digs going back to 1000 BC and beyond. In a perfect world, such excavations could conceivably tell us whether the accounts of historians were accurate. But all archaeology unearths is material remains. It does not give us the stories (unless we dig up texts). The best it can do is provide a series of snapshots of material trends and developments. These can, for example, tell us whether people were becoming richer or poorer, or urbanized, or whether they came into contact with other cultures. The Romans knew nothing of this discipline.

So, a warning here: any account of Rome up to *c*. 300 BC needs to be taken *cum grano salis* (with a grain of salt).

WHEN ROME WAS JUST ANOTHER TOWN

We are accustomed to associate Rome with world domination – the Roman Empire, the Roman Catholic Church and so on. So it is easy to forget that *c*. 1000 BC Rome was just a smattering of settlements made up of a few thatched huts, scattered round the tops of hills, including the Palatine Hill. These would, in time, make up the famous Seven Hills of Rome. Rome's hilltop defensibility was its strength, as well as its position in the middle of a very fertile plain of volcanic soil and its location on the Tiber. This river gave it easy access not only to the sea, but also to the Tiber Valley inland and across the Tiber to the north, because the river could be forded at this point.

Rome was, in other words, a frontier town. No one at that time could conceivably have imagined that this hill people would one day dominate and unify the whole Italian peninsula – let alone the known world. It is as if the world were now being ruled by the local council of Newcastle upon Tyne, UK, or Buffalo, USA.

THE SEVEN 'HILLS' OF ROME

Rome was built on volcanic soil and its Seven Hills were steep and craggy. Most of them were not really hills but rather ridges cut out by streams flowing from high ground into the Tiber Valley. Traditionally, the Seven Hills were the Palatine, Capitoline, Quirinal, Viminal, Esquiline, Caelian and Aventine. But there were so many of them that even Romans had difficulty deciding which to include. There were also smaller hills and ridges leading off from these, such as the Oppian, Fagutal, Cispian and Velian. Janiculum Hill was across the river, and the hill beyond that was the Vaticanus. Livy says these hills were settled by local people who were later conquered by the Romans and subsequently welcomed as Roman citizens. This whole complex was eventually walled in *c.* 386 BC.

THE NAME OF ITALY

Italy was at this time a hotchpotch of different, strongly independent tribes, all with their own identities, language and levels of culture. About 40 mostly Indo-European languages have been identified there. Rome was in Latium; it was flanked by Etruscans (from Etruria) to the north, and Sabines and Samnites (from Samnium) to the east. So how did the whole peninsula come to be called Italy? *Italia* originally referred only to the Greek-colonized bottom quarter of Italy. So Romans reckoned the name was invented by the Greeks. There was in fact an early dialect word *vitelia* ('young bull', Latin *vitulus*); Romans thought Greeks turned that into *Italia*, probably to reflect the south's rich fertility. Slowly the name caught on. By the third century BC *Italia* covered all modern Italy except for the far north; under the Roman emperor Augustus (first century BC) it finally included all territory up to the Alps.

WHY 'LATIN'?

'Latin' comes from *Latini*, 'Latins'. This was the name of the people who occupied the area known as Latium, in which Rome was situated. But why is it called Latium? Romans had a story that the ancient Roman god Saturnus was driven from power by his young son Jupiter. He fled to Latium and hid there – and the Latin for 'hid' is *latebat*. So Romans thought Latium was connected with hiding. This derivation is complete drivel – like nearly all the derivations the Romans dreamed up – but is also historical in the sense that they believed it.

THE SPREAD OF LATIN

The earliest Latin inscription is on a pot and dates from the eighth century BC. It says: *Manios med vhevhaked Numasioi*; or in classical Latin: *Manius me fecit Numerio* – 'Manius made me for Numerius'. The number of early surviving Latin inscriptions suggests that Romans had become literate by about the seventh century BC (pp. 25, 79); and as Rome spread its power the Latin language went with them, slowly driving out local languages. As a result, Latin would become the *lingua franca* of all Italy by about the first century BC, and eventually the Western half of the known world, as the Romans slowly conquered it. French, Spanish and Italian are all dialects of Latin. The Romans also conquered Greece, but it was never going to shift *that* ancient and revered tongue.

LATIN PRONUNCIATION

We have good evidence for the individual sounds of Latin letters. For example, Greek historians transcribed Latin names into Greek. Assuming we know how Greek was pronounced, we can expect their transcriptions to tell us something about Latin. Thus *Cicero* was transcribed as *Kikerôn*, not *Siserôn* (the *-ôn* being a Greek ending), i.e., the Latin 'c' was pronounced hard. Greeks also transcribed *Valerius* as *Oualêrios*, again suggesting that 'v' was pronounced as a semi-vowel, more 'w' than 'v'. So Julius Caesar's *veni, vidi, vici* would have come out 'ouaynee, oueedee, oueekee'. But when it comes to treatment in English, we follow our own conventions of pronunciation and spelling.

21 APRIL 753 BC

It was important for Romans to determine as exactly as they could everything about Rome's foundation, especially its date. The first person known to have proposed a date is the Greek historian Timaeus (p. 6). He used Greek dating methods to put it at 814 BC. This seems to have got contemporary Romans thinking about an actual date, and 748, 728 and 751 were all proposed. The traditional date is one that the Roman antiquarian Varro espoused: 21 April 753 BC. How he arrived at it we do not know. Nor does it bear any relation to what the archaeology reveals about Rome's development. This makes it clear that the Palatine was inhabited from 1000 BC.

LUPINE SOLUTIONS

According to tradition, Romulus and Remus, adrift on the Tiber, were cast ashore at the point where the Romans subsequently celebrated a festival called the Lupercal. *Lupa* is the Latin for 'she-wolf'. So perhaps *lupa* was inserted into the story of the twins' rearing in order to explain the festival's name. But some Romans were sceptical of the idea that the twins were the children of the god of war and Rhea Silvia. So they toyed with the idea that they were rather the offspring of a prostitute – because that is what *lupa* also means in Latin. We are right to be doubtful about any of the historical accuracy of this. The Romans were making it up as they went along.

ROMULUS AND REMUS

We have no idea what the real derivation of the word *Roma* is. Ancient Greeks called *Roma* '*Rhômê*', which in Greek meant 'strength' or 'might'; so one can see why Romans jumped at that derivation. *Romulus* means 'little Roman'; and because 'e's and 'o's are often linguistically associated (e.g., 'foot' and 'feet'), *Remus* may just be another form of the *Rom-* stem as well. They are both obviously invented names for mythical characters, designed to make a strong connection with *Roma*.

OPEN DOORS IN ROME

Romulus, Romans were told, found the site of Rome completely deserted. He therefore turned the Capitoline Hill into an asylum and invited immigrants or asylum seekers to come in: runaway slaves, exiles, paupers, debtors, all were welcome. Now it may be that something like this did in fact happen at some time in Rome's early history. Near the Capitol, votive offerings (thanks to the gods for prayers fulfilled) have been found dated to a time *before* that area was ever settled. Was it, then, an asylum area? If so, it might have become part of the Romulus myth, because it would 'explain' the origins of one of Rome's most unique features: its 'open-door' policy to non-Romans. Indeed, later Rome so swarmed with 'foreigners' that the most common language heard there would not have been Latin but Greek, the universal Mediterranean language. Rome, indeed, would in time become the world's first global city, where as many foreigners lived as Romans. So while the *story* of Romulus and Remus is clearly invented, it may still refer to incidents that Romans at the time, or later, felt were significant.

FROM SLAVE TO CITIZEN

Romulus' invitation to expand Rome's population 'explained' another uniquely Roman phenomenon: its liberal attitude towards citizenship. From early times, Romans regularly extended citizenship to peoples they had subdued. Further, slaves, once freed, *automatically* became citizens (p. 34); and in the centuries to come, aristocrats from slave stock, and freed slaves (freedmen) who made good, would be commonplace in Rome (p. 149). Extraordinarily, more than half the ancient funerary monuments ever found in Rome commemorate ex-slaves, rather than freeborn Romans: they were proud of what they had achieved and of what this meant for their families (who always feature large on these monuments). This willingness to make people citizens stands in strong contrast to the Greeks, who jealously guarded that privilege, and in time it resulted in the concept of the 'citizen of the world'.

ROMULUS AND THE 'RAPE' OF THE SABINES

Male immigrants were all very well, but they needed women to breed Romans and there was a desperate shortage. Romulus' appeals to local villages met with a cold response: who would want to marry that riff-raff? So he decided to tempt in some of the local Sabine people (inhabiting the Quirinal Hill, p. 8) by putting on a religious festival featuring horse races. They flocked to the show and at the same time were drawn to admire the fine new town that was growing in their midst. At a given signal, however, the Romans seized the young Sabine women – note that the word used, *raptus*, means 'seizure' or 'abduction', not 'rape' – and promised to make honourable women of them. The Romans managed to hold off revenge attacks; and in the final battle against the Sabines, the women themselves intervened successfully to plead with their former families to desist, saying that they had been well treated and were happy in their new homes. The result was a peace agreement, and the Sabines were made welcome as Romans. That, at any rate, is Livy's wonderful version, which caught the imagination of later artists such as Poussin and David.

FIGHTING IN SEASON

Romans always did a lot of fighting. In the early years this probably consisted of brief raids or revenge attacks carried out by clans under their leaders. After a campaign of a day or so, they returned to work their farms. They were, in other words, an irregular farmer-citizen army. Further, since one cannot live by fighting, only by eating, they fought between March and October, i.e., when food was more likely to be easily available. The result was that most fit Roman males had military experience – a tradition that did not change for hundreds of years.

TARPEIA THE TRAITOR

The Romans punished traitors by flinging them from the Tarpeian rock, a cliff on the Capitoline Hill (p. 8). This was named after Tarpeia. She was a Vestal Virgin and the daughter of the Roman commander. During the Sabine siege of Rome she was bribed by the Sabines 'with what they had on their left arm' (their gold armbands) to give them access to the citadel. But they also had shields on their left arms, and once they were in, they crushed her to death with them. She was buried near the Tarpeian rock, which was named after her. That's the story, anyway.

PATRES, PLEBS AND SENATE

Romulus, Livy tells us, created 100 *patres* ('fathers' or 'patricians'), a circle of advisers consisting of wealthy members from the clans (*gentes*). Each king of Rome subsequently chose the *patres* he wished to advise him. Eventually, this body would transmute into a full-blown Senate (Latin, *senex*, 'old man', but see p. 179), Rome's venerable advisory body. Members of *gentes* that had *not* produced *patres* were called 'plebeians', from *plebs*, 'people'. At this time, however, 'plebeian' carried no class connotations; the term simply distinguished the clans that had not won royal favours from the rest. In time even that distinction would disappear (Pompey, Crassus and Cicero were all, technically, plebs). Here, then, is an important Roman institution, the Senate, which the Romans assumed Romulus had invented. Useful things, myths.

DEATH OF ROMULUS

While one story had it that Romulus parted from this life by being taken up in a cloud to heaven, the other had it that he was assassinated, torn to pieces by *patres*. The tabloids or their equivalents were at work even then. But minds were put at rest, Livy tells us: one Julius Proculus, a man known for his wisdom, announced that Romulus had appeared to him and told him it was heaven's will that Rome should rule the world. From the very start, the gods had marked out Rome for world domination.

II

753–509 BC

TIMELINE

753–509 BC   Part-legendary rule of (six) kings of Rome

Rome developing into a large town

Power spreads over local Latins

Hills of Rome populated

Salt works developed

Bridge built over the Tiber into Etruscan territory

Forum area drained (start of the Cloaca Maxima)

Story of the Sibylline books

509 BC   Building of temple to Jupiter Optimus Maximus

NOT A ROMAN IN SIGHT, BUT ROME IN OUR SIGHTS

The Early Kings

Early Romans did not emerge untouched by outside influences. Archaeology and myth tell us that Greek traders from abroad had a strong influence on Rome's neighbours the Etruscans, and both, in turn, on the Romans.

After Romulus came a series of kings, none of whom was Roman. This is so bizarre it gives credence to those stories about an ancient 'open-house' policy towards local peoples like the Sabines, Latins and Etruscans. Nor were the kings hereditary. After the death of a king, Livy explains, there was a brief *interregnum* during which a successor was discussed. After due consideration the *patres* elected a new king and the people ratified him by popular vote. This was done by a people's assembly called the Comitia Curiata. Already, Livy is suggesting, there were strong popular influences at work – preparing the way for the later transition to a republic.

In their traditional order and dates the kings were: Numa (716–674 BC: Sabine), Tullus Hostilius (673–642 BC: Latin), Ancus Martius (641–617 BC: Sabine), L. Tarquinius Priscus (616–578 BC: Greek-Etruscan), Servius Tullius (578–534 BC: uncertain) and L. Tarquinius Superbus ('The arrogant', 534–509 BC: Etruscan). Not a Roman among them – open house, indeed.

Whatever the truth about these kings, there is good archaeological evidence that Rome at this time quickly began to develop into a proper urban centre. Further, Livy stresses another point: during this period Rome began to expand by defeating and absorbing its neighbours. Under Tullus, defeated tribes were welcomed onto the Caelian Hill, doubling Rome's population; under Ancus, the Aventine was opened to some Latin tribes, as was the Janiculum Hill over the river. Meanwhile, Superbus brought all the other Latins under Roman control.

Because of the Etruscan king Tarquinius Superbus and the various Etruscan-style practices that Romans seem to have adopted at this stage (such as auguries: see p. 21), some suspect that Etruscans took over the control of Rome. But Livy offers not even the slightest hint of this, and 'influence' is a very different thing from 'control'.

REAL HISTORICAL NAMES?

It is noticeable that the earliest figures of Roman history have only one name: Romulus, Remus, Numitor, Amulius. Later figures have two: Numa Pompilius, Tullus Hostilius, Ancus Martius; even later figures have three: Lucumo Tarquinius Priscus and Lucumo Tarquinius Superbus. This may reflect a historical reality. Before the foundation of Rome single names were used because they were all that was needed.

But with the development of a large community, the two-name system was adopted, identifying people by clan as well as family. There was a personal name (e.g., Numa, the *praenomen* or 'before-name') and a clan name (e.g., Pompilius, the *nomen*). This eventually developed into the full-blown republican three-name system, when an inherited family name was added (e.g., 'Cicero', see p. 81). So the early single and double names may possibly reflect accurate historical memories.

AUSPICIOUS BEGINNINGS

Livy tells us that Numa wanted his reign to be validated by the gods. So auspices were instituted (*auis* 'bird' + *specio* 'I inspect') – that is, the will of the gods was determined by looking for signs, usually in the flight of specific birds. The ritual, which anyone could perform, was similar to Etruscan versions and became the standard for all later bird auspices. The *auspex* sat on a stone, facing south. Then he veiled his head, holding in his right hand the augur's staff, uttered a prayer and marked out an east-west space in the sky. He declared the southward section to be 'right' (good) and the northward 'left' (bad). After that he fixed his eyes on a point in front of him, as far ahead as he could see; transferred the staff to his left hand; and named the signs he hoped to see (the nobler the birds the better: eagles were best of all). Naturally, the requested auspices usually appeared. They became so important that no serious proceedings could be undertaken – war, assemblies and so on – without them. Many aspects of Roman public and private life had a ritual attached. That is what religion meant to the Romans.

THE TEMPLE OF VESTA

Vesta was the goddess of the hearth, the centre of the home. As an object of state cult, she was located in the king's hearth, where the eternal fire burned, a guarantee of Rome's permanence. Later a sanctuary in the shape of a hut was built for Vesta, made to look like a private dwelling. It contained only the fire and other 'sacred things', including an erect phallus.

FASCINATING PHALLUSES!

The Latin for the representation of an erect phallus was *fascinum*. Its basic meaning was 'evil spell' or 'bewitchment' (Latin, *fascino*, 'I bewitch' or 'put a spell on'). It is the root of our 'fascinating'. The phallus was held to be 'apotropaic' (Greek, 'turning away'), i.e., it averted evil. This was its most common function throughout the Roman world. Roman generals enjoying their triumphal procession carried a model of a phallus in their hand to ward off envy. It has nothing to do with 'fascists' – not linguistically, anyway (see p. 73).

THE VESTAL VIRGINS

According to tradition, the cult of the Virgins of Vesta was already established in the city of Alba (Rhea Silvia was one, see p. 4). Numa brought the cult to Rome. Vestal Virgins had to be six to ten years old, with both parents living, and they served for thirty years. The six of them lived near the Vesta temple and were present on major state religious occasions. Their main job was to protect the eternal fire. If it went out, it proved that a Vestal was not a virgin. That signalled danger for Rome, and burial alive was the penalty (as it was for losing their virginity). The Vestals' other task was to mix grain with salt and make a cake used at public sacrifice (the cake, *mola salsa*, sprinkled on the head of sacrifices and burned in the fire, gives us our 'immolation'). They were expected to behave decorously. But there were advantages: they lived in considerable luxury and were the only ones, except for the empress, allowed to drive around in carriages; also they could own and administer property and were deeply revered.

SACRIFICE AND RITUAL

The literal meaning of sacrifice is 'I make [something] sacred' (Latin, *sacer*, 'sacred' + *facio* 'I make'), that is, I hand something over to a god so that humans can use it no longer. The more precious the item made sacred and removed from human use, such as a bull, the greater the sacrifice and the more pleased (one hoped) the god would be. All it took at the other end of the sacrifice 'scale' was leaving a piece of bread or a cake on an altar or splashing some wine on the ground before drinking. But it was the ritual of acknowledging the god in this way that was the important thing, the theory being that the deity would respond with a *quid pro quo*. Ancient religion did not require dogmatic *theological* belief in a deity – only acknowledgement of his or her power, and the performance of the correct ritual on the right occasions.

VESTAL LIFESTYLE

Any Vestal who did not live a sober, modest and discreet life was regarded with some suspicion. In 420 BC one Vestal, Postumia, was put on trial for a sexual offence. In fact she was innocent, but she dressed quite fashionably and talked rather too amusingly. She was acquitted, but reprimanded by the *pontifex maximus* (see below) and told to cut the jokes and *haute couture*. The Vestal Minucia (337 BC) was not so lucky. She too dressed more elegantly than was deemed appropriate, was found guilty on a slave's evidence and buried alive. The Vestal Tuccia, we are told, accused of fornication, asked Vesta to allow her to carry water in a sieve to prove her innocence: 'O Vesta, if I have always brought pure hands to your secret services, bring it about now that, with this sieve, I shall be able to draw water from the Tiber and bring it to your temple.' Vesta agreed. Tuccia duly carried the water and was reprieved.

RELIGIOUS LAW: THE *PONTIFEX MAXIMUS*

As the name suggests, the *pontifex* (*pons* 'bridge', *facio* 'I make') was originally a minor official in charge of bridges and roads. But Numa ascribed to him all the functions with which the *pontifex maximus* would later be endowed as the most important priest in Rome: determining the time of a public sacrifice, its location and cost; the proper conduct of all religious observances, public and private; proper ways of burying the dead and propitiating spirits; and deciding what portents (such as lightning) should be acted upon. Note that the *pontifex maximus* was not like an archbishop, more like a lawyer of ritual procedure. Further, he was elected and held office for life. Julius Caesar, a virtual atheist but knowing the political importance of the role, was elected (at vast personal expense) to this post in 63 BC, spent ten years conquering Gaul, defeated Pompey in a civil war, made himself dictator and was assassinated. He gave no moral or spiritual guidance, laid on no coffee mornings. He just performed the rituals for all to see.

ROMAN ALPHABET

Our alphabet ultimately derives from the Phoenicians. Greeks in the eighth century BC modified Phoenician symbols to produce the (highly economical and efficient) first alphabet to consist of vowels and consonants; they then imported this alphabet into Italy. It consisted, as the Greek did, of capital letters. Sentences largely lacked punctuation and gaps between words until the sixth century AD; at that time minuscule letters (small versions of capital letters) were also invented, soon after the codex (book rather than roll) became common (p. 255). It is this alphabet and orthography that we have inherited. Incidentally, the order of the letters in the alphabet has remained largely unchanged for thousands of years.

A LUNATIC CALENDAR

The Roman year originally ran to ten months, beginning in March (hence our *Septem*-ber, *Octo*-ber, *Novem*-ber, *Decem*-ber from the Latin for seven, eight, nine, ten). The twelve-month year, common elsewhere round the Mediterranean, was perhaps officially introduced to Rome in 153 BC. But Romans had exactly the same trouble as all other nations in aligning the solar year with the lunar year. The problem was that the earth's 365.25-day orbit of the sun controlled the seasons; but the lunar year of twelve months was marked by the waxing and waning of the moon, and each lunar month lasted only 29.53 days = 354 days a year. This shortfall of 11.25 days a year on the solar year caused chaos. For example, after three years, the calendar was more than a month behind the seasons; after six years, two months, and so on. This was no good at all.

Ancient man was aware of the terrifying forces of nature. If he was to survive, these mysterious powers needed to be won over – even more so when man took up season-dependent agriculture. Obviously, the god of harvest would be insulted and likely to withdraw his favours if his harvest song was raised in the winter, for example. Hence the importance of getting the calendar aligned with the seasons, thereby ensuring that the right rituals took place at the right time (this is why control of the calendar in the ancient world was nearly always in the care of the priesthood). Romans did this by occasionally and unpredictably adding a month when things had got too far out of kilter (so Roman calendars added space for a thirteenth month, just in case). Julius Caesar finally got it all sorted out in 46 BC (p. 176).

GODS OF AGRICULTURE

Since farming was a major source of livelihood and wealth, Romans invented a range of gods to oversee its smallest details. There were the gods of ploughing (e.g., *Vervactor*, *Imporcinator*), weeding (*Runcina*, *Suruncinator*, *Spiniensis*); the gods who protected against mildew and rust (*Robigo*, *Robigus*); even *Stercutus*, a god of muck-spreading (Latin, *stercus*, 'excrement')!

HORATII 1, CURIATII 0: A CLOSE-RUN THING

The third king, Tullus Hostilius (673–642 BC), was aptly named because he thought the Romans were going soft. So he declared war against Rome's father state, Alba. However, both sides, feeling threatened by the surrounding Etruscans, decided not to weaken themselves by all-out conflict. So they settled the issue by matching champions against champions in battle – the three Roman Horatii (all called Horatius) versus the three Alban Curiatii. The Romans were soon two-nil down, but the last Horatius ran for it, leaving the Curiatii strung out behind him. He then turned and, as they caught up with him, killed them one by one. However, this champion's sister Horatia was engaged to one of the Curiatii. Seeing her grieving, the infuriated Horatius killed her as a traitor. Romans were appalled, and the young man was brought to trial. Condemned to death, he appealed to the people, who acquitted him. This story has had a rich afterlife, inspiring painters, writers and composers from Corneille to David, Honegger and Brecht.

CRIME . . .

Livy calls Horatius' crime of killing his sister a case of *perduellio*, 'treason'. This was defined as any act inimical to the interests of one's country. But was not the crime Horatia's, since she was guilty of betrayal for mourning the death of an enemy? Therefore, Horatius was justified in doing what he did. Possibly, but Horatius had killed her before the case had come to court. In so doing, he also committed parricide (murder of a father or near relative) – a dreadful crime in the eyes of family-loving Romans. Hence the uproar. Brutal the Romans may have been, but even at this early stage, Livy suggests, the law was the law and its strictures keenly felt. Ultimately, however, the Roman people had the final say: the law was made for them and in their eyes its spirit was more important than its letter. Horatius had killed Horatia in the heat of the moment. He was too good a man to lose.

. . . AND PUNISHMENT

In the course of a war against the town of Fidenae the Roman troops were badly let down by their Alban allies under Mettius Fufetius. In the whole of Roman history, Livy says, no punishment of such inhumanity was ever meted out to anyone as it was to Mettius. Tied between two four-horse teams, he was ripped apart as they galloped off in different directions. This *precise* punishment was never inflicted again (to our knowledge), but by our standards Roman retribution was very nasty and often staged as entertainment. Nero (see p. 224), we are told, dressed Christians in animal skins and had them torn to pieces by dogs; or crucified them and set them on fire to serve as lamps when night fell. Parricides were sewn into a leather sack with a dog, a monkey, a snake and a cockerel, and thrown into the sea or a river.

THREE STEPS FORWARD, ONE BACK

War was a serious matter and Romans had an ancient, three-step formula for declaring it, back-dated to Tullus by Livy: (i) *denuntiatio*, delivered by delegates to the enemy: give us satisfaction – usually the cattle or similar you have stolen – in 30 days or else; (ii) *testatio deorum*, again delivered in front of the enemy, calling on the gods to witness that the enemy had done wrong; three days after that (iii) *indictio belli*: a messenger threw an iron-tipped spear into enemy territory, hobbling his power (iron, being magnetic, was thought to have magical powers). When the enemy surrendered, the one-step ritual of *deditio* was enacted: the enemy first agreed that they were free to make the decision, then they formally handed over themselves, their land and their property 'into the sovereignty/good faith of the Roman people'. The whole purpose of this was to prove that the war was just and properly concluded. Inevitably, elements of this procedure (such as the 30-day rule) were used less as Roman power spread across the globe. But they kept the spear-throwing ritual by declaring a piece of land in Rome in the Campus Martius (pp. 67, 233) to be foreign, and, when necessary, throwing a spear into it!

SALT SAVOUR

Rome's fourth king Ancus (641–617 BC) set up salt works in the future harbour area Ostia (Latin, *ostium*, 'mouth of a river'). It was Rome's first attempt at commerce. Salt was a very profitable item. Until the invention of refrigerators and canning processes it was the most freely available and effective preservative of all, especially for meat; it was also highly valued for flavouring. The technique for gathering it – by evaporating shallow 'flats' of salt water – was no secret and went back to at least 6000 BC. Incidentally, Roman soldiers were not paid their salaries (*salarium*) in salt (*sal*); that is a myth, derived from Pliny the Elder (p. 6), trying to explain why it was called a *salarium*.

BRIDGE OVER THE TIBER

Rome was a left-bank river (the term always applies to the direction downstream). The right bank was Etruscan territory and Ancus took two initiatives designed to encroach on that territory: he constructed the first bridge over the Tiber – the all-wooden *pons Sublicius* (*sublica*, 'pile') – and guarded its Etruscan entrance by fortifying the nearby Janiculum Hill. This was done with a specific purpose in mind: to open up the way for Rome to trade its salt into Italian territory, by way of the old gravel 'Salt road', *via Salaria*, which eventually reached 150 miles (240 km) across Italy to the Adriatic coast.

ROME'S FIRST PRISON

An expanding population, Livy notes, resulted in a blurring of the distinction between right and wrong, and therefore crime. So Ancus had a prison built, right next to Rome's main public square, the Forum. This was the notorious Tullianum. It consisted of two cells, the lower of which was reached through a hole in its roof. An ancient writer describes this underground horror: 'about twelve feet deep, with strong walls and a stone vault, filthy, dark and foul-smelling, it makes a hideous and loathsome sight'.

Imprisonment was not, in fact, a punishment recognized in Roman law; the prison was a place where people were held prior to trial or execution, though they could be held for some time. Vercingetorix, a Gallic chief captured by Julius Caesar, was held in the Tullianum for five years before being executed in 46 BC. Tradition has it that St Peter was imprisoned there too.

THE (NOT A) CIRCUS MAXIMUS

The fifth king Lucumo Tarquinius Priscus (616–578 BC) was Greek, the son of an émigré from the Etruscan city of Tarquinii (hence his name). Livy assigns to him the planning of the Circus Maximus, Rome's favourite entertainment centre. It was not a circus as we know it, but a race circuit.

Patres and the other rich, we are told, had special seating reserved for them, raised twelve feet from the ground, but this is an obvious anachronism: such reservations for senators did not appear until 194 BC, and then for the other rich in 74 BC. The earliest entertainment there consisted of horses and boxers, but in time the Circus Maximus would become the site of *Ben Hur*-style chariot races, which provided luxury entertainment for the wealthy and were hugely popular with the people (see p. 233).

CATCHING THE TOWN DRAIN

Rome's Cloaca Maxima started out as a river running through the original Forum and the marshy Velabrum below it into the Tiber. One story had it that Romulus and Remus' basket was stranded at the point where the river issued into the Tiber (p. 4). Priscus developed the system for draining the region with a series of small ditches. But in time, the river came to be covered over and built into the superbly engineered drain that is still used in part today. Note 'drain': it eventually served as a sewer, too, with outlets from baths, public toilets, etc., feeding into it, but its main function was always drainage (see aqueducts, p. 287). Pliny the Elder comments: 'for 700 years from the time of Tarquinius Priscus the sewers have survived almost completely intact'. They even had a goddess, Cloacina.

THE SIBYL

Priscus was thought to be the Roman responsible for getting hold of the 'Sibylline books' from the Sibyl at Cumae, near Naples. The Sibyl (Greek, *Sibulla*, derivation unknown) was originally a Greek prophetess, speaking under her own or a god's inspiration. Her name became the usual term for a large number of prophetesses all over the ancient world. They were well known for producing sacred books that could be consulted in times of trouble. The antiquarian Varro (p. 6) listed ten such 'Sibylline books', including those from Persia, Libya, Delphi, Samos, Phrygia, Cumae and Tibur (Tivoli), while other sources talk of Egyptian and Hebrew examples.

A BARGAIN: ONE FOR THE PRICE OF THREE

The Church historian Lactantius (*c.* AD 250–325) tells the story of how Priscus came by the Sibylline books:

> They say that Amalthea, the Sibyl from Cumae, brought nine books to the king Tarquinius Priscus, and asked 300 gold pieces for them. The king refused, saying it was far too much, and derided the woman, saying she was mad. So in the sight of the king, she burnt three of the books, and demanded the same price for the remaining six. Tarquinius thought her even madder. When she burnt three more, but persisted in demanding the same price, the king was thrown into turmoil and bought the remaining books for the original price.

ROME'S SIBYLLINE BOOKS

The Sibylline books did not divulge the future; rather, they gave instructions as to how to placate the gods in times of disaster or unexpected and ominous natural events (comets, showers of stones and so on). The books were put in the care of two patricians. In 367 BC they were transferred to a college of priests. They had orders to consult the books only on the command of the Senate and to add to them if any further books worthy of the honour came to hand. They were kept in the Capitoline temple, but were destroyed by fire in 83 BC. In 76 BC the Senate ordered a team of three to make a new collection from available sources in Africa, Sicily and elsewhere. Their destruction was, apparently, ordered by Stilicho, an Arian Christian, *c.* AD 400.

SIBYLS AND CHRISTIANS

Christians scoured pagan literature for signs of early Christian beliefs. In his fourth *Eclogue* (40 BC) the poet Virgil talked of the Sibyl prophesying the 'ultimate day' when the world would return to a golden age with the birth of a child. This probably referred to the expected birth of a son to Marc Antony and Octavia – the child was Octavian (p. 188). Christians, however, saw a reference to Jesus, and turned the Sibyl into an important figure in Christian literature and art. The *Dies irae*, a thirteenth-century hymn once used in the Catholic Requiem Mass to describe the day of judgement, features the Sibyl as one who foresaw that final day:

> Dies iræ! dies illa
> Solvet sæclum in favilla,
> Teste David cum Sibylla!

> Day of Wrath! That day
> Will dissolve the age in ashes,
> On the testimony of David with the Sibyl!

Christians were especially interested in the collection known as the 'Sibylline Oracles'. This was a mishmash of arbitrary texts from different times, places and authors, which could be reinterpreted to apply to the Christian god. Christians fell on Sibylline oracular utterances such as

'One God, who is alone, most mighty, uncreated' or 'but there is one only God of pre-eminent power, who made the heaven and sun and stars and moon and fruitful earth and waves of the water of the sea' or 'I am the one only God and there is no other God'.

SERVING SLAVES

The Latin for 'slave' is *servus*. On those grounds alone, it seems, Rome's sixth king Servius (578–534 BC) was believed to be the first ruler to declare that freed (*libertus*) slaves automatically became full citizens. Historically accurate or not, this was a quite extraordinarily liberal act at a time when people were enslaved across the Mediterranean (p. 145).

ROMAN NUMBERS

It is a relief that we do not use Roman numbers. Just try dividing MDCCCXXXVIII by DCCCXLIX and see how far you get. But it is at least a decimal system: I = 1, V = 5, X = 10, L = 50, C = 100, D = 500 and M = 1,000. Just add them together as economically as possible, largest first, e.g., CCCXXXVI = 3 hundreds, 3 tens, a 5 and a 1, i.e. 336. There is one wrinkle: a letter standing *before* a larger letter, e.g., IV or XC, is taken away from it. So while VI means 6, IV mean 4; CX means 110, but XC means 90. That said, it is not uncommon to find the adding system here too, e.g., 4 represented by IIII = 4. There is no zero (see p. 360).

Where these symbols came from is not known. One guess is that they were of Etruscan origin and were originally notches on a stick. So 'I' was a single notch, every fifth notch a double-cut 'V' and every tenth notch a cross-cut 'X'. This would explain how IV for 4 arose: it was the notch before the V in the sequence I II III IIII V. And so on. Incredibly, this system was used in Europe until the twelfth century, when the Arabic system – based on the Indian system and complete with zero – replaced it. This important revolution was largely down to Leonardo Fibonacci's pioneering work *Liber Abaci* 'The Book of Computation' (early thirteenth century). Incidentally, the 'Exchequer' derives from the chequered tablecloth, squares in an alternating pattern, on which counters ('checkers') were placed to denote the different values of the Roman numerals. It was a way to simplify working out accounts in the rebarbative Roman number system.

THE CRIME OF TULLIA

Servius' ambitious daughter Tullia was determined to gain power, come what may. Married to a placid nonentity, she organized a coup against her father. Her means to this end was the (grand-?) son of the fifth king Priscus – Tarquinius Superbus ('the arrogant, proud, haughty'). She persuaded him to kill her husband and sister, then marry her and drive out Servius. This Tarquinius did, ignoring all conventions of an *interregnum* and election (p. 19). Worse was to come. Tullia was being taken back from the Forum when she came across her father's body lying in the road. Livy takes up the story:

> Then, the tradition runs, a foul and unnatural crime was
> committed, the memory of which is preserved in the road name,
> 'Crime Street'. It is said that Tullia, goaded to madness by the
> avenging spirits of her sister and her husband, drove right over her
> father's corpse, and carried back some of her father's blood, with

which the car and she herself were befouled, to her own and her husband's *penates* (household gods). As a result of their anger, a reign which began in wickedness was soon brought to an equally evil end.

No wonder Livy painted Tarquinius Superbus and his wife as tyrants of the worst sort.

THE HOUSEHOLD GODS

Even the humblest house was a holy place for Romans, generating a strong emotional pull. The threshold, door and lintel, as well as the hearth – the centre of the house where the fire burned – were considered to be under divine protection. The god *Limentinus* protected the threshold, *Forculus* the doors and *Cardea* the hinges! Each house had its own household gods: the *Lares* (derivation unknown; they acted as guardians), *Penates* (*penus*, 'provisions', associated with the inside of the house) and *Genius loci* (the male spirit of the family's tribe, *gens*, personified in the head of the family). They were all worshipped with their proper rituals. Rome, too, had its state *Lares* and *Penates*, with the emperor as its *Genius loci*. When Aeneas left burning Troy, he is said to have taken with him on his shoulders his crippled father Anchises, the head of the family, and the images of the state *Lares* and *Penates* – emblems of Troy itself.

THE TYRANT KING (534–509 BC)

Tarquinius Superbus was portrayed by Livy as the typical Greek-style tyrant. He refused even to bury Servius on the grounds that Romulus had not been buried either (p. 14). He tried capital cases on his own, executing whomever he liked or ruining them and taking their money; he reduced the number of *patres* and executed those who supported Servius; and he declared war on anyone he disliked. Tarquinius Superbus was so unpopular he had to have a bodyguard. For Romans, that was almost a definition of the tyrant: someone so hated that he could rule the people only by fear. The Capitoline Hill was a religious centre, dominated by the gigantic temple of Jupiter Optimus Maximus, the largest of its kind in the Italic-Etruscan world. Its original platform still exists (it was burned down and rebuilt several times), measuring 186 x 174 feet (56 x 53 m). An emperor said of a much later version that 'beside it, everything else is like earth compared to heaven'. Tradition says it was dedicated on the first day of the Republic in 509 BC. It was dedicated to three gods: the famous 'triad' of Rome's patron, protecting deities – Jupiter, his wife Juno and Minerva. It was a major centre of ritual in Rome. Here consuls offered sacrifice when they took up office on the first day of the year; provincial governors took vows before leaving to take over their provinces; and military triumphs (see p. 144) reached their triumphant conclusion, with white bulls sacrificed to Jupiter.

ROME WITHOUT END

While the site of the new temple of Jupiter was being cleared, two omens occurred of the highest significance. One was a clear indication from the auspices (p. 21) that the shrine of the god Terminus (a rough stone) on the site should remain untouched. Terminus was the god of boundary stones which, once in place, could never be moved. As a result he became the immovable god and his stone was left inside Jupiter's temple – a sign of the stability and permanence of all things Roman.

The next omen was that workmen dug up a man's head (*caput*), fully intact, on the site where the foundations of the temple were to be laid. Hence, the hill on which the temple was built was called the Capitoline – while the *caput* proved that Rome would be the 'head' of the world for ever.

THE SIZE OF ROME

By the end of the regal period about one-third of old Latium was in Roman hands – nearly 350 square miles (906 square kilometres) – and Rome had a population of *c.* 40,000. This made it far larger than any other city in the region and well over twice the size of its closest rival Tibur, which occupied 135 square miles (349 square kilometres). Rome was already the major regional power.

III

509–264 BC

TIMELINE

509 BC   Rape of Lucretia and expulsion of last king, Tarquinius Superbus

Horatius holds the bridge; defeat of Lars Porsena

Founding of Roman Republic

507 BC   Carthage signs treaty with Rome

493–270 BC   Rome's treaty with Latin tribes and expansion

458 BC   Cincinnatus

395 BC   Veii surrenders. Rome's power spreads

386 BC   Gauls pillage Rome

c. 320 BC   Greek Pytheas circumnavigates Britain

312 BC   Appian Way built; Rome's first aqueduct

309 BC   Etruscans come to terms with Rome

290 BC   Rome finally defeats Samnites

280–270 BC   Rome defeats Pyrrhus; Egypt's treaty with Rome

Rome the master of Italy

WHAT IT MEANT
TO BE ROMAN
(I)

From Rape to Conquest

Romans told how in 509 BC (traditional date) King Superbus' son Sextus Tarquinius, overcome with lust, raped Lucretia, the wife of a Roman noble. Lucretia committed suicide out of shame. Her husband Collatinus and Lucius Junius Brutus raised a force to expel Tarquinius and remove the kings from Rome for ever. The Roman Republic was, Romans believed, the direct result. The Etruscans under Lars Porsen(n)a tried to take advantage of this chaos to reinstall Superbus, but failed because of the heroism of Horatius, who held the bridge.

In 507 BC Carthage – an ancient, established Mediterranean power in North Africa with whom Rome would in time come into deadly conflict – signed a treaty with the fledgling republic. They agreed to be friends and not act contrary to each other's interests. It signalled that Rome was respected, even at this early date.

Romans were soon in conflict again with the Latins, but in 493 BC they united and extended their influence among the surrounding tribes. This brought Rome into serious further conflict with the Volsci, Aequi and northern Sabines. These mostly took the form of border raids, but occasionally turned into something more serious. The town of Veii was especially troublesome. A nine-year siege brought it to heel in 395 BC. Further, the victory over Veii and subjugation of the other towns involved considerably extended the Roman area of control. They colonized newly conquered towns with their own citizens and imposed Roman forms of government.

But Rome now almost met with disaster. Gauls (a Celtic people from France, Belgium, most of Switzerland and parts of the Netherlands and Germany) had long been settling in northern Italy. In July 386 BC they marched on Rome, entered the city and burned and pillaged parts of it. Rome finally bought them off with gold. More trouble with the Etruscans, Volsci and Aequi ensued, but by *c.* 351 BC the Romans had gained the upper hand.

Now Rome moved further inland and south, encountering their most formidable enemy yet: the Samnites, who were often aided by Rome's old foes such as the Etruscans and Gauls. After three fierce wars (343–341, 326–304 and 298–290 BC), Rome finally prevailed. When the central Etruscans came to terms in 308 BC, Roman domination of Italy was almost complete.

But not quite. There was still the deep south, colonized by Greeks hundreds of years earlier (p. 3) and still dominated by them. Many Greek cities were happy to come over to the Romans, but Tarentum was not. In 280 BC it called in the help of the brilliant Greek general

Pyrrhus, who had 35,000 professional troops and 20 elephants. It was a close shave, but Pyrrhus was defeated at the battle of Beneventum and returned to Greece in 275 BC.

This was a sensational result: a famous Greek general with a professional army had been beaten by some dim little Italian city-state. Rome was now very seriously on the Mediterranean's military map. In 272 BC Egypt, then at the height of its influence, promptly offered an accord. It was the first power to acknowledge this major realignment in the geopolitics of the Mediterranean. The Romans ended any further resistance in the south and by 270 BC the Italian mainland was theirs – although, as ever, Italian tribes were not averse to rising up against their master.

FROM LUCRETIA TO JULIUS CAESAR

When Lucretia committed suicide, one of the witnesses was Lucius Junius Brutus. On the bloody blade with which she had killed herself, he swore – and made the others swear too – to drive out Tarquinius and his family and rid Rome of kings for ever. And so it was. It is no coincidence that the driving force behind the assassination of Julius Caesar on the Ides of March 44 BC (p. 180) was Marcus Junius Brutus, of the same family (note clan and family name, see p. 81). Cicero tells us that a statue of Lucius stood in Marcus' house. So while Lucius Brutus in 509 BC had driven out a king to initiate the Republic, Marcus Brutus in 44 BC would assassinate a man whom many feared wanted to be king, so as to restore the Republic.

RAPE AND SUICIDE: LUCRETIA'S ARGUMENT

Livy invented the following dramatic dialogue:

COLLATINUS (*her husband*)

Are you all right?

LUCRETIA

No! What can be well with a woman when her honour
is lost? The marks of a stranger, Collatinus, are in your
bed. But it is only the body that has been violated. My
conscience is clear; death shall bear witness to that.
(*She calls on him to avenge her. They try to console her
by turning the guilt from the victim of the outrage to the
perpetrator, and urging that it is the mind that sins, not the
body, and where there has been no intention, there is no guilt.*)

LUCRETIA

It is for you to see that he gets his deserts. But although
I acquit myself of the sin, I do not free myself from the
penalty. No unchaste woman shall henceforth live and
plead Lucretia's example.
(*She commits suicide.*)

This raises a major question: if Lucretia was innocent (as she and her
relatives agree she was) why did she commit suicide? Ancients argued
that certain acts polluted a person irretrievably, and this might transfer
itself to the family, putting everyone at risk, especially if an illegitimate
child were born. Death alone could solve the problem. But at the root of
Lucretia's response was a powerful Roman sense of shame and honour,

irrespective of responsibility. Another man had entered her bed. That was that. Though she was a woman and therefore 'weak' (by definition, in Roman eyes), Lucretia's heroism was the equal of any man's.

Later Christians thought in terms of sin, rather than shame or honour. One branch of this tradition praised her for refusing to live without her chastity. But St Augustine argued that no crime was worse than suicide, since life was uniquely at God's disposal. Besides, to value something as ephemeral as chastity over life was to commit the sin of pride. The subject has been endlessly reworked in art and literature: Shakespeare wrote the *Rape of Lucrece*, Benjamin Britten composed an opera on the subject, and it has been depicted by artists such as Cranach, Titian and Rubens.

ANCIENT GODS

> Lars Porsena of Clusium,
> By the Nine Gods he swore
> That the great house of Tarquin
> Should suffer wrong no more ...

So begins 'Horatius', the most famous of Lord Macaulay's *Lays of Ancient Rome* (1842). Among the nine (Etruscan) gods were Juno, Minerva, Tinia (Jupiter), Vulcan, Mars, Saturn and Hercules. But these were also Romans gods. Ancient peoples were very happy to absorb gods from other cultures. In Roman Britain, for instance, you will find Jupiter, Mars, Mercury and Hercules mixing it on altars with Baudihillia, Friagabis, Fimmilena, Useni Fersomeri and other baffling local deities. No one could be certain which gods were powerful and which not, so people hedged their bets.

HOW HORATIUS KEPT THE BRIDGE

Livy is brilliant at turning out *exempla* of noble behaviour for Romans to admire, learn from and emulate – a central purpose of Roman historical writing. Lars Porsena, besieging Rome, managed to capture Janiculum Hill on the Etruscan side of the Tiber. The Roman army, in headlong flight, poured towards the *pons Sublicius* – the one bridge over the Tiber at that time – to escape. Horatius, on guard at the bridge, rallied them and said he would hold the bridge on the Etruscan side while the Romans destroyed it behind him. He was supported by Spurius Lartius and Titus Herminius. They held off the Etruscans until the bridge started to totter. Horatius ordered the other two back – and the bridge fell. Offering a prayer to the god of the river Tiber, he plunged in, fully armed, and finally made it to the Roman shore.

MUCIUS SCAEVOLA, THE LEFT-HANDED HERO

Another great example of real Roman guts was the youthful Mucius Scaevola. As Porsena's siege took its toll, he asked permission from the *patres* to assassinate the Etruscan. They agreed, and Mucius, a dagger hidden in his clothes, worked his way to where Porsena was holding court. But he could not distinguish between Porsena and his secretary, who was taking all the questions. Afraid to ask who was who, he stabbed . . . the secretary. Porsena ordered him to be burned alive. 'Then take a look at this,' Mucius shouted, 'and understand how worthless the body is to those who have great glory in their sights!' With these words, he plunged his right hand into the fire and held it there, allowing it to burn as if he felt nothing at all.

Amazed, Porsena freed him, but Mucius warned him that there were 300 young men queuing up to kill him. Porsena, shaken by this, made a peace treaty with Rome and withdrew. Or so Livy claims. From then on Mucius was known as *Scaevola* – 'left-handed'. It is another Roman incident much depicted by later artists.

WILD WEST WORLD

Since we associate Rome with military might, order and control, it is important to understand that in these early years Romans were basically engaged in a series of turf wars over territory. No truce or treaty was expected to last. It merely represented a breathing space while sides gathered themselves for the next encounter. The point is this: Sabines, Samnites, Etruscans and all the rest were as determined to beat the Romans as the Romans were them. Romans, in other words, did not have a monopoly on aggression. The people they came up against would love to have been able to do what the Romans were doing. So when we say that Rome dominated the Italian peninsula in the third century BC, old rivalries were never far from bursting out again, given the opportunity.

THE PERKS OF POWER

In the absence of the industrial revolution, there were only two sources of wealth in the ancient world: agricultural and mineral. Given the relative shortage of accessible minerals, the rich were rich by virtue of their huge land holdings and the rents that could be raised from them. Since Roman politicians were not paid, only the rich could afford to stand for office, and as Rome expanded its territory across Italy, so it came to control more and more land. This was denoted as *ager publicus*, 'public land', for the state (in theory) to dispose of as it saw fit. Much of it was rented out to families to farm. But much of it also, one way or another, ended up in the possession of the wealthy senatorial classes, depriving the poor of the means of living. However, reforms to divide up land more fairly, as Livy said, 'have never been done without serious disturbances'.

CINCINNATUS: FARMER AND DICTATOR

The story of Cicinnatus gave Livy the perfect excuse for encouraging the Romans to believe that status and ability were not dependent on wealth. In 458 BC Rome was faced with a double threat from the Sabines and the Aequi. The attack on the Sabines was successful, but the consul Minucius and his army were trapped by the Aequi. By universal agreement of the *patres*, Cincinnatus was summoned to Rome. He was found ploughing a three-acre (1.2 hectares) farm west of the Tiber. When the envoys approached and asked him to put on his toga, 'he was surprised and asked if everything was all right, before telling his wife Racilia to run to their cottage and get it. The toga was brought and, wiping the grime and sweat from his hand and face, he put it on' and was told he was dictator.

The next day he summoned his troops, called on each to add twelve stakes to the usual kit and made for Minucius' besieged camp. By night he ordered his men to encircle the Aequi, build a palisade with their stakes and dig a trench. Next they raised the battle cry. Minucius' men, realizing what had happened, attacked and the Aequi were trapped, crushed between the two forces. Cincinnatus turned the booty over to his own men, giving nothing to Minucius. After the triumph, having been dictator for 15 days, he resigned and, we are told, went back to find his plough where he had left it.

THE INVENTION OF TAX

The nine-year war against the Veii, which ended in 395 BC and kept the army engaged for years at a time, was a turning point. Under such unprecedented conditions, soldiers had to be paid, fed and equipped. But where should the money come from? The answer was an annual property tax (*tributum*), perhaps introduced in 406 BC (p. 68). Further, it became more and more common to demand recompense from defeated enemies, including military supplies such as clothing and equipment.

AN HONOURABLE LESSON

Romans endlessly debated the pros and cons of 'honourable' as opposed to 'self-interested' behaviour. They claimed to prefer the former, because as well as being glorious it invariably turned out to be more in their interests. History bore this out. In 394 BC the Romans under Camillus were engaged in a lengthy siege of Falerii. A Falerian schoolmaster, however, who still regularly exercised his boys outside the walls, saw his chance and led his charges right into the Roman camp. Since the children were all the sons of Falerii's great and good, the schoolmaster announced that Falerii was now at the Romans' mercy. He obviously thought this would be in Camillus' interest, who would eagerly accept the offer. Far from it. Camillus called him an unprincipled swine. Rome and Falerii may have no political ties, he said, but 'we are bound together none the less, and always shall be, by the bonds of common humanity'. He had the traitor stripped and bound, gave the boys sticks and told them to beat him back into Falerii. The Falerians, moved by Roman honour and Camillus' justice, at once gave in to their besiegers, and in their submission to the Roman Senate said, 'From this war, two things have emerged which the world would do well to take to heart. You preferred honour to an easy victory. We now recognize your sway.'

THE GALLIC SACK OF ROME: DIGNITY IN DEATH

Virtus was displayed by both young and old in Livy's account of early Roman history. When the Gauls conquered and entered Rome in 386 BC, most of the population – apart from an armed force on the citadel of the Capitoline – had already fled. But some ex-consuls decided to stay, offering themselves as a sacrifice on behalf of Rome (see *devotio*, p. 53). Dressed in their finery, as if for burial, they sat on their ivory-inlaid chairs of office and awaited death, clutching their beards in the ritual *devotio* gesture. Cowed by these awesome, statuesque figures, one of the Gauls touched the beard of Marcus Papirius – worn long, as was the custom – who responded by striking him over the head with his ivory staff, because the Gaul had interrupted the ritual gesture. At that, the Gauls, inflamed, massacred every one of them and set about their work of looting and burning.

SAVED BY THE GEESE

In Roman religion the gods moved in mysterious ways, their wonders to perform. Man had to be sensitive to their whims and respond accordingly. When the Gauls took and sacked Rome in 386 BC, they did not know what to do about a small army of Romans taking refuge on the steep

Capitol. They tried an assault and were thrown back, but then noticed an easier route up. By starlight they managed to reach the top unnoticed by guards or dogs – but not by the geese, sacred to Juno, that the Romans used for auspices. Their cackling awoke Marcus Manlius, who gave the alarm and attacked. The Gauls were repelled, and the next day the Roman soldier on guard who should have heard the Gauls attacking was thrown from the Tarpeian Rock (p. 14). Every year from then on the event was commemorated: geese were carried about in litters on gold and purple cushions, while dozens of guard dogs were crucified on the Capitoline.

The point is the geese were sacred to Juno. In rewarding the geese, you were honouring her; in punishing the dogs whose ancestors had once let you down, you were giving them fair warning not to do it again. In ritual terms it made perfect sense. As has often been said, religion is like a language, comprehensible only to those who speak it.

'WOE TO THE VANQUISHED'

The language of power is universal. When hunger finally took its toll on both sides in the Gallic siege of Rome in 386 BC – though Romans threw bread down from their defensive position on the Capitol to the Gauls to suggest otherwise – the two sides made a truce. The Gallic chieftain Brennus agreed to be bought off with a thousand pounds weight in gold. But the Gauls used weights heavier than the standard, so the Romans complained.

Vae victis! ('Woe to the vanquished!'), exclaimed Brennus, throwing his sword onto the scales as well.

It was, as Livy says, *intoleranda Romanis vox*, 'a pronouncement intolerable to Romans'. The biter bit, we might say; but the Romans never, ever, took defeat on the chin. The language of power was for them to wield, and no one else.

THE PRICE OF DISOBEDIENCE

Discipline was felt to be one of the defining features of the Roman character. In 340 BC, near Mount Vesuvius, the Romans were up against a superb Latin army which they had previously trained when they were allies. The military council argued that discipline was now at a premium, and no man must leave his position to fight the enemy. But Manlius disobeyed. He rode his cavalry squadron so close to the enemy that one of them, Geminus Maecius, challenged him to single combat. Manlius killed him, gathered the spoils and rode back in triumph to the camp, where he offered them to his father, a consul. His father said nothing, but summoned an assembly, which Livy says he addressed as follows:

'Manlius, you have shown respect neither for a consul's authority nor a father's standing and, defying my orders, have left your position to fight the enemy. You could not have done more to subvert military discipline, the very heart of Rome's success to this day. So you have made it necessary for me to forget either the Republic or myself... If you have a drop of my blood in you, I believe that you yourself would agree that punishment is necessary to restore the military discipline which you are to blame for undermining. So go, lictor, bind him to the stake.'

And there and then Manlius was decapitated.

DEVOTIO TO DEATH DUTY

The willingness to sacrifice oneself for the common good was another much-admired Roman virtue. The night before the battle referred to above, two consuls, Decius Mus and Titus Manlius, had the same dream: one side would be losing the battle, but one of its generals would offer himself up as a sacrifice to the gods, charge into battle and be killed (the term for volunteering to do this was *devotio*); as a result, his side would win. When the consuls offered sacrifice before the battle, the priests inspected the animals' livers. They found that Titus Manlius' was perfect, but Decius' had a cut near the top, though it was still acceptable.

'If my colleague's sacrifice is favourable,' said Decius, 'all is well.'

Battle was joined and the Romans were put under such severe pressure that Decius summoned the state *pontifex* and told him to recite the prayer that a man made before offering himself up to the gods to save his people. This ended:

> On behalf of the Republic of the Roman nation and of the army,
> the legions and the auxiliaries of the Republic of the Roman nation,
> I devote myself and the legions and auxiliaries of our enemies to
> the gods of Underworld and of Earth.

With these words, Decius galloped into the thick of the action. He died under a hail of missiles, and the Romans eventually emerged victorious.

SAMNITE DYNAMITE

The Samnites were a tough, uncouth, sheep-herding and cattle-droving, village-based hill people, used to raiding and plundering on the say-so of the local landowning chieftain. Because of population growth they had expanded from central southern Italy into the areas where Romans were now advancing. Livy is eloquent about the iron resolve of the Samnite tribes. Writing of the year 295 BC, he says:

> We have now been covering the Samnite wars continuously in the last four books, and in the next forty-six years more were to come . . . In the past year, using their own and allied troops, they were cut to pieces by four Roman armies under four Roman generals. They lost their nation's most distinguished commander; saw their allies in the same position as themselves; and could carry on no longer. Yet they refused to give up. Far from tiring of the liberty they had been unable to defend, they preferred to be defeated rather than not try for victory.

Worthy foes indeed, who cannot have known that they were shaping Rome's future.

First, they gave Romans an idea of what Rome might achieve if it wanted to. Second, they hardened the mentality of the citizen body, turning them into a fighting force that would not be denied, whatever the cost. Finally, they forced the Romans to think hard about the sort of relationship between themselves and the peoples they conquered that was most likely to help them stay on top.

POISONOUS WOMEN

Romans thought of women as compensating for their lack of physical strength by secretiveness and treachery. Poison was often thought to be their weapon of choice. Livy tells how in 331 BC a nasty plague broke out in Rome. But a slave girl went to the *aedile* (see p. 73) and told him that it was not a plague at all – it was an outbreak of poisoning.

The accused women were rounded up in the Forum and charged. Two of them, Cornelia and Sergia, both from patrician families, insisted the 'poisons' were wholesome medical cures, presumably from herbs lovingly tended in their gardens. So the slave girl challenged them to drink it. They did, and died. About 170 women, Livy tells us, were found guilty of these practices. The case was regarded as an ill omen, and it was judged the women were possessed by evil spirits rather than depraved. A religious ritual was then performed to negate the effects of this ill omen.

FROM PRETANNIKÊ TO BRITAIN

In about 320 BC, a Greek called Pytheas wrote *On the Oceans*. It survives only in fragments quoted by other authors. Pytheas records his voyage around the islands that we know today as Britain. He says they were called *Pretannikê* (as he puts it in Greek) by the locals. From this it is likely that the original inhabitants called themselves *Pretani* or *Priteni*, i.e., 'Painted people' or 'Tattooed people' (the term that Romans translated into Latin to apply to the *Picti*). *Pretannikê* became *Pretannia* in the first century BC, whence *Britannia*. Pytheas calculated the circumference of Britain at 4,600 miles (7,400 km), which is not bad, given it is actually 4,700 miles (7,563 km). Further, he let us know that the south-east corner of the country was called *Kantion*: Kent.

THE ROAD TO POWER

Appius Claudius, a censor in 312 BC and a man who tended to get his way, was responsible for commissioning the famous 132-mile (212 km) *via Appia* from Rome to Capua. The first Roman road worthy of the name, it came with foundations and closely paved surface, bridges and a raised section across marshland. Appius, who later went blind, was said to have walked it, feeling with his feet whether it had been properly put together; and he was buried in a large tomb alongside it, setting a fashion. The road was extended under Trajan (starting in AD 114) and eventually reached Brindisi, a total of 366 miles (589 km). A column he set up marking the road's end still stands there.

Appius' idea was a significant moment. Rome had just captured the important town of Capua from the Samnites. It needed to be able to keep a grip on the south and roads were the way to do it. All roads may have led to Rome, but far more importantly they gave the Romans easy access to all points in their Empire. As ever, the main purpose of roads was military: quick and easy passage for messengers on horseback and the wheeled back-up accompanying the army. However, once roads were in place, they also brought economic advantages.

NOT ROME'S FIRST AQUEDUCT

It is an indication of the growing wealth of Rome that in 312 BC Appius Claudius also initiated the construction of Rome's first aqueduct, the ten-mile (16 km) *aqua Appia*. In fact, it was not an aqueduct. It was a water-leat, a channel carrying water along the surface or in an underground tunnel big enough for human access – the commonest sort of 'aqueduct' in the Roman world. This was developed from the qanat, the Middle Eastern channels or tunnels driven into a mountain to tap water, probably for draining mines originally. 'Qanat' gives us Greek *kanna*, Latin *canna* 'reed', the origin of our 'canal' and 'channel'.

WATER SUPPLY

Since water is so basic, no town in the ancient world was built where it was not easily available, with springs, lakes, rivers, (private) wells and cisterns to serve its drinking needs. So a town in the ancient world did not suffer water shortages unless things went wrong with the supply, or its expansion outstripped its ability to provide for the population. London, for example, never had an aqueduct.

ARMIES AND THE MEN: FROM PHALANX TO LEGION

The Roman army started out as a Greek-style hoplite 'phalanx', i.e., a solid and rather inflexible wedge of heavy-armed infantry. But after all that fighting against the hill tribes of Italy, it underwent a major change to make it more mobile. It consisted of three lines of soldiers. Each line had a series of units called a *maniple* ('handful') of 120 men. The men in the front two lines each wielded a short throwing spear and stabbing sword; the third line was made up of veterans with long thrusting spears. The front line charged, threw their spears and followed up at close quarters with the sword. The second line moved up with them to take over when they fell back, while the third waited in reserve if needed. 'It's come to the third line' was a common expression, meaning things had become serious. In 311 BC the army was divided into four *legiones*, meaning 'division of troops'. We hear of battles lasting from fifty minutes to three hours. It is an indication of Rome's commitment to warfare at this time that between 6 and 19 per cent of Roman adult males were under arms at any one time, rising to 25 per cent when things became critical. These figures remain unprecedented before the industrial era.

NO BITING ON SAMNITE BRIBES

Historians liked to present the Good Old Roman like Cincinnatus (see p. 48) as a man contemptuous of worldly goods. It is said that in 290 BC the consul Manius Curius Dentatus – the cognomen *dentatus* being explained by the antiquarian Pliny 'because he was born with teeth' – was approached by Samnites with a massive bribe of gold. They found him seated on a rough bench by his hearth in his farmhouse, eating from a wooden dish or roasting turnips. They invited him to take the bribe, but the incorruptible Manius, despising wealth for himself, laughed out loud, calling them 'ambassadors on a superfluous, not to say incompetent, mission', and said, 'There is no glory in possessing wealth, but only in controlling its possessors.'

IN THE SHIT

The flames of independence still burned brightly in the Greek city of Tarentum in southern Italy, and they strongly resisted any Roman approaches. Roman ambassadors sent to the people's assembly there were mocked for their bad Greek and for their togas with purple stripes. When the Greek Philonides bared his backside to the Roman leader Postumius and shat all over him, Postumius replied that he would clean it with Tarentine blood.

PYRRHUS – MAN OF AMBITION

When the people of Tarentum invited the highly rated general Pyrrhus in 280 BC to help them drive the Romans out of southern Italy, his wise adviser Cineas asked him what he would do if he conquered the Romans.

'Why,' said Pyrrhus, 'conquer Sicily.'

'And what next?'

'Take Libya and Carthage.'

'And next?'

'Recover Macedon and Greece.'

'And next?'

'Take it easy, drink every day and talk to our heart's delight,' replied Pyrrhus.

'If that is the ultimate aim of all this effort,' replied Cineas, 'then what is stopping us enjoying it now? We can do it at once, without any bloodshed, toil and danger of the sort you propose, which will entail harm for others and much suffering for ourselves.'

Pyrrhus, we are told, saw the point but 'could not bring himself to abandon his ambitions'.

PYRRHIC VICTORIES

Pyrrhus was victorious in his first battle against the Romans at Heraclea (280 BC), but was unable to persuade them to make peace. In the second at Asculum (279 BC), he won again, but lost 15,000 of his own men, many friends and generals, and could not persuade the Italian tribes hostile to Rome to replace them. He was much impressed by the Roman army, saying he could have conquered the world with such soldiers; but he also ruefully commented: 'If we win one more battle against the Romans, we shall be completely done for.'

ELEPHANT TRAPS

Pyrrhus' surprise weapon was the Indian elephant, large enough to carry a howdah and some missile-bearing soldiers, as well as the mahout. The

Romans had never seen such beasts before and called them 'Lucanian cows' after their first encounter with them at Heraclea in Lucania.

These 'cows' caused chaos in the Roman ranks, and when Pyrrhus was later negotiating a settlement (in vain) with the Romans, he first tried to bribe the negotiator Fabricius, and then he attempted to frighten him by withdrawing some hangings to reveal an elephant.

'Your gold made no impression on me yesterday,' said Fabricius, 'nor your beast today.'

ELEPHANTINE RISKS

The problem with elephants was their unpredictability. At the battle of Asculum they routed the terrified Roman cavalry and broke the infantry line, even though the Romans used fire and ox-led chariots, equipped with long spikes to wound them. But at Beneventum, when Pyrrhus had returned from his Sicilian expedition, the elephants were attacked with spears by the Roman camp guards; the beasts panicked, turned and trampled their own lines. That was one lesson the Romans learned. The second was that, having captured some of the elephants, they found that horses, which had previously been terrified of them, could in fact be trained to face them.

WINNING OVER THE LOCALS

Romans saw it to be in their interests to draw into alliance the communities they defeated in battle. There were different categories of relationship: full Roman citizenship, with or without the right to vote; autonomous citizen colonies planted by Rome across Italy; independent communities with various more or less compulsory ties to Rome; and communities encountered in Rome's expansion, usually in a defensive alliance with Rome, either voluntary or non-voluntary. All supplied manpower for the Roman army, and could expect Roman protection if attacked; likewise, communities could change status if Rome felt they deserved it. This flexible system of incorporations and alliances was to prove one of Rome's great strengths in maintaining control and keeping their armies manned. Manpower was the *sine qua non* behind Rome's expansion, even more so in the lengthy war against Hannibal.

THE SIZE OF THE ROMAN STATE

To indicate the speed at which the Roman *state* grew over this period (i.e., land occupied by citizens with full Roman rights, though some without the right to vote), it has been estimated that in the mid-340s BC Rome occupied 775 square miles (2,007 square kilometres; Greater London is 607 square miles) and by 280 BC 5,900 square miles (15,280 square kilometres, almost the size of Yorkshire). So in 60 years the Roman *state* nearly octupled in size. The census figure for 265 BC tells us that the number of adult male Roman citizens was 292,234; figures from the historian Polybius (p. 110) suggest that the total manpower available to Rome from across Italy, allies and all, was 730,000.

IV

509–287 BC

TIMELINE

?509 BC   *Comitia centuriata* develops

494 BC   Plebeian revolt; Plebeian Assembly; Tribunes of plebs

493 BC   Gaius Marcius earns courtesy title Coriolanus

451 BC   Twelve Tables legal code

449/287/227 BC   Gradually Plebeian Assembly's laws applied to all

447 BC   Tribal Assembly established

443 BC   Censors appointed to take census

?406 BC   Tax on property introduced

?400 BC   All magistrates become senators

c. 300 BC   Coinage develops

WHAT IT MEANT
TO BE ROMAN
(II)

The Rise of the Republic

I n 509 BC, with the kings thrown out, Rome set about defining a new way of ruling itself. The details are very hazy and much debated, but over time something like the following may have occurred. At some stage Rome replaced the kings with two annually elected consuls (though to start with, they were called *praetors*); and people's assemblies were established to appoint ruling officials (*magistratûs*, 'magistrates') and pass laws.

But the problems typical of a peasant society would not go away – poverty, lack of land, debt and so on. This affected many plebeians, who decided they wanted their own say. After a military strike in 494 BC they won a right to have their *own* law-making assembly (the Plebeian Assembly, 'a state within a state') and to appoint 'Tribunes of the plebs' to protect their interests in the Senate. Over time, further settlements advantageous to them were made, e.g., the production of Rome's first legal code in 451 BC (the 'Twelve Tables'); from 449 BC most laws passed by the Plebeian Assembly applied to the whole people (with the last minor restrictions abandoned in 287 BC); and eventually all official posts that the patricians regarded as their own became open to plebeians.

A cautionary note: we rather tend to divide Roman citizens into patricians (rich, powerful toffs) and plebs (poor, struggling peasants) and pitch the two against each other. But that distinction is far too polarized. There were plenty of Romans in between these two extremes.

THE CLASS IN CLASSICAL

The Roman 'class' system is literally that: the Latin is *classis*, meaning 'a body of citizens summoned for military service', because it was (wrongly) ascribed to the earlier King Servius as a means of selecting men for military service. This class system divided citizens into seven groupings by wealth:

- The (unnumbered) top group: the 'equestrians' were the richest men in society, owning property worth 400,000 *ss*. From their ranks would come the senators, the advisory body once to kings and now to consuls.

- Then came five numbered *classes*, from the first *classis* (i.e., the next richest) and graded by wealth down to the fifth *classis*.

- The last, again unnumbered, *classis* was those with no wealth at all. All they had was children. Hence their name – *proletarii* (Latin, *proles*, 'child'). Another name for them was *capite censi*, 'counted by head', because they had nothing else to be counted by.

Regular censuses – organized by the new post of *censor* – took place to determine which *classis* you went into. Punishment was severe for those who tried to avoid it. Incidentally, the term *classici* was restricted, we are told, to members of the first class. Hence 'classic' and 'classics' – only the very best.

CENSUS

Taxes, military duty and voting rights: all these were determined by your *classis* and registered in the citizenship records gathered every four or five years by the censors. Every man had to state in public his full name, age, the name of his father or guardian, his place of residence, occupation and amount of property. Censuses in the provinces were organized centrally from Rome.

FIXING IT FOR THE RICH

The *class*-ification described above later formed the basis of the system for electing consuls and *praetors* ('magistrates'). The citizen body that did this was the *comitia centuriata*. This *comitia* ('an assembly of the people for judicial and legislative purposes') met in the Campus Martius. It was called *centuriata* because each *classis* was divided into groupings called *centuriae*, 'centuries' (but there was no link to the number 100). The rule was that each 'century' had one vote, no matter how many people it contained. The richest 'equestrian' group was turned into 18 *centuriae* (18 votes) and the first *classis* into 80 *centuriae* (80 votes) – 98 votes in all. The whole of the remainder of the Roman citizens, vastly outstripping those two groups in number, became 95 *centuriae* – 95 votes! So the system was fixed in favour of the rich:

if they unanimously voted for or against something, the matter was settled.

PAYING TRIBUTE

The *classis* system also served another function: the payment of tax (*tributum*). This tax may have come in around 406 BC, probably to help pay for the army (p. 49). It was not a tax on income, but on property. The total amount of *tributum* required annually (if any) was determined by the Senate as a proportion of your wealth. So the higher your *classis*, as determined by the 'Servian' rating, the more you paid.

VOTES FOR TAXES

'One man, one vote' is for us a given of democracy. But it was not for Livy, who could not understand why the rich, by being placed in the highest *classes*, were willing to pay tax as a proportion of their wealth, and therefore much more than those poorer than they. His explanation was that it was a *quid pro quo* for the voting system. This gave the rich almost complete political control over the conduct of affairs on which the state spent their money. So not one man = one vote, but instead one rich man = the equivalent of many votes, and one poor man = only a portion of a single vote. 'No tax without representation,' we say. Livy might emend that to: 'No more-than-anyone-else's tax without more representation.'

THE PRICE OF SERVING ONE'S COUNTRY

In 495 BC (Livy informs us) a distressed and emaciated old soldier gathered a crowd about him in the Forum and described what had happened to him: he had served his country faithfully in war, but in his absence the Sabine enemy had burned his crops, taken his cattle and destroyed his cottage. He fell into debt, losing his land and all his other possessions. Finally his creditors reduced him not to slavery, but to an underground slave prison, a death sentence. This was the eternal problem of a peasant society, created by the gap between the wealthy and the rest. The kings had not solved it. Surely the Republic should! The Roman poor and dispossessed came back to the problem time and time again.

POWER TO THE PLEBS!

In 494 BC the very poor plebs in the army, tired of the Senate's continued refusals to deal with their debt problems, went on strike and withdrew under their leader Sicinius to the Sacred Mountain, three miles (5 km) from the city. Without the plebs, Rome's army was paralysed. The Senate sent Menenius Agrippa, a plebeian, to negotiate with the strikers. He addressed them with the famous parable of the belly of the body politic.

Once upon a time, he said, the members of the body (plebs) got tired of working themselves to the bone every day while the belly (Senate) did nothing but just lounged about, being stuffed full. So the hand said it would no longer carry food to the mouth, and the mouth and teeth refused to accept or chew anything that was offered. The result was that the whole body wasted away to almost nothing. Conclusion: the belly *did* do work. It nourished the whole body by digesting food. This made blood, sent through the body by veins, on which life and health depended. Menenius' speech won the day and the subsequent negotiations ended the strike by creating two 'Tribunes of the plebs' and a new assembly dedicated to plebeians alone. Military might, in other words, gave the plebeians some hold over the patrician elite. A refusal to fight left the patricians no option but to talk.

THE PLEBEIAN ASSEMBLY

This Plebeian Assembly could at first pass measures binding only on the plebs (the *plebiscitum*, whence our 'plebiscite'), but in 287 BC *plebiscita* were given the force of law over the whole people. The Tribunes of the plebs (*tribuni plebis*) had two main functions: they were automatically members of the Senate and had the power of veto, so they could bring public business to a halt; and they could intervene to protect any Roman citizen from the action of a politician. They were also immune from any sort of physical harm and coercion. This whole development created a theoretically alternative political voice in Roman society. In the second century BC, theory would become fact.

VOTING FOR LAWS

Every Roman citizen was a member of one of Rome's 35 tribes or clans. In 447 BC a tribal assembly was set up: the *comitia tributa* (*tribus*, 'tribe'). This assembly elected officials known as *quaestors* and *aediles* and passed laws. It met in the Forum and, unlike the *comitia centuriata*, every citizen was treated *equally*: each tribe had one vote, determined by the majority vote of their members. Romans in this assembly, however, did not debate issues. Any debate would take place in the Senate and in public in the Forum, between the opposing magistrates. This would give them the chance to gauge the mood, adjust the proposal and so on – these debates could be very rowdy affairs – before deciding whether it was worth going ahead. The people simply voted to turn into law (or not) a single, pre-existing proposal put before the assembly by one of the magistrates – rather like a modern referendum or plebiscite.

POLITICAL MAGISTRATES

'Magistrate' to us usually means a Justice of the Peace. To a Roman, *magistratus* (pl. *magistratûs*) referred to the highest elected officials of the state. It derived from Latin *magis-ter*: *magis* 'greater' + the suffix *-atus* indicating a functionary. Ironically, *minis-ter* (Latin, *minus*, 'one lesser', 'servant', 'attendant', 'subordinate') is the term we use. Such officers of state were appointed by the two people's assemblies. All were subject to audit when their term of office ended. But none was ever paid. This restricted membership to the very few, very wealthy families that could afford it.

(*Note*: in our system, there is in theory a 'separation of powers': Parliament is the legislature, making the law; the goverment departments and civil service are the executive, putting it into action; and the courts are the judiciary, checking that it is legal. Each is (in theory) the master in its own field, and the judiciary certainly is, ever ready to hold Parliament to account at all costs; but Parliament and government are to a large extent identical, though the function of the House of Commons Select Committees is to hold government to account. But in Rome, the past and present *magistratûs*, individually or *en masse* in the Senate, could be the lawmakers (assemblies willing), executive and judiciary all in one.)

IMPERIUM: THE ULTIMATE AUTHORITY

The origin of our 'imperial' and 'emperor' is *imperium*, 'the right to give orders', which derives from the Latin *impero*, 'I give orders' with the added implication of orders 'which I have the authority to enforce'. It was the ultimate power vested in selected *magistratûs* by the community, giving them supreme authority over any individual; it was wielded only by consuls, *praetors*, dictators and others in special circumstances, e.g., governors going out to their provinces.

CONSULS

Two *magistratûs* were elected to serve as consuls. They were absolute heads of state for one year only, each with equal authority (see *imperium* above), each able to veto the other – the very opposite of the single king with absolute power. If a consul died, another was immediately elected. They were responsible for carrying out the rituals that would keep the gods onside (*pax deorum* – the gods' peace), and with the Senate they controlled the diplomatic, military and political process (they had the right to declare war and summon the Senate and the *comitia centuriata*). Eventually, one of them had to be a plebeian, and in time both could be (p. 103).

PRAETORS

The term *praetor* derives from the Latin *praeeo*, 'I go before, precede (into battle)', and it was originally applied to the two heads of state. But in 367 BC these were re-named *consules*, and *praetor* became the term for the next great office of state, head of the legal services and with military authority. The *praetors* took control in Rome when the two consuls were away. The number of *praetors* fluctuated, rising briefly to 16 under Julius Caesar.

QUAESTORS

With a title derived from the Latin *quaero*, 'I investigate', *quaestors* originally had legal duties, but over time they came to have a primarily financial function, mainly running the state treasury under the control of the Senate, or helping a provincial governor run his financial affairs (p. 157). But they had some legal and military duties as well. There were as many as 40 *quaestors* under Julius Caesar.

AEDILES

The title derives from the Latin *aedis*, 'room' or 'temple'. Originally in charge of common temples and the cults of the plebs, *aediles* came to take over the fabric, running and good order of Rome, e.g., streets, markets, water supply, public order, corn supply and administration of public games (gladiators, chariot races, etc.).

'FASCIST' POWER

By the republican watchword *libertas* ('freedom'), a word regularly invoked in imperial times to recall the days of the Republic, Romans meant 'controlling those in office'. Celebrating the *libertas* that Romans enjoyed, Livy observed:

> You could reckon that liberty lay rather in the restriction of the consuls' powers to one year of office rather than in any diminution in the power that kings had held. The first consuls had all the

> rights and insignia of kings, but here, too, precautions were taken:
> the [twelve] *fasces* were not held by both at the same time.

The *fasces* consisted of a bundle of rods about five feet long, bound by red thongs and containing single-headed axe(s) when displayed in war. Regarded as symbols of the right to punish, they were carried by twelve *lictores* (lictors), the consul's attendants. These lictors preceded the consul everywhere he went – inside and outside Rome – in single file, each with one bundle over his left shoulder. Their job was to clear his way and enact his rights to arrest and summons people. The right to carry the *fasces* swapped between the consuls every month. Some other magistrates were also entitled to lictors with *fasces*; a *praetor* had six.

DICTATOR

Emergencies call for special measures. The creation of a *dictator*, authorized by the Senate, was one such. In the early days a dictator was appointed to deal with a specific military crisis, with a maximum tenure of six months. Once the crisis had been dealt with the dictator resigned. Other magistrates remained in office during that period but, to indicate his supreme authority over everyone, the dictator was given 24 lictors, as if he were two consuls rolled into one.

CENSORS

From the Latin *censeo*, 'I register/enrol', the two *censors* (positions established in 443 BC) were responsible for drawing up the official citizen roll. This was regarded as a very important job – usually held by ex-consuls – because it determined what *classis* you were in (p. 66), and therefore your duties and privileges. The term of appointment was four or five years. Censors also became guardians of the moral health of the state, with the power to strike citizens off the roll if their conduct seemed in any way reprehensible (hence our 'censor'). Finally, censors came to have a financial role. They leased out the rights to work state-controlled properties such as mines and forests, and the rights to collect taxes (both of which produced revenue); they also let out contracts for public works, such as road building or aqueduct construction. The post of censor disappeared after 22 BC under the emperors, who took the responsibility into their own hands.

GRADUATES OF EXPERIENCE

Up until now the Senate had consisted of a king's or consul's chosen advisors: always wealthy patricians. But at some stage, perhaps around 400 BC, all Roman magistrates automatically became members of the Senate. It continued to be a purely advisory body, as it had been under the kings (p. 14), but the experience of its members now gained it the authority to become a key player in Roman politics; though it could not pass laws itself, it effectively controlled military command, finance, Italian and foreign relations and proposals for new laws for the assemblies to pass (or not). Eventually numbering 300 (sometimes more), senators wore special shoes and sported the broad purple stripe (perhaps two stripes) on their togas. But because senators signed off state spending, they were *not* themselves allowed to win state contracts or deal in large-scale shipping (they got others to do it for them). Their wealth 'officially' lay in land and rents.

TOGS AND TOGAS

For everyday use, Roman males and females wore a range of clothes: cloaks, mantles, tunics, shifts and loin clothes. The toga, the traditional Roman free-male garment, with a purple border on the upper edge, was worn only on ceremonial or official occasions. It was quite impractical for every day. It was a clumsy garment: a large semi-circle of woollen cloth, 20 feet by 10 feet (6 x 3 m), wrapped round the body in such a way as to require the left arm to support it all. It was an emblem of civilian, not military, power, of a world at peace (it was not worn by soldiers), and it came in various colours. The toga was taken up by some provincials in the West, but it was *not* a Greek garment (so a Greek toga party is a contradiction in terms). The Roman antiquarian Varro derived it from *tego*, 'I cover'. Unusually for Roman etymological assertions, this is correct. Incidentally, the toga was also said to have been worn by prostitutes and women divorced for adultery!

NOBLEST ROMANS

The Latin *nobilis* means 'well known' (*[g]nosco*, 'I know'). It was the term that became applied for the most part to those families, whether patrician or plebeian, one of whose members had at some stage been a consul. In terms of top-status value, *nobilis* replaced 'patrician' and came to be the distinction to have. A member of a non-noble family who managed to become consul and join this club was called a *novus homo*, 'new person'. To give some idea of the discrimination they faced: over any lengthy period of time, between 70 and 90 per cent of consuls came from a noble family.

A CONSUL'S IMAGE

Display was important to Romans. The Latin *imago* refers among much else to the wax image or funeral mask of an ancestor who had made it to the top in Roman politics. This was kept on display in the family shrine, with a record of the man's ancestry and honours. At family funerals and public sacrifices, actors in full ceremonial gear wore the family *imagines* (pl.), impersonating their great men. Families with a long string of consuls in their history must have made an extraordinarily powerful impression on the public as their ancestors were paraded before them.

SPQR

The origin of our 'republic' is two words, *res publica*, the two words meaning, literally, 'people's property' or 'people's business'. It was so called because, in theory, the people could always have the last word through the various people's assemblies. Displayed on army insignia and inscriptions all over the Roman world, SPQR, *Senatus Populusque Romanus* ('Senate and Roman People'), made the point: the people were as important as the Senate in the running of the state. After all, who did the fighting?

A MACHIAVELLIAN LESSON FOR A ROMAN HERO

In 493 BC the aristocrat Gaius Marcius earned the courtesy title of Coriolanus after an almost single-handed assault on the Volscian town of Corioli (p. 42). However, he was bitterly opposed to the success of the common people in gaining the right to their own all-powerful Tribunes and Plebeian Assembly (p. 69). The following year there was a famine, and it was proposed to keep down the price of imported grain to a level that the people could afford. Coriolanus opposed this strongly. He was put up for trial by the furious Tribunes, but fled into exile without appearing before the court. He joined the Volsci, vowing vengeance against his country. His Volscian army seized many of the towns that Rome had won from them, and went on to threaten Rome itself. Livy put a quite magnificent speech into Coriolanus' mother Veturia's mouth, pleading with him to desist. It ends:

> Had I not been a mother, Rome would not be under attack; had I not born a son, I would be dying a free woman in a free land. As it is, I have nothing to suffer that could bring greater disgrace on you, or misery on myself. But *I* shall not remain miserable for long; for these, however [she means Coriolanus' wife and children], understand that, if you remain fixed of purpose, nothing but early death or long enslavement is in store.

Kissing his wife and son, Coriolanus sent them home and dismissed his army – and that was the last anyone heard of him. The family had won: in attacking your own city, you attacked *them*. This was not *pietas* (p. 5). But there was a further lesson: Coriolanus' action united Rome against him. As Machiavelli was later to point out, people pull together when danger threatens; it is the easy life that creates discord in a state. Shakespeare based his *Coriolanus* (*c.* 1608) on Plutarch's *Life of Coriolanus*.

THE IMPORTANCE OF THE TWELVE TABLES

Cicero claimed that every Roman child learned by heart the *si in ius vocat* ('if he summons to law') – the first words (presumably meaning the whole) of the legal code known as the Twelve Tables of 450 BC (an expansion of the original Ten Tables of 451 BC). This was Rome's first attempt at such a 'code'. In a dialogue, Cicero makes a speaker say:

> They can all moan, if they like, but I shall say what I feel: you can take the library-loads of books of every philosopher in the world, but if one is looking for the origins and sources of the law, the one little book of the Twelve Tables seems to me to surpass them all in weight of authority and fertility of usefulness.

THE LANGUAGE OF THE TWELVE TABLES

The Twelve Tables are the first examples we have of Roman literature, though they survive only in part and only in later quotations (the original bronze copies were probably destroyed in the Gallic sack of Rome 386 BC, see pp. 42, 50). But we can be fairly confident that what we have is genuine, because the language is often so stilted and obscure, unlike later, classical Latin, e.g., 'If he summons to law, he is to go. If he does not go, he is to call to witness. Then he is to seize him.' Presumably this means: 'If [the plaintiff] summons [the defendant] to law, [the defendant] is to go. If [the defendant] does not go, [the plaintiff] is to call [someone else] to witness.' The language struggles to express abstract concepts: 'If the weapon flew from hand rather than threw it, he must pay a ram', for example, is attempting to distinguish between the intentional and unintentional. At this time, fifth-century BC Athenians were expressing themselves with supreme eloquence in elegant and subtle philosophical treatises, political analyses and legal orations, as well as in tragedies from such masters as Aeschylus, Sophocles and Euripides. Romans still had a long way to go.

THE CONTENT OF THE TWELVE TABLES

The Twelve Tables did not deal with the constitution: that was felt to be too hot a topic and better left to the assemblies to determine. Private law seems to have been the main target, occasionally touching on the relationship between the individual and the community: family, marriage and divorce; inheritance, ownership and property; assault and injury relating to people and property; debt, slavery and debt-bondage (when the debtor remained a Roman citizen and could not be sold abroad). Here are some further samples:

> If a man is mad, his nearest male kinsman is to take control of him and his property.

> An obviously deformed child must be put to death at once.

(Exposure of babies was common: we have a father's instructions in a letter saying 'If the baby is male, keep it; if female expose it'. Bodies of babies were regularly buried in gardens or under floorboards.)

> If someone breaks another's bone by hand or club, he is to pay 300 ss; if a slave's, 150 ss; if he's just done an injury, 25 ss [see p. 75].

> If a man commits theft by night and is killed, let the killing be lawful.

In the way of all ancient law codes, the wording is brief, practical and stark.

THE PATERFAMILIAS

By *familia* Romans meant the whole household, property and people, including slaves. All power over the *familia* lay in the hands of the *paterfamilias*, the father of the family, technically the oldest surviving direct male descendant. However old his sons, officially speaking they had no independent status until he died. They could not go to law, make a will or buy or sell property. Indeed, the money which a father gave his son was called *peculium* – the term used of money or property owned by a slave. Further, if the *paterfamilias* so determined, he could kill them or sell them into slavery. In reality, the situation was not so inflexible. Incidentally, the very word *familia* itself makes the point about the *paterfamilias*: it is cognate with *famulus*, 'slave'. The *familia* was in principle, if not practice, a body enslaved to one man.

MONEY

Since the Twelve Tables talk about transferring property by means of 'bronze and scales' (i.e., bronze by weight) and compensating certain types of injuries by payments in bronze, it is clear that metal money had entered the equation by the fifth century BC. This was not coinage (that was developed *c*. 300 BC), but rather metallic units of fixed value – the really important step in establishing a currency. Bronze ingots, a relatively easy way to carry wealth around with you, have been found dating from the sixth century BC.

THE NAMING SYSTEM

In republican times the traditional naming system worked as follows:

1. Personal name, *praenomen*: e.g., Gaius or Marcus. There were

surprisingly few personal names, by far the most popular being Gaius, Lucius, Marcus, Publius and Quintus. Gaius, incidentally, was usually abbreviated to C. (not G.) and was pronounced as three syllables: Ga-i-us (long 'a', short 'i').

2. Clan name, *nomen*: [Gaius] Julius or [Marcus] Tullius.

3. Inherited family name, *cognomen*: e.g., [Gaius Julius] Caesar or [Marcus Tullius] Cicero. These covered a huge range, often denoting various qualities, e.g., occupations (*Agricola*, 'farmer'), capacities (*Clemens*, 'merciful'), physical qualities (*Longus*, 'tall') and other characteristics (e.g., *Leo*, 'lion'; *Sagitta* 'arrow'; *Felix* 'lucky'). Incidentally, *Caesar* (p. 154) became in German Kaiser, in Russian Tsar/Czar, and 'sherry' – from Xeres, a city in Spain named from *Caesaris* 'Caesar's [city]'.

Women usually took on the feminine form of their father's clan name. Thus Cicero's daughter was *Tullia*. Some names were simply 'honorific'. The Roman general Pompey was given one: Gnaeus Pompeius *Magnus* ('the great'); so too was the Scipio who defeated Hannibal in Africa (Publius Cornelius Scipio *Africanus*).

V

810–146 BC

TIMELINE

810 BC   Traditional date for founding of Carthage

264–241 BC   First Rome vs. Carthage Punic War

254 BC   Mythical story of Regulus

249 BC   Publius Claudius drowns the chickens

229–146 BC   Roman interventions in Greece

218–202 BC   Second Punic War (Hannibal)

217 BC   Battle of Lake Trasimene

216 BC   Battle of Cannae

211 BC   Marcellus takes Syracuse; Hannibal besieges Rome

207 BC   Battle of Metaurus: death of Hasdrubal

203 BC   Hannibal leaves Italy

202 BC   Scipio beats Hannibal at Zama

199 BC   Cato the Elder consul

182 BC   Hannibal commits suicide

180 BC	Laws for ages of magistrates passed
167 BC	End of direct taxation of Romans
c. 151 BC	No one can be consul more than once
146 BC	Carthage razed to the ground (Third Punic War)
	Corinth sacked; Greece semi-provincialized
	Rome the Mediterranean superpower

THEIR FINEST HOUR

Carthaginians, Hannibal and Empire

The great maritime state of Carthage on the North African coast was a long established power. From the eighth century BC it had been colonizing grain-rich, centrally placed Sicily to the north. In 264 BC Rome, remembering Pyrrhus' recent foreign incursions, saw Carthaginian encroachment east across Sicily as a potential threat to southern Italy, and the First Punic War began. The seas being crucial for victory, Rome built its first standing naval fleet and, with new tactics, incredibly, won. By 241 BC Carthage had had enough and sued for peace. Sicily became Rome's first province. The Empire had begun.

Carthage built up its finances again by expanding into mineral-rich Spain under the powerful Barca family. In 218 BC Hannibal Barca crossed a Roman-claimed territorial boundary in Spain and began the Second Punic War. He took his army over the Alps – Rome immediately sent one into Spain – and by 216 BC Rome was on the brink of defeat. But much of Italy remained loyal. Hannibal was not reinforced, nor could he capture an Italian harbour. Gradually, Rome clawed its way back.

Meanwhile the Scipio family in Spain was having great success. Hasdrubal Barca, however, did slip past the Romans there in 207 BC, but was defeated in Italy before he could join his brother. Then, one of the Scipios – later to be nicknamed 'Africanus' – crossed into Africa. In 203 BC Hannibal returned to Carthage, and Scipio defeated him at Zama in 202 BC. Spain, too, was now slowly brought under Roman provincial control.

Because King Philip V of Macedon (Greece) had supported Hannibal, Romans moved their armies east into Greece. In 183 BC, during a further conflict against King Antiochus (Syria), they finally (and almost accidentally) caught up with Hannibal scheming against them in Bithynia. Romans left Greece briefly, but returned again and in 146 BC they destroyed Corinth and made Greece a province. They also razed Carthage to the ground after a Third Punic War (149–146 BC). North Africa became another province.

All this ushered in a period of rapid artistic and cultural enlightenment, driven by contact with Greek culture, while military conquests generated incredible riches for Rome's senatorial classes and their families, from whom their generals were drawn. But where did this leave those back home, who did not share in it?

PHOENICIANS, PHOENIXES AND PUNIC WARS

The Carthaginians were originally a Phoenician people from the Lebanon region. We do not know what 'Phoenicians' called themselves. The Bible called them Canaanites; they tended to call themselves by the names of their cities – 'inhabitants of Tyre/Sidon/Byblos' and so on. Why, then, 'Phoenician'? It comes from the Greek name for them: *Phoinikes*. *Phoinos* in Greek meant 'red' and *Phoinikes* probably refers to their expertise in the purple dye industry. The Romans changed the Greek *Phoi-ni-kes* to the Latin *Pu-ni-ci* or *Poeni*. Note that in Greek *ph* was not pronounced *f* but is aspirated *p*, as in to*p-h*at; and the Latin plural ending is in –*i*. Hence 'Punic' war. Incidentally, the date palm is also called *phoenix*, and so is the bird – both, it was believed, originating from that area.

DYEING FOR A NAME

The dye which probably gave the Phoenicians their Greek name was the famous and very expensive Tyrian purple (from Tyre). This was the colour that identified senators, emperors and, later, royalty. It was made from the shells of the *murex* genus of shellfish. These were collected and killed instantly to preserve their secretions; then opened or crushed. They were left in salt for three days, extracted with water and inspissated to a sixteenth of their volume. Depending on the mix of shellfish, a range of indelible colours was possible, from violet-scarlet to bluish-green. If you come across a pile of small, smashed shells on Mediterranean coasts, it is probably the result of this ancient industry. In Sidon there is one 130 feet (40 m) high.

THE FOUNDING OF CARTHAGE

The Phoenicians, expanding west, established a colony in North Africa called, appropriately, *Qart-Hadasht* ('New City'), which Greeks Hellenized to *Karchêdôn* and the Romans Latinized to *Carthago*. The expedition to found a new city was led in 810 BC (traditional date) by a queen, Dido (others called her Elissa). She was the wife of Pygmalion of Tyre and the grand-niece of Jezebel, the biblical 'wicked queen' who married the Israelite king Ahab (they both come to bad ends in the Bible). When Dido arrived in Carthage, according to the ancient Greek version of the story, the local inhabitants said she could have as much territory as she could cover with an ox-hide (Greek, *bursa*). Choosing the largest *bursa* she could find, Dido proceeded to cut it up into thin strips, making it embrace quite a sizeable chunk of territory. So by 264 BC the Carthaginians were not upstart barbarians trying their luck against those nice Romans. A sophisticated, cultured people, they had already been a power in the region for some 500 years before the Punic Wars; indeed, as early as 507 BC Carthage had acknowledged Rome's growing importance by signing a bilateral trading agreement with it (p. 41).

BURSAR ERROR

Greek *bursa* means 'ox-hide'; late Latin took it over, giving us purse, bursar (who holds the purse strings), disburse, French *bourse* – and possibly even sporran. But ancient Greek is not Phoenician. Carthage's walled citadel was called *Byrsa*, probably from Akkadian *birtu*, 'fortress'. When Greeks heard this, they possibly associated it with their word *bursa*, 'ox-hide'; and that may be how the bizarre story of ox-hide being cut into strips was invented.

HARBOURING AMBITIONS

Ships need harbours. The problem for peoples at the eastern end of the Mediterranean was that the winds in the summer came predominantly from the north-west. Since ancient ships did not tack efficiently it was a struggle to sail west; they also ran the constant risk of being blown onto the dangerous African lee shore, riddled with sandbanks and not well served by natural harbours. This explains why Carthage, having a superb harbour, was so important; and why Carthage was always seeking to implant itself in places further north and more propitious for sailing, like Sicily, Sardinia, the Balearics and so on – even, given the chance, southern Italy.

RAVENOUS FOR VICTORY

When the First Punic War broke out, Rome had very little experience of fighting at sea, particularly not against Carthage's huge oared *quinqueremes* with five decks of oars either side. So the Romans decided to build their first standing fleet and train sailors for the task. A Carthaginian ship, attacking Roman transport ships, ran aground and fell into Roman hands. Using this as a model, they built a fleet of 100 *quinqueremes* and 20 *triremes* (three banks of oars) in an incredible 60 days (later beating even that record, according to the antiquarian Pliny the Elder, by building a fleet of 220 ships in 45 days!). Meanwhile, the rowers trained on benches set out on dry land to resemble the deck.

However, the Romans soon realized that – unsurprisingly – they could not match the Carthaginians for skill. So they thought up a way to minimize any skill involved: the 'raven'. This was a gangway 36 feet high and 4 feet wide (11 x 1.2 m), with rails either side, and a large spike at the outward end. It was fixed onto a rotating base in the bows of the ship and hauled up by a pulley system. Ignoring tricky marine manoeuvres, the Romans rammed their ships directly into the enemy and slammed the 'raven' hard down onto the enemy deck. This locked the two ships together, allowing Roman soldiers to pour over the gangway and fight a land battle at sea. The point of the rotating base was that, from whatever quarter the contact was made, the gangway could be swivelled round to form a bridge onto the Carthaginian ship. The Roman sterns, where the 'raven' could not be brought into play, were protected by a second line of ships.

ROMAN CAN-DO

Romans refused to be beaten. Their determination was second to none. During the First Punic War, Rome not only built its first fleet of 120 warships and beat their far more experienced enemy at sea, but they also rebuilt that fleet again and again as gales and losses at sea took their toll. While the census of 247 BC suggests that the male population had declined by 17 per cent since the start of the war, we hear of ship losses numbering 140 (255 BC), 120 (250 BC) and 200 (243 BC). In all, the total, according to our sources, comes to more than 1,000 ships, the majority being large *quinqueremes*, all funded from state coffers. The strain on the system was such that the last tranche had to be part-funded by wealthy private citizens.

INVENTING HEROISM

In 254 BC the Roman general Regulus was sent to wage war in North Africa. He was defeated by the Carthaginians and taken prisoner, then sent back to Rome to negotiate the ransom of Roman prisoners or the return of Carthaginian ones. He promised to return if he failed. In Rome he argued against the negotiations and, keeping his promise, he returned to Carthage, knowing he would be put to death. His eyelids were cut off, and he was kept in a spike-filled cage in which rest was impossible, under the blazing sun; finally he was trampled to death by an enraged elephant. A later source has it that his wife in Rome was given two of the Carthaginian captives, and when she learned that her husband had been killed she treated them with such brutality that one of them died. Romans made much of Regulus' heroism – the poet Horace ended one of his *Odes* with the story – but since there is no mention of it in our best source, Polybius (p. 110), it is almost certainly a useful invention.

CHICKENING OUT

In 249 BC the consul Publius Claudius wanted to carry out a surprise attack on the Carthaginian Adherbal's fleet in the harbour at Drepana (Trapani in Sicily). Poor weather foiled the element of surprise, and Publius took the auspices (p. 21) to see what to do next. But the sacred chickens refused to eat. This was a bad omen. Publius determined to see the matter through, however. 'So they refuse to eat, eh?' he said. 'Then they can drink' – and he hurled them overboard. By now Adherbal had sailed out of harbour and had the Roman trapped against the shore. Publius lost virtually every ship, returned to Rome in disgrace and was exiled – not for being defeated but for sacrilege (p. 23). That was the point: since Roman religion was ritualistic, it was no surprise that the gods would turn against you if you got the rituals wrong or ignored divine warning signs.

HANNIBAL'S HOWDAH-DO

Pyrrhus, summoned by the people of Tarentum to defend them against the Romans, had brought with him the easily trained Indian elephants (p. 59). It seems unlikely that Hannibal could have got his hands on any of them in the Second Punic War. Further, while African elephants from below the Sahara are bigger (10 to 13 feet (3–4 m) high), they are very difficult to manage. Though African forest elephants from the Congo Basin are relatively small (8 feet maximum (2.4 m)) and less imposing, they were probably the ones used by Hannibal, equipped with howdahs and mahouts as required. Each mahout evidently carried a spike to drive into the elephant's head and kill it, if it panicked. But in the event, none of the 30 or so survived the 15-day crossing of the Alps.

FLOATING ELEPHANTS

To get his elephants across the Rhone, Livy tells us that Hannibal had a float built 200 feet long and 50 feet wide (61 x 15 m). It was held firmly in position beside the riverbank and covered in soil to make it look like solid land. To this, however, was attached a large raft, suitable for towing across the river. The first batch of elephants, complete with riders, was driven onto the float and then ushered onto the raft. The mooring lines were promptly cast off, and it was towed by rowing boats to the other side. There was some shoving and jostling when the elephants got into midstream, and a few fell in, but eventually they all got across.

MOUNTAINOUS LOSSES

Hannibal's men were attacked by local tribes as they crossed the Alps, while also contending with treacherous icy conditions and rough terrain. On the descent they split huge rocks, we are told, to create a path through. They felled large trees, created huge piles of timber and set fire to it. When the rocks were sufficiently heated, Livy tells us, the men's rations of sour wine/vinegar were poured onto them. This made the rocks easier to split, and the soldiers, getting to work with pickaxes, were able to open a slightly easier zigzag track down the mountain. Only about half the army of 50,000 foot and 9,000 cavalry survived this crossing, but none of the elephants. However, Gauls in northern Italy did join Hannibal against the Romans, while many Italian and Greek towns less than enthusiastic about their Roman masters, especially in the south, also signed up after his early victories.

HANNIBAL, MASTER OF DISGUISE

Though Hannibal had made allies of the tribes to the north of Italy, he was not at all convinced of their reliability. He therefore had a number of wigs made for himself, each indicating a man of a different age. These he constantly changed, choosing at the same time different styles of dress to suit the age of the wig. This, apparently, made him hard to recognize, even by those who knew him well.

SPY NETWORKS

After Hannibal crossed the Alps into Italy (218 BC), he set up extensive spy networks in Roman camps in Italy and in Rome itself. His spies used hand gestures to help them recognize each other. His great rival Scipio 'Africanus' learned such tricks. On one occasion, laying siege to a Carthaginian camp, Scipio sent an embassy to discuss terms. The slaves accompanying it, however, were trained centurions, with instructions to check out the camp's design, sentry rosters and so on, while terms were being discussed. Thus informed, Scipio took the camp in a night attack.

ROMAN GRIT

The first three years of Hannibal's attack on Italy were the stuff of nightmares for the Romans: perhaps one in six adult males eligible to serve died on the battlefield. In the three major set-piece battles of 218–216 BC, Trebia probably saw about 18,000 casualties; at Lake Trasimene in June 217 BC the total was 15,000 with 10,000 taken prisoner; at Cannae in August 216 BC, 50,000 were killed, 4,500 captured and 17,000 surrendered (on the first day of the Somme, 1 July 1916, British losses amounted to 19,000 killed, 35,000 wounded and 7,000 missing). The elite, too, was badly hit: a third of the Senate was killed. But still Rome would not yield. Rome was like that. Winning a big battle outright usually brought a war to an end. Winning a big battle against the Romans guaranteed that the war would continue.

MASTER TACTICIAN

Hannibal was a master of battle tactics. First, he knew how important military intelligence was; second, he tried to ensure that he fought his battles in locations he had chosen, at the time he had chosen; third, when it came to battle, he knew the importance of surprise and the unexpected (he was a highly imaginative military thinker); and, finally, he knew how to exploit the strengths of the whole army, especially in combining infantry with cavalry. This combination of careful advanced preparation, surprise and flexibility left the Romans baffled. Their idea of battle was immediate contact with the enemy, head down and attack them. It took many defeats before they learned the lesson.

MASTER OF PSYCHOLOGY

Human intelligence (HUMINT is the modern acronym) is one of the keys to success in warfare, and Hannibal had informants in Rome and every Roman camp. He took great care to understand the mindset of the Roman generals he came up against. He knew that Flaminius, for example, though ignorant of the arts of war, was a good showman who thought himself unbeatable. Hannibal therefore concluded that he could easily be lured into a trap – as proved to be the case at Trasimene. Polybius summed up as follows:

> There is nothing a general should value more than knowledge of his opponents' principles and character . . . rashness, excessive audacity, blind impetuosity, vanity, foolish ambition – all can be easily exploited . . . such a general will fall easy prey to all kinds of trickery . . . So the general who knows his enemy's precise weak spot and exploits it is most likely to secure a decisive victory.

FABIUS SAVES THE DAY – EVENTUALLY

Knowing your enemy – what he can and cannot do – is a basic military maxim. It took Rome some time to work out that Hannibal was no ordinary general, and that radically different tactics were required to deal with him. After the disaster at Trasimene, Quintus Fabius Maximus, nicknamed *Verrucosus* ('full of verrucas'), became dictator and put in place the much-needed new policy – one of attrition, not open conflict.

The idea was to hound Hannibal's army, following it every step of the way: skirmishing and cutting it off from supplies (what Romans later called 'kicking the enemy in the stomach'), but always refusing battle, however much Hannibal invited it. The Romans, however, had still not learned their lesson. After nearly a year of this, Fabius was overruled, and in 216 BC Rome's gung-ho party took to the field against Hannibal at Cannae with what they thought of as an invincible force of 120,000. It was massacred. The message now finally sank in, and from then on Fabius' policy was followed. His nickname became the rather less disagreeable *Cunctator* – 'Delayer'.

HANNIBAL'S WEAKNESS?

After Cannae, we are told, Maharbal, Hannibal's master of the cavalry, urged him to march immediately on Rome, promising that within five days they would be dining in the Capitol. Hannibal appreciated Maharbal's enthusiasm, but asked for time to think about it. Maharbal famously replied: *vincere scis, Hannibal, victoria uti nescis* ('You know how to win, Hannibal; you do not know how to use your victory'). Livy added, 'That day's delay is generally credited with being the salvation of Rome and its empire.'

NICE VS. NASTY

To win round the locals, Hannibal made a point of treating Italians generously in defeat. This policy and his early military success persuaded many to join him. But when he moved on to his next target, Fabius was waiting to follow up and make it quite clear to the now defenceless defectors their punishment for disloyalty to Rome:

executions, enslavement, destruction of crops, trees, livestock, farm buildings and equipment, and confiscation of land, turning it into *ager publicus* (publicly owned land) for Roman use. Capua, for example, lost all of its territory and autonomy. By contrast, the loyal were well rewarded. Two could play at that game.

ARCHIMEDES SCREWED

In the Second Punic War Syracuse, theoretically a Roman province, sided with Carthage. When Rome finally took Syracuse (*c.* 211 BC), a Roman soldier came across one of the world's most brilliant mathematicians: Archimedes, who had lived there most of his life, hard at work. He was credited with inventing all sorts of (largely impossible) weapons for use against the Romans – huge catapults or cranes to lift enemy ships out of the water or concave mirrors to set fire to them, and so on – but at this time he was sketching a geometrical diagram of some sort in a sand tray or in sand on the ground (so much cheaper than ink and papyrus). When a Roman soldier confronted him, Archimedes, without looking up, ordered the man not to ruin his diagram. The soldier killed him. Educated Romans had a very high regard for Greek intellectuals, so the Roman general Marcellus, mortified at what had happened, made sure that Archimedes received a grand burial.

Much later, Cicero tells us that he looked for Archimedes' tomb in Syracuse (p. 157) and found it only after a long search. On it was a model: a ball dropped into a cylinder that perfectly enclosed it. Archimedes proved that the sphere had two-thirds of the volume and surface area of the cylinder – the calculation of which he was most proud. The monument no longer survives.

AUCTION IN ROME

In 211 BC Hannibal marched on Rome and camped outside its walls in an attempt to draw the Roman army away from its siege of Capua. Tradition has it that the Romans at the time were holding an auction of land outside Rome – including the land on which Hannibal's army was currently encamped. Far from being driven down in value, it sold for the expected price! When Hannibal heard of this, he was so outraged by the Romans' conceit that he held an auction among his own troops. The winners were to own the rights to the money-lending operations based around the Roman Forum, when he captured Rome. When . . . Incidentally, his diversionary tactic failed, and the Romans took Capua.

BRING ME THE HEAD OF HASDRUBAL

In 207 BC Hannibal's brother Hasdrubal finally managed to evade Scipio's clutches in Spain (p. 86) to bring reinforcements to Hannibal. By now the Romans were almost at the end of their resources. But they made one last, desperate heave. Mobilizing massively yet again, they had a lucky break. They intercepted dispatch riders sent by Hasdrubal and learned that he intended to link up with Hannibal at the river Metaurus. The two Roman armies dashed to that point. The double bugle call from the Roman camp told Hasdrubal the Roman armies had united. Outnumbered, he tried to escape by night to join forces with his brother. The army lost its way in the dark, and Hasdrubal died fighting, along with almost all his men. The following day his head was thrown into Hannibal's camp. The game was up.

SPANISH SILVER

Hannibal's family (the Barcas) had originally moved into Spain to get their hands on its fabulous mineral wealth, especially silver and iron. Indeed, a Greek author claimed that rivers of silver ore streamed down the mountains during forest fires. Phoenicians had been exploiting this for centuries from the magnificent Spanish harbour of Cadiz (ancient Gades); indeed, huge smelting furnaces have been uncovered at the port of Huelva (north of Cadiz), producing almost industrial quantities of metal ingots.

When the Barcas moved in they developed new production methods. Slaves working in dreadful conditions did the manual labour; new technology pumped water out of the shafts. The rock was crushed in running water and then sieved several times to get out the ore. This was then heated up in a kiln to separate the silver from the lead and stones. By Roman times, some 40,000 slaves worked these mines, producing around five tons (5.08 tonnes) of silver a day; even so, it barely covered the cost of pacifying the region. War was as expensive then as it is now. At Rio Tinto, some 6.7 million tons (6.8 million tonnes) of mainly silver slag date from that period. The result of all this metalworking here and across the Empire is that levels of pollution during the Roman period, uncovered in Greenland's ice cores, were unmatched until the nineteenth and twentieth centuries.

SLAVING IN MINES

The historian Diodorus wrote of working in mines in Egypt:

> The kings condemn to the mines all criminals and prisoners of
> war . . . They work unceasingly – a great multitude, all bound

in chains – both night and day, with no respite and cut off from all means of escape . . . The operations are under the charge of a skilled worker who picks out the gold-bearing rock and directs the labourers to it . . . the physically strong break the rock with iron hammers, applying no skill to the task, but only force, cutting tunnels through the rock wherever the gold may lead. Working in darkness as they do . . . they carry lamps on their foreheads . . . they throw the blocks of stone on the ground as they cut them, and they labour ceaselessly beneath the sternness and blows of the overseer. The boys . . . go in through the tunnels into the galleries formed by the removal of the rock and take out the pieces. The men over 30 years old take this stone from them and pound it with iron pestles; then the women and older men take it and grind the stone in mills to the consistency of flour. And since no opportunity is afforded them to look after themselves, and they have no clothes to cover their nakedness, no one can look upon the unfortunate wretches without feeling pity for them . . . They labour without respite . . . until through ill-treatment they die in the midst of their tortures.

HOW DID THE ROMANS BEAT HANNIBAL?

When Hannibal finally left Italy for Carthage in 203 BC, he boasted of destroying 400 towns and killing 300,000 Italians. How, then, did Rome come out on top? Rome's fleet dominated the Italian coastlines and held Sicily and Sardinia, vital stopping-off points between Africa and Italy (which is why Hannibal went via the Alps in the first place). Carthage, consequently, could not resupply Hannibal with troops from Spain or

Africa. It was essential, therefore, that he win over local Italians, and he made a point of treating them well.

But Hannibal needed to break his enemy militarily, and though he came close to doing so, Rome would not be defeated. After Cannae in 216 BC, for example, not merely did the Romans immediately raise a new army, but they also reinforced their army in Spain. Further, Fabius' manner of dealing with traitors had proved effective (p. 96). Finally, the Scipios in Spain – especially Africanus – learned tactics from Hannibal and, applying them brilliantly, ensured that Spain would eventually be theirs. In the end it was sheer Roman determination and manpower that did it: Italy was theirs, given them by the gods, and no one would take it from them. Sons of Mars indeed (p. 5).

EXPLOITING THE LAND

After the defeat of Hannibal there was even more 'public land' available for Rome to use, especially in the south. Naturally, the rich were always keen to get their hands on it. So a theoretical limit was put on how much any one citizen could hold – 500 *iugera* (325 acres (131 hectares); say 185 football pitches). But this was never enforced, and over time many families – especially senatorial ones – won control of far more. It was to cause major problems for Rome's poor (p. 118).

ROMAN MEMORIES

If you wanted to be a real Roman, you had to know about Hannibal. He helped the Romans understand themselves – and he became a key figure in Roman historical memory. So there were three statues of him in Rome. At antique markets, it always raised the price to say that Hannibal had owned the item for sale. True, Hannibal ended up as part of someone else's story – the 'other man' in the Scipio Africanus legend – rather as we think of Rommel as part of Montgomery's story and Napoleon as part of Wellington's. But as a later Scipio (Aemilianus) once observed, Carthage was the whetstone of the Romans – it kept them sharp.

THE DEATH OF HANNIBAL

One version of Hannibal's death in 182 BC goes as follows. Some ambassadors from King Prusias of Bithynia (north-west Turkey) were in Rome, and one of them remarked over dinner that Hannibal was in Bithynia. The Roman Senate immediately sent an embassy to Prusias, demanding to know Hannibal's whereabouts. Prusias, aware of the laws of hospitality, did not tell them, but said they would easily find him if they searched – which they did, in a castle designed with exits all around, in order to offer the best chance of escape. The Romans surrounded it.

When a slave on watch from the castle reported what was happening, Hannibal asked if every exit from the castle had been covered. Learning that he was completely surrounded, as a historical source for this story says, 'he realized this was no accident, but that they were after him, and he could cling on no longer. Not wanting to put his life at anyone else's disposal, he took the phial of poison he always kept with him and, calling up his ancient valour, drained it dry.'

RESTRAINING THE POWERFUL

It is a law of human nature that the more one attempts to hold people back, the harder they will try to find ways around the restrictions. The

Punic War had given certain talented individuals the chance to shine with almost supernatural glory. Scipio Africanus, for example, had been given proconsular *imperium* in Spain, and then held a string of consulships and proconsulships from 205 to 201 (a 'proconsul' was a Roman general who was not actually a consul, but had been granted consular *imperium*). This was resented by those who felt they were owed a share of the glory. So in 180 BC the *lex Villia annalis* was passed. This ruled that anyone who wanted to be consul had to have held the posts of *quaestor* (minimum age about 25), *aedile* (36), *praetor* (39) and consul (42), with two years between each post. Further, in 172 BC it was decreed that *both* consuls could be plebeians; and *c.* 151 BC a law was passed that no one could be consul more than once.

It didn't work. Whatever the law said, voters might in certain situations want X to lead them rather than Y. Once X, for example, had been appointed consul several times on the trot, the precedent was established, and others could take advantage of it. This exploitation of the spirit of the law was to become more and more common, with disastrous consequences (p. 128).

ROME AND GREECE

Rome had been on nodding acquaintance with Greeks and their culture for hundreds of years, but it was only during the third century BC that they came to see just what Greeks had achieved, especially in literature, philosophy, art and architecture. In 240 BC Livius Andronicus, a 'half-Greek' freed slave from Tarentum, was said to have been the first person to compose Greek-style poems in Latin, including tragedies, comedies and a translation into Latin of Homer's *Odyssey*. This was to be the start of a hugely influential and fruitful Roman 'love affair' with Greek culture. As the later Roman poet Horace famously said:

> *Graecia capta ferum victorem cepit, et artes*
> *intulit agresti Latio.*
> Captured Greece took captive its savage victor and
> introduced culture to rustic Latium.

Greek philosophers, playwrights, teachers, doctors, poets and craftsmen arrived in Rome, as did Greek art. New styles of building – basilicas and porticos – appeared; street paving was widely used from 174 BC; fine stone-like marble and travertine also began to make an appearance. Luxury indeed: but was it corrupting, too, as many Romans argued? It was a massive cultural and artistic revolution for this tribe of fighting farmers. Soon the sons of the elite were being educated in Greek; Greeks designed and decorated buildings in Rome and Italy; Romans dressed as Greeks and held Greek-style drinking parties (*symposia*). But that does not mean they liked or admired Greeks. One can admire a Toyota without feeling compelled to idolize the Japanese. At the same time, the poor were also flooding into a flourishing Rome, looking for work of any sort – construction, street trading, sex-working and so on. Presumably they could survive, but for many it must have been an existence always on the edge.

ART COLLECTING AND THE 'WORK OF ART'

Romans had been bringing cult statues back to Rome for a long time, to dedicate as thank-offerings in temples (they removed 2,000 from Etruscan Volsinii in 264 BC). But the game changed after they went to Greek-dominated Sicily and Tarentum in southern Italy. When Marcellus sacked Syracuse in 211 BC (p. 97) he brought back to Rome Greek art of a quality and a quantity that staggered the Romans and began a revolution in Roman aesthetic sensibility. The historian Plutarch says of that defining moment:

> Marcellus was at length recalled by the people of Rome to the immediate war at home; and to illustrate his triumph and adorn the city, brought back with him a great number of the most beautiful ornaments of Syracuse. For, before that, Rome neither had, nor had seen, such fine and exquisite rarities; nor was any pleasure taken in graceful and elegant pieces of workmanship. Stuffed with barbarous arms and spoils stained with blood, and everywhere crowned with triumphal memorials and trophies of battle, Rome was no pleasant or delightful spectacle for the eyes of peaceful or refined spectators. [Some did not approve of this development, because] Marcellus had diverted to idleness, and trivial chat about sophisticated arts and artists, the common people who, bred in war and farming, had never tasted luxury and sloth.

Aemilius Paullus also returned from his conquests in Greece in 167 BC with 'statues, paintings and colossal images, carried on 250 chariots, for which a whole day was barely sufficient to appreciate'. When Corinth was sacked in 146 BC we are told of a flood of decorative 'Corinthian' bronzes that entered the Roman market and were collectors' items for years to come. So was born the concept of the 'work of art', removed from its original functional context to be displayed elsewhere for purely 'artistic' reasons.

AN END TO TAXES

Romans paid direct taxes on the value of their property, assessed at a variable rate every year (p. 68). But as the Empire expanded, more money flowed into Rome from the taxes it could levy on provincials; and this would continue for many centuries to come. The result was that in 167 BC, direct taxation of Romans came to an end. Why indeed should Romans pay taxes when others would do it for them? However, indirect taxes (e.g., harbour dues and so on) would continue.

CATO – THE OLD ROMAN WAY

The Elder Cato (234–149 BC, 'Cato the Censor') fought in the Second Punic War, served in Sardinia and Spain and became consul in 199 BC. Known for his enthusiasm for the courts, he composed speeches, wrote on farming (how best to make money out of it), warfare and morals – he virtually invented Latin prose – and became the epitome of the stern old Roman, frugal in life and severe on decadence. Never afraid to speak his mind, he made his name as censor (p. 74), reviewing the citizen rolls and being especially strict in removing those of dubious morals. Under him, luxury attracted high taxes, and state contracts benefited the state, not the contractor. When he visited Carthage in 153 BC, he became convinced it would be an eternal danger if not destroyed. He is said to have ended every speech with '*delenda est Carthago*': 'Carthage is to be wiped out.' In 146 BC, it was.

BACK STREET ROMANS C. 200 BC

The Roman comic poet Plautus here describes the shady sorts of character you would see hanging round the Roman Forum at this time:

You want a perjurer? Go to the Comitium. For a liar and braggart, try the temple of Cloacina; for rich, married crooks, it's the Basilica; you'll find whores there too – pretty shagged-out ones – and members of dining clubs in the fish market. In the lower Forum the respectable wealthy take a stroll; in the middle Forum, near the Canal, the flash set; by the Lacus Curtius there's the boastful, spiteful lot spreading their nasty, lying rumours about others, and liable to have the compliment repaid. For money-lenders, try the Old Shops; behind the temple of Castor are people you wouldn't touch with a bargepole; and in the Tuscan quarter the male prostitutes, offering their arses or propositioning yours.

Not much sign of Cato's noble Romans there.

MEN ON WOMEN

As with most things Roman, one may generalize only about the upper classes, for literature was composed by them and for them. The story was told of Cato that when he saw a young man coming out of a brothel he congratulated him for satisfying himself there rather than 'grinding away' at other men's wives; however, when Cato saw him visiting the brothel repeatedly, he reprimanded him for his lack of self-control. Prostitutes, then, and slaves were fair game for the Roman male, but free women, especially other men's wives, were dangerous prey. Only poets seem to have boasted regularly about sex with them. We have no idea what women made of this behaviour, though we hear of plenty of men complaining about their wives' watchfulness over them.

ACTING THE MAN

For the Roman male the question of sexual identity was wrapped up in what he was doing to the other person. The *real* man did nothing but penetrate, whether female or male, slave or free. If he was in any way penetrated, he was no man at all. So when one Valerius was accused by Suillius of corrupting his troops, having an affair with a society lady and being effeminate (i.e., on the receiving end), he erupted: 'Suillius, ask your sons: they will tell you I am man enough', the suggestion being that *he* had penetrated *them* – thus defending himself and humiliating them, and Suillius, with the same insult.

MEN ON MEN

Livy told a story of one Quinctius Flaminius, distinguished proconsul in Gaul, who summoned from Rome, at great expense, a young male prostitute. This boy had missed a big gladiatorial match to fulfil his professional obligations, so to make up for it Flaminius had a Gaul slaughtered at the dinner table. Cato, as censor, had Flaminius expelled from the Senate – *not* for his homosexuality, but because of his drunken destruction of a human life *over dinner*. It is telling that other versions replace the boy with a female prostitute, i.e., the gender of Flaminius' bought companion was simply not relevant.

Males, then, were fair game for the aristocratic Roman. The point is that Flaminius' activities in the bedroom did not (in the modern western style) proclaim a lifestyle choice or personal identity. The only issue was one of moderation, the proper self-control befitting a Roman. For later Christians, drawing on the Judaic tradition, the aim of all sexual activity had to be the production of legitimate children (a view exemplified by the Catholic Church's concerns about contraception). The consequence was that anything other than intercourse for that purpose, and within marriage, became immoral or taboo.

LIMELIGHT ON CONCRETE

The ancient world knew all about burning limestone to generate the white, caustic crystals known as quicklime. Mixed with water, this produced 'slaked' lime that could be mixed with sand or rubble to produce mortar or concrete. But this took a very long time to dry and would not dry under water. This all changed in the second century BC when some Romans mixed lime with a pink volcanic ash, assuming it was sand. But it was much better than that. It contained alumina and silica; and this mixed chemically with the lime to produce a cement that not only dried extremely quickly, but was very strong and durable and could even set under water. It is now known as *pozzuolana* cement, because it was discovered at Pozzuoli (Roman Puteoli, near Vesuvius). It revolutionized Roman building techniques. Incidentally, heated quicklime glows intensely and was used to light stage productions before electricity became available: hence being in the 'limelight'.

CARTHAGE ASSAULTED, NOT SALTED

When the Romans took Cato the Elder's advice and destroyed Carthage in 146 BC – the Carthaginian defence was absolutely heroic – it is not true that they sowed it with salt to make the land infertile (this is a twentieth-century invention). Much more sensibly, its land was divided up and distributed among local farmers and Italians. Nor did Carthage stay destroyed. It was far too valuable as a harbour. Julius Caesar started to rebuild it 100 years later (p. 206).

POLYBIUS ON THE ROMAN STATE

When the Romans were moving into Greece, the Greek historian Polybius (*c.* 200–118 BC), who came from a powerful diplomatic family, was taken to Rome in 167 BC as a hostage. There he made friends in high places and became a great admirer. In his 40-book history of Rome (only five survive in full) he analysed the reasons for the dynamic growth of Rome and put it down to its 'balanced constitution' – a combination of elements monarchic (consuls), oligarchic (Senate) and democratic (people's *comitia*). He summarized their three functions as follows: consuls with absolute military power; Senate in charge of expenditure and revenue; and the people passing laws and controlling the law courts (for capital offences) as well as elections to public office. He argued that neither could act without the broad consent of the others and, as a result, each felt an obligation to the other. Likewise, if one element tried to expand its powers, the others reined it in. The result was a sense of public and private cooperation across the system. This made the Romans capable of doing almost anything they wanted; furthermore, when danger threatened, it gave them almost unbreakable strength of purpose. Romans, too, were immensely proud of their republican system, believing it to be the key to their success. (For an alternative view, see p. 142.)

GOING FOR GROWTH

This is a period of astonishing change. About 320 BC the Romans controlled most of central Italy. By 268 BC they were masters of it all.

By 146 BC they had defeated well-established armies and monarchies in North Africa, Greece and Asia (west Turkey), established provinces there and elsewhere, and were a major – arguably the sole – Mediterranean superpower. The only parallel for this rate of expansion in the Mediterranean is to be found in the spread of Islam after the death of Muhammad in AD 632, which by AD 750 saw Islam established westwards across North Africa and into Spain, and to the east as far as the borders of India.

VI

146–78 BC

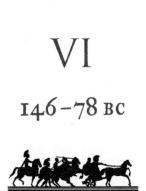

TIMELINE

133 BC   Tiberius Gracchus' land reforms

Scipio Aemilianus brings Spain under control

Attalus III bequeaths Asia/Pergamum to Rome

123 BC   Taxes in Asia to be collected by *publicani*

111 BC   Jugurtha (North Africa) usurps power

109–101 BC   The rise of Marius

107 BC   Marius recruits from the poorest classes

106 BC   Marius defeats Jugurtha

101 BC   Marius defeats Germans

91–87 BC   Social War: citizenship for Italians

88–84 BC   Mithradates' 'Asiatic Vespers'; Sulla defeats him

83–81 BC   Sulla returns and defeats forces loyal to Marius' son

81–79 BC   Sulla dictator, then resigns

THE PROBLEM
WITH NO
SOLUTION

From the Gracchi to Sulla

Three big names dominate this climactic period. First, Tiberius Gracchus of the Scipio family. He realized there was a problem: the rich were exploiting the absence of soldiers on campaign to increase their land-holdings. So in 133 BC he used his position as Tribune of the plebeians to ignore the Senate's will and pass his bill for land redistribution *via the Plebeian Assembly*. It would change the rules of the political game for a hundred years. From now on, and for the most part, the term *optimates* was used of those who wanted to maintain control through the Senate, and *populares* of those who sought to win power through the Plebeian Assemblies. These were not parties (in our sense), but rather two basic strategies for gaining and holding on to power. Ambitious members of the ruling classes opted, generally, for one or the other.

Second, Marius, an ambitious *popularis* general. He began to build up his army from anyone who wanted to join, and armed them himself – it was the germ of the *idea* of an army loyal primarily to its general, rather than to the state. With this army he defeated the African rebel Jugurtha in 106 BC and then a dangerous invading force of Germans in 101 BC. He also broke all the rules by being consul every year from 104 BC to 101 BC, and seven times in all.

Third, Sulla, another ambitious politician and general, but an *optimate*, determined to use *his* army to restore proper senatorial control – and he did so by launching a bloody civil war against Marius. This was the first time an army had been used by a Roman for personal ends. Sulla succeeded, made himself dictator in 81 BC and retired before dying in 78 BC. His reforms included strengthening the Senate and weakening the powers of Tribunes of the plebeians.

But nothing had been solved. Power could now be won by anyone with money and an army at their back. The clash between the *popularis* supporters of Marius and the pro-senatorial *optimate* supporters of Sulla would set the scene for more big beasts like Pompey and Caesar – and bring the Republic to an end.

These developments all took place within the context of big social and military upheavals. Alongside the general problem of debt and dividing up land more fairly, the soldiers now demanded, as the price of their loyalty to the general, that they retire with a piece of land as their 'pension' – and they expected their generals to provide it.

Further, Italians who had fought alongside Romans against Hannibal, and again in the East, started to demand equal political rights. In 91 BC it came to war (the Social War), which Sulla settled (against Marius), yielding to the Italians' demands. According to census figures, the rise in the number of Roman citizens went from *c.* 320,000 around 150 BC to *c.* 910,000 soon after the Social War.

On the foreign front, war against tribes in Spain continued, exacerbated for the Romans by the mountainous terrain in which it was fought. It was finally ended by Scipio Aemilianus in 133 BC and most of Spain was now under Roman control. In Numidia in North Africa, Jugurtha slaughtered the pro-Roman ruling family and in 111 BC Rome retaliated. Amid rumours of bribery, this conflict achieved nothing, until Marius was sent to sort it out, returning in time to deal with a Germanic invasion. Trouble also flared in the East: Mithradates, king of Pontus (north Turkey), wanted to drive out all Romans from Asia. Sulla, consul in 88 BC, was sent to deal with him – leaving Marius to seize power in Rome – but foolishly he allowed Mithradates to live.

In 83 BC Sulla returned to fight his way into Rome against Marius' forces and make himself dictator. Among his lieutenants was a promising young man. His name? Pompey. As dictator, Sulla removed the property of his enemies (and sometimes had them murdered). One of them was, not unnaturally, a nephew of Marius. His name? Julius Caesar.

SOLDIERS AND THE LAND

Romans lived in extended families. If a father and his sons were soldiering abroad for years on end, as was now beginning to happen, it made maintaining their land – the source of their subsistence – extremely difficult. If the family had to borrow its way out of trouble, debt could ensue and their land be seized by the local wealthy landowner, to be farmed cheaply by slaves. The rich could gobble up a lot of land that way because of the booty that such families, especially senatorial ones, had accrued during Rome's expansion. Further, the population was growing. So the old land problems were back. Hence Tiberius' proposals in 133 BC: to enforce the original limit of 325 acres per family (131 hectares; see p. 101), plus an additional 150 acres (61 hectares) per son, and distribute the rest in 14-acre (5.6-hectare) plots among the poor. A commission was set to work, but Tiberius was murdered by a mob of senators and their friends before he could reap the political benefits.

LEGAL VIOLENCE

Given the scope of Roman law (see p. 346), it seems remarkable that the flagrant murder of a politician – even the the assassination of Julius Caesar – did not result in any legal action (indeed, having murdered Caesar (see p. 180), Brutus and co. then dined with Antony to discuss the matter, and the Senate agreed an amnesty!). The reason is that (unlike in our world) there were no police acting on behalf of the state, and the state prosecuted no one. All prosecutions were brought by private individuals. So the question had nothing to do with 'the public good': the question was whether a prosecution was worth it for the person bringing it: what was in it for him, and what were his chances of winning? In high political circles that was a political, not a moral, question. Further, at the street level, cases would probably be settled not by a jury but by a local bigwig called in to reach a conclusion. Imagine the possible consequences for you and your family of bringing a case against the intimidating leader of (say) a gang of thugs who had assaulted you – especially as it took two to make a fight, and the law basically agreed that force could be met with force, no questions asked.

EXPLOITING PLEBEIAN POWER

Over the years since the foundation of the Republic in 509 BC, more and more plebeian families had gained the consulship and become *nobiles* (see p. 103). But Plebeian Assemblies were now able to pass laws binding on all the people, whatever the Senate thought about it; and the position of *Tribunus* of the plebeians (see p. 70) was a very influential one. Here, then, was a way to wield power for any ex-plebeian noble; become Tribune of the plebeians and do what you want to do via the Plebeian Assembly. This was the constitutional route taken by Tiberius Gracchus.

SOLDIER POWER

The connection between plebeians and power – and therefore a further assault on traditional senatorial politics – was strengthened in 107 BC when Marius started recruiting into his army from the poorest classes. Lacking the resources to buy the gear, they were not, technically, allowed to serve at all, except in emergencies, when the state armed them (p. 66). But now Marius chose to recruit them quite openly and then to arm them *himself*. Further, Marius *kept* the men in arms, offering them a 'pension' of money and land after 16 years' service, and therefore began the process by which soldiering would eventually become a full-time career. An army committed not to the interests of the state but to their own interests, in the name of the man leading them, opened the way for the idea of someone using such an army to advance his own cause by force. Here, then, was another way in which a politician could work himself into a position of power – by raising a personal army, outside state control and directed against his rivals. The precedent had been established, intentionally or not. Where was Polybius' 'balance of powers' now (p. 110)? Incidentally, in 104 BC Marius abandoned four of the animals traditionally displayed on military ensigns or standards (wolf, minotaur, horse and boar) in favour of the fifth – the eagle.

CORN DOLE

Handouts of grain – introduced by Tiberius' brother Gaius Gracchus – now became a common feature of life in Rome, at first at minimum cost, and then for free. They went only to those who had a fixed address in Rome, but fraud was common. Cicero complained that men working on his villa twelve miles (19 km) from Rome had left it to claim their corn ration in the city. The real problem was registering those qualified for it. In 46 BC Julius Caesar revised the list of claimants, district by district. Illegal claimants were struck off. The number of recipients dropped from around 320,000 to 150,000. Once your name was on the roll, however, you 'owned' it and could bequeath or sell it, if you chose. So it guaranteed an income. In the later Empire, olive oil, wine and meat were added to the benefits of living in Rome.

ROAD-THRILL

Tiberius' brother Gaius was a great road builder. Here Plutarch describes his achievement:

> His most especial exertions were given to constructing the roads, which he was careful to make beautiful and pleasant, as well as convenient. They were planned across the fields, exactly in a straight line, partly paved with dressed stone, and partly laid with

tamped-down gravel. When he met with any valleys or deep watercourses crossing the line of the road, he either filled them up with rubbish, or built bridges over them, all levelled off so that the work presented a beautiful, symmetrical appearance. Besides this, he had the roads measured in Romans miles, and erected stone pillars to mark the distances. He also set up other stones at shorter intervals on both sides of the road, so that horsemen should be able to mount from them without help.

Incidentally, the Roman mile was 1,000 paces, *mille passus*. Our 'mile' derives from the *mille* ('1,000') part.

ROMAN ROADS

Rome constructed 272 trunk roads, covering 53,000 miles (85,000 km) across the Empire, and all of them (of course) 'led to Rome': an expression of Rome's control over the Empire's landscape – river, marsh, desert and mountain alike – and populace. Designated public roads were constructed at state expense, sometimes with help from local landowners. Other roads were public-private partnerships, funded by a combination of state subsidy, imperial donation and local financing from townships and roadside inhabitants. Their original purpose was primarily to provide a firm surface for the army, its wheeled vehicles and the imperial messenger service on horseback. But roads also sped cultural and economic exchange. Further, distances *en route* were signposted only *to* Rome, but not *from* it, so as you approached Rome they got shorter, and as you left Rome, longer – a brilliant way of emphasizing Rome's centrality.

KNOWING WHO'S BOSS

Many foreign kings, aware of Rome's growing power, realized it was sensible to keep Rome onside. In the second century BC Pergamum's king Attalus II wrote as follows:

> It became apparent that to start something without the Romans involved considerable danger. For in the event of success we would become objects of envy, detraction and suspicion, while failure would be a simple disaster, because the Romans would be pleased – not sympathetic – at our plight, since we had started something without them . . . I decided, therefore, to keep Rome fully in contact with what was at stake.

His son Attalus III, in fact, went one better. When he died in 133 BC he bequeathed his whole kingdom to a surprised Rome. It became the province of Asia and was Rome's entrée into the Hellenized world of the East – 'Hellenized' because Alexander the Great had spread Greek culture throughout the region during his revenge attacks on Persia (334– 329 BC) and the Greek generals he had left in charge turned themselves into kings when he died.

BIDDING TO BECOME A PUBLICAN – AND SINNER?

Rome did not have what we think of as a civil service. There were no such things as government offices or Whitehall. All government services – construction, repair of public buildings and so on – were put

THE PROBLEM WITH NO SOLUTION 123

out for tender under public contract. Thus wars were fought, troops fed, roads built and mines worked on the back of service contracts offered out to hopeful bidders; and the right to gather dues from harbours and toll-stations was also sold off. Wealthy contractors, known as *publicani*, formed themselves into consortia (*societates*) to win the tenders. When in 123 BC Gaius Gracchus won the agreement for the taxes in Asia to be collected by these consortia, he proposed that the contracts should last for five years. The censors (p. 74) worked out how much tax that should raise for the state and invited bids for the privilege of collecting it; the winner would pay all five years' worth up front. Obviously, only a consortium could do that. The great advantage to Rome was that it got its money all at once, in advance, without any need for a huge state-run collection service. The total take might have been less than was theoretically possible, since the *publicani* had to be allowed their cut, but Rome wisely preferred its bird in the hand.

Inevitably, *publicani* were charged with corruption and extortion, but for the most part only when they worked hand-in-hand with corrupt provincial governors on the make themselves. Under the Empire, however, they were phased out, and the unpopular job was left to local bigwigs: *they* could take the blame, and make up any shortfall in the take!

NO NATIONAL DEBT FOR ROME

In 1816 the American president Thomas Jefferson argued that the banking system was 'more dangerous than standing armies . . . the principle of spending money to be paid by posterity, under the name of funding, is but swindling futurity on a grand scale'. There was no such swindling in the ancient world, because minted coin (*c*. 300 BC) was the sole monetary instrument. Second, it was worth its weight: it did not simply represent symbolic value, as it does today. Third, there was no machinery for creating credit. So in the innocent days before banks, you could spend only what you had, and borrow only against existing assets (see below). As a result, if Rome ran short there was no question of public borrowing or running to international banking consortia for a bail out. For example, in 216 BC Rome exhausted its funds during the war against Hannibal. It asked for money and wheat from an ally, Hieron, king of Syracuse; it deferred payments to those who had won contracts to supply the army in Spain and to carry out building works; it sold off assets; it equipped its fleet through a special tax on the rich; and it appealed for contributions. So there was no such thing as 'national debt' hanging over Rome.

BANKING ON BORROWING

Individuals who ran short of money could do a credit deal with moneylenders against the value of existing assets. This money was for immediate use. There was no concept of individuals using it to further economic investment, for example. We have a typical credit note from the time of emperor Tiberius:

> 18 June, AD 37. I, Novius, have written that I have received a loan from Hessucus. I am therefore in debt to the sum of 10,000 *ss*, which I will return on request and for good reason, as stipulated between Hessucus and me, Novius, and I hereby formally obligate myself. For the 10,000 *ss*, I have given as collateral . . .

On the next page the document lists Novius' collateral goods: 7,000 *modii* (over 40 tons or 40.6 tonnes) of Alexandrian grain and 4,000 *modii* (25 tons or 25.4 tonnes) of chickpeas, lentils and spelt contained in 200 sacks, deposited in the public granaries of Puteoli. True wealth was in agriculture.

RICH DUTY

Personal financial deals between friends were a matter of honour, and wealthy aristocrats felt obliged to make them when friends were in need. Transactions were marked by the absence of securities, interest or even written agreements, because that implied distrust. In his *On Duties*, Cicero distinguished two categories of givers: those who squandered their money on public banquets, food doles, gladiatorial shows and wild-beast fights (to gain political credit), and those who took over friends' debts, helped in providing dowries for their daughters or assisted them in acquiring property. Crassus, whose total wealth exceeded that of Rome's annual revenues, funded Caesar throughout his early spendthrift career. Caesar conquered Gaul in the hope of making gazillions and paying off his debts.

MATTERS OF LITTLE INTEREST, OR NONE

Today we take it for granted that loans involve paying interest. Romans knew about interest, though (strangely) it is never mentioned in private credit transactions. However, other financial conditions could be attached. Here Novius (see p. 124) did another deal with Hessucus. Novius had received a loan of 1250 *ss*, which he had to repay on 1 November. He writes: 'If on that day I do not respect my obligation, not only must I be considered to have perjured myself, but as penalty I must pay 20 *ss* for every day of delayed payment.'

STATUS GAMES: FROM SLAVE TO FINANCIER

Who were these moneylenders? Novius was dealing with Hessucus, who was, in fact, a slave working on behalf of a man called Primianus. Who was Primianus? He *had* been a slave belonging to the emperor Tiberius, but he was eventually freed. He was now in the business of moneylending. Presumably Primianus had dealt with finances as an imperial slave, and was now exploiting his old contacts. But as a freedman, he owed his first duty to serve his old master, the emperor. So for his other clients he used Hessucus, a Greek slave who was presumably just as financially astute. The document tells us that Hessucus was, in fact, one of Tiberius' slaves, presumably lent to Primianus for the purpose. Wheels within wheels, emperor, slave and freedman working in consort (see p. 147 on slavery).

COIN OR CREDIT?

If money equals coins, how on earth did Cicero buy a house worth 3.5 million *ss*? Did he present the seller with 3.5 tons of silver coin? How were the legions in various provinces around the Empire paid? How did the citizens of Nicomedia in Asia Minor transfer the 3,318,000 *ss* they spent on building an aqueduct? (It was abandoned, unfinished, then demolished.) Did they carry the money about in carts? Who guarded it? Were they never ambushed? Furthermore, shipwrecked trading vessels rarely have any coins on board. We know that in 48 or 46 BC the Romans started minting gold coins, which would have made transfers slightly less cumbersome. These coins were certainly popular – in Pompeii (destroyed AD 79) 69 per cent of the coins found are gold. However, it seems that credit was also available, and we hear frequently of the use of credit notes. This was surely the only way to do big business, provided one's credit was good. This must have had some effect on the total money supply, but how much and with what consequences it is impossible to judge.

TOFFWATCH

It is not unknown for people who have made good today to claim virtue for being 'working class' and to contrast their honest endeavour with inherited wealth and privilege. The soldier Marius felt much the same. Here the Roman historian Sallust (who composed a history of the war against Jugurtha) puts into Marius' mouth emotional words addressed to a public meeting in 107 BC, when he had gathered his army to take on Jugurtha:

Compare me, the 'new' man, with these high and mighty ones. What they know only from hearsay or reading, I have seen with my own eyes or done with my own hands. What they have learned from books, I have learned on the battlefield. It is for you to judge whether words or deeds are more to the point . . . The truth is that ancestral glory is like a torch that sheds a revealing light both on a man's virtues and on his faults. I admit, citizens, that I have nothing of this kind; but I have something much more glorious – deeds that I can claim are my own. The privilege *they* claim on the strength of other people's merits, they will not allow

> me in right of my own merits, just because I have no family
> portraits to show and am a newcomer to the nobility of office. Yet
> surely it is better to have ennobled oneself than to have disgraced a
> nobility that one has inherited . . . and I shall not have my soldiers
> go short, while I bathe in luxury, nor win my own glory and leave
> them all the toil. That is the proper way to lead fellow citizens;
> for to live in luxury oneself but subject one's army to rigorous
> discipline is to be a master of slaves, not a commander.

And so on. The People's General meets Tom Paine's 'no-ability nobility'.

But that is the rhetoric the 'new man' had to deploy: personal virtue versus the accumulated merits of the long-established noble families.

THE THREAT THAT NEVER WENT AWAY

Germanic and Celtic tribes from northern Europe regularly tried to migrate south into Italy. Their sack of Rome (386 BC: see p. 50) left a lasting mark on the Roman imagination. So there was panic when the Cimbri and Teutoni, who came from the Jutland peninsula (Denmark and German Schleswig-Holstein), appeared in southern Gaul and defeated Roman armies in 110 BC and then again in 105 BC. These Germanic tribes briefly turned west towards Spain – they clearly had no fixed destination in mind – but were driven out and moved back towards Italy. By now Marius had returned from the Jugurthan campaign in Africa. He had also won the consulship successively from 104 to 100 BC (theoretically against the rules: see p. 103), and defeated the Germans in battle in 101 BC. When Julius Caesar turned all Gaul into a Roman province in the 50s BC he never failed to boost his own image by magnifying his exploits against the northern menace, such was the terror these tribes induced. They were eventually to prove the undoing of the Western Roman Empire (p. 339).

IN TOUGH-GUY VEIN

Marius was renowned for his hardiness. His biographer Plutarch tells us that he was embarrassed by the ugly varicose veins in his legs and asked a surgeon to take them out. During this excruciating operation, Marius did not flinch or utter a sound. When the surgeon had finished one leg, he asked Marius if he should do the other. Marius inspected what had been done and replied, 'No. The improvement does not justify the pain.'

SPREADING CITIZENSHIP

Where did the Romans get their huge armies from? About half were Roman citizens and half Italian allies. As allies, Italians were obliged to serve in the Roman army, but they did not have the same rights as Roman citizens. 'Popularis' politicians – i.e., those, like Marius, keen to exploit the people's grievances – saw this as an opportunity to gain power by demanding equal rights for Italians. The result was much political violence and eventually, when the Italians did not get their way, civil war – or, as it is usually called, the Social (*socius*, 'ally') War. This was a dreadful moment in Rome's history, and the pattern would become all too familiar: Italians and Romans, who had fought alongside each other against Hannibal and in the East, now turned against each other. Rome suffered badly, but largely managed to bring the Social War to an end in 89 BC by granting citizenship to all Italians south of the river Po.

MITHRADATES VI

The northern coastal region of Turkey/Asia Minor (Pontus) was ruled by a Persian family, whose founder king was Mithradates I (306–266 BC). (The name means 'given by the god Mithra[s]'; 'Mithridates' is the Roman spelling.) Subsequent kings had struck up friendly relations with Rome – Mithradates V had supported Rome against Carthage – but the aggressive Mithradates VI (120–63 BC) had other ideas. Roman control over Greece and Asia was not popular. The *publicani* in particular took their pound of flesh in taxes (p. 123), and then some. Mithradates saw his chance.

THE 'ASIATIC VESPERS'

In 89 BC Mithradates took full advantage of Rome's entanglement in the Social War in Italy to move his troops into Asia Minor (Bithynia and Cappadocia) and then into Greece. In early 88 BC he took the final step. He wrote to all the non-Roman regional and city leaders, telling them to slaughter all Romans and Italians along with their wives, children and freedmen. They should throw out their bodies and leave them unburied. He offered to free slaves who killed or informed on their masters, and said he would share the property of the dead, half and half, with those who did the killing and informing. So it was done, and 80,000 were slaughtered. It guaranteed that any city that had perpetrated this outrage would now have to be in league with him against Rome.

(*Note*: The term 'Asiatic Vespers' is used to mark the parallel with the 'Sicilian Vespers' of Easter Tuesday (31 March) 1282, when Sicily rose up against Charles I of France, starting with the slaughter of 2,000 Frenchmen in Palermo. In all about 8,000 were massacred.)

LIBRARIES

Athens was the glory of ancient Greece, home of its greatest philosophers, playwrights, orators and historians in the 'Golden Age' of the fifth to fourth centuries BC. When Sulla took Athens in 86 BC (it was held by a pro-Mithradates tyrant) he got hold of a fantastic prize: Aristotle's library.

Personal libraries as we understand them were known in fifth-century BC Athens. The comedian Aristophanes mocks the tragedian Euripides for being an intellectual and a book (papyrus roll) collector. The West's first scholarly library was founded in Egyptian Alexandria in the third century BC by the Greek king Ptolemy (p. 122). Here papyrus rolls were kept, consulted and copied, though never lent out. Ptolemy wanted to outdo Athens as the intellectual centre of the Mediterranean, and his wealth ensured that he did. Acquiring or copying texts went on at a phenomenal rate. Eventually the library in Alexandria held nearly 500,000 rolls.

One of its directors, Zenodotus, was the first person we know of to order books alphabetically; his successor Callimachus was the first to produce a detailed bibliography of all Greek literature – author, brief biography, works – along with its shelf-number, a vital reference tool. Other Greek kings got the idea, and rival scholarly libraries sprang up in Antioch and Pergamum, poaching the top directors. The Romans, thrilled by Greek culture (p. 104), keenly took on the idea of a library. Julius Caesar planned – but did not live to see – Rome's first (again non-lending) public library (39 BC). Emperors endowed them in large numbers, and by AD 350 there were 29 in Rome alone (many attached to public baths, the Roman equivalent of leisure centres). Lending libraries were an eighteenth-century invention, but public lending libraries were not created until the nineteenth century.

PAPYRUS

Papyrus (the origin of our word 'paper') was made from the stem of the papyrus plant. The main source of papyrus was Egypt. The inner pith, sticky and fibrous, was laid bare by stripping away the outer rind, then cut into thin strips of about 16 inches (40 cm) long. These were laid side by side with another layer on top at right angles. The two layers were then hammered together, mashing them into a single sheet. This was pressed and dried, producing a very flexible papyrus sheet. It was then rubbed down to produce a fine surface. Sheets were placed side by side, slightly overlapping, and glued together, all fibres parallel with the roll's length. That was the side that was written on. This made a roll from 10 to 22 feet long (20 sheets to a roll maximum, says Pliny). Various grades of paper existed in Roman times. The first grade came to be called 'Augustus', the second 'Livia' (his wife), the next 'hieratic' (sacred), and so on to the bog-standard 'emporitic' – scraps good enough for nothing but commercial documents.

ORGANIZING A PRIVATE LIBRARY

Since worms and damp did their worst on the vegetable papyrus, rolls constantly needed repairing; and in time the text would need copying onto new papyrus. The Greek scholar Tyrannio was one of Rome's top librarians. Cicero used him, and in 56 BC in a letter to his old friend Atticus, Cicero urged him to visit:

> You will see Tyrannio's wonderful organisation of my library
> . . . Could you send me a couple of your own library people too?
> Tyrannio could use them for gluing and other jobs. Tell them to
> bring some parchment for the tags.

Cicero was referring to gluing papyrus pages together to make the rolls, and sticking tags on the ends for identification.

Atticus had a fabulous, well-staffed library. Cicero frequently borrowed books from it for his own clerks to copy. The point is that – in the absence of printing, publishers and sometimes booksellers too, and with no system of royalties, let alone copyright – anyone who needed a book could only beg, borrow or steal a version from somewhere else, and get a slave to copy it. So the main job of the library, public or private, was to reproduce existing texts, whether to preserve a crumbling text or get one in the first place. It all meant a great deal to Cicero. As he commented on one occasion: 'Now that Tyrannio has arranged my book-rolls, the house has a soul.'

YOUR PROSCRIPTION IS READY

When the 'optimate' Sulla made himself dictator, the Senate voted him immunity from prosecution for any actions, past or future. He then set about dealing with his political enemies by 'proscribing' them. The Latin *proscribo* means 'I make a public announcement in writing', particularly to announce the sale of something, often the enforced sale of confiscated property. Sulla went further. He declared his enemies outlaws as well as confiscating their property. As a result they could be killed on the spot. Teams of soldiers went about this business in Rome and across Italy, dangling rewards in front of potential cooperators (including slaves), and threatening punishment on those helping the victims. Up to 4,000 people may have been targeted (the figures are disputed). One day the Senate, while being addressed by Sulla, expressed concern about the screams coming from outside. He suggested it would be quite a good idea to listen to *him*. One person who survived was the young 'popularis' Julius Caesar.

SYMPTOMS, NOT CAUSES

Sulla thought the way to solve the Republic's problems was to go back to the good old days: boost the Senate (he doubled numbers to 600) and severely restrict the powers of the plebeian Tribunes. He did this by legislating that all plebeian Tribune proposals had to be agreed by the Senate; he also barred ex-Tribunes from other magistracies (so there was no career path for them). He strictly enforced the age qualification for magistrates too (p. 103), and gave the Senate greater control over holders of *imperium* outside Italy (e.g., governors could not move troops out of a province without the Senate's agreement).

However, Sulla had been so ruthless in exercising murderous force to seize power that his supporters were unlikely to have the best interests of republicanism at heart. Further, his reforms did nothing to tackle the real problem – the use of personal armies by the powerful in their own interests. Sulla had also let Mithradates in Asia go free, and there was to be a lot more trouble from him. Nevertheless, Sulla did at least pull the state together again, if by brutal means. In doing so, however, he set the pattern for dictatorship, and later the Empire.

EARLY RETIREMENT

In 79 BC, to universal amazement, Sulla gave up the dictatorship. Plutarch tells us that he did it because – as Sulla revealed in his memoirs (finished two days before he died) – astrologers prophesied that 'after an honourable life, he ought to die at the peak of his good fortune'.

So he retired to his villa in the bay of Naples with a new young wife. There he hunted, fished, drank and spent time in the company of his artistic friends – the actors, harpists, ballet-dancers, comedians, female impersonators and other riff-raff of whom he had always been so fond. It was said that he dismissed his bodyguard and walked as a private citizen about the Forum, challenging anyone to hold him to account. Such a retirement was almost unheard of in the ancient world (compare Marius, who struggled on to the bitter end). Julius Caesar said of this decision 'Sulla did not know his ABC.' But Sulla was soon dead of a ghastly disease: ulcerated intestines, which, we are told, turned his flesh to worms.

ORACULAR CYNICISM

In his *On Divination*, Cicero defines oracles as 'the foreknowledge and foretelling of events that happen by chance'. He comes out firmly against them. First, he says the definition is illogical. If something happens 'by chance' it cannot, by definition, be predicted: otherwise it could not be said to have happened 'by chance'. If an event were truly to happen 'by chance', Cicero goes on, even the gods would not be able to predict it: so how could a diviner? So what if divination, then, means 'dealing with everything that is fated'? In that case, *divinatio* can hardly bring any advantages: for if something is fated it will happen, come what may. He gives the example of Julius Caesar, fated to die on the Ides of March 44 BC – and so it happened. Cicero ends by contrasting religion, which he associates with 'the knowledge of nature', with 'superstition, which must be torn up by the roots: for it is at your heels all the time, pursuing you at every twist and turn – when you listen to a prophet or an omen, offer sacrifice, watch the birds, consult an astrologer, see lightning. Since these signs are given all the time, no one who believes them can ever be at peace.'

VII

81–44 BC

TIMELINE

81–70 BC   Rise of Pompey: from triumphs to consul

81 BC   Sulla gives Pompey triumph

Julius Caesar, proscribed, leaves to fight in the East

80 BC   Pompeii becomes a Roman colony

73–72 BC   Pompey defeats Sertorius in Spain

73 BC   Spartacus leads slave revolt

71 BC   Pompey finishes off Spartacus: second triumph

70 BC   Pompey and Crassus consul

69 BC   Caesar elected *quaestor*

67 BC   Pompey sorts out the pirates

66–62 BC   Pompey conquers Mithradates and most of the East; third triumph

65 BC   Caesar elected *aedile*

63 BC   Cicero (consul) deals with rebellion of Catiline

61 BC   Pompey's fourth triumph

c. 60 BC   Poets Catullus and Lucretius at work

60 BC	Caesar, Pompey and Crassus' 'triumvirate'
60–49 BC	Pompey, Senate and Caesar in struggle for control of Rome
59 BC	Caesar consul; given Gaul as his province
c. 55 BC	Cornelius Nepos aligns Roman with Greek history
55–54 BC	Caesar's incursions into Britain
53 BC	Crassus killed on expedition to Parthia
51–50 BC	Cicero governor of Cilicia
49 BC	Caesar refused consulship; crosses Rubicon
49–46 BC	Civil war against Pompey
48 BC	Pompey murdered in Egypt
48–47 BC	Caesar trapped in Egypt: affair with Cleopatra
46 BC	Caesar mops up rest of Pompey's troops
45 BC	Caesar made dictator; rafts of legislation
44 BC	Caesar assassinated; Octavian his heir

THE END OF
A WORLD

Pompey and Caesar

This period is dominated by two big beasts: Pompey and Caesar. They used popular support and personal armies to get their way, sometimes involving the Senate, sometimes not. It was a case of whatever worked – for *them*.

Pompey's rise to power began when he used his father's private army to fight for Sulla against Marius' men. He was given a triumph by Sulla in 81 BC at the absurdly early age of 25. He was handed a second triumph for dealing with an anti-Sullan exile, Sertorius, who was causing trouble in Spain (73 BC), and then for finishing off the slave rebellion led by Spartacus (71 BC). Now a power in the land, he and the billionaire Crassus, who had done most of the hard work against Spartacus, were made consuls in 70 BC – Pompey well below age and never having held any magistracy!

Pompey's star rose yet higher in 67 BC when he sorted out the Mediterranean pirate gangs in three months, and from 66 BC when he dealt with Mithradates in the East, and then, off his own bat, brought most of it under Roman control. A third huge triumph in 62 BC followed, and Rome's income rocketed from around 200 million *ss* a year to 340 million *ss*. But trouble was looming: the Senate began to see Pompey as a threat – was he another potential dictator?

In Rome, meanwhile, the senator Catiline was building support for change among the debt-laden, landless poor. When he resorted to military force, the consul Cicero, in a series of brilliant speeches, characterized Catiline as an unprincipled, power-grabbing revolutionary, put down his army and executed (without trial) his leading allies (63 BC).

All this time a poor but ruthlessly brilliant young man was on the rise: Julius Caesar. A 'popularis', he lost all his money during Sulla's proscriptions (81 BC). For the next ten years he earned his spurs fighting against Mithradates in Asia Minor, then came back to work his way up the greasy pole in Rome. In 60 BC, while the Senate led by Cato the Younger tried desperately to impose its will, Pompey (with huge popular support), Crassus (the money) and Caesar (the brains) informally banded together to impose *their* will on Rome.

Caesar, made consul in 59 BC, was given a special command in Gaul, whose conquest he completed in 51 BC, with some incursions into Britain in 55 and 54 BC. Pompey took over Spain as governor, but stayed in Rome and got others to run it (quite unprecedented); Crassus took over Syria, but was killed on expedition there against Persia in 53 BC. It all raised the question: who controlled policy? Clearly not the Senate. The traditionalist Cicero, seeking a *concordia* between competing factions to solve Rome's problems, was appalled by these events.

In Caesar's absence the Senate won Pompey to their side. When Caesar's tenure in Gaul came to an end, he demanded the consulship of 49 BC so that he could leave Gaul safe in the knowledge that he could not be prosecuted when he returned. Pompey and the Senate refused. Caesar crossed the Rubicon with his army to enforce his claims. It was civil war – again.

Pompey, rightly fearful of Caesar's Gaul-hardened veterans, promptly abandoned Italy to raise an army in Greece and his old stamping ground, the East. Caesar defeated his army at Pharsalus in 48 BC and pursued Pompey to Egypt. Egyptians, after pondering whom to support, decapitated Pompey on the beach where he landed. The pursuing Caesar, trapped in a local dispute, became involved with Cleopatra. She knew exactly what she was doing: joining the 'master race'. Caesar established her on the Egyptian throne and left her with child when he finally departed in April 47 BC. By 46 BC he had mopped up the rest of Pompey's followers from all over the Mediterranean, and in February 44 BC he appointed himself dictator in perpetuity. Torrents of legislation followed, aimed at solving Rome's many problems, but Republicans, led by Brutus and Cassius, feared Caesar's ambition. He was assassinated a month later on the Ides of March 44 BC. So much for dictators. What next? The Republic restored?

THE COMPETITIVE LIFE

It was partly the intense competitiveness of Roman life that made Rome a power. Our best insight into it is given in a funeral oration. This was spoken by Quintus, the son of Lucius Caecilus Metellus, who founded one of the great noble houses of Rome and died in 221 BC. Metellus was a *pontifex*, twice consul, dictator, master of horse and *quindecimvir* (member of a group of 15) for the distribution of land; he was the first to lead elephants in a triumphal procession, during the First Punic War. In the funeral oration his son Quintus said:

> He achieved the ten greatest and best things, which wise men spend their whole lives seeking. He wished to be the first of warriors, the best of orators and the most valiant of commanders; to be in charge of the greatest affairs and held in the greatest honour; to possess supreme wisdom and be regarded as supreme in the Senate; to come to great wealth by honourable means; to leave many children; and to be the most distinguished person in the state. These things he achieved, and none but he achieved them since Rome was founded.

Admirable. But this desperate need to come out and stay on top by whatever means was also one of the reasons for the ultimate destruction of the Republic.

SMOKING OUT CORRUPTION

The Latin for 'electioneering' was *ambitio*, and its cognate *ambitus* meant 'bribery'. Since vote-winning was an honourable pastime, bribery did not automatically mean corruption. It meant doing favours by offering gifts for something in return, which could be interpreted to be in the public interest. Such a culture was at the heart of all social, political, legal and business relationships in the Roman world. It is not unknown in the modern either.

The general public also played the game, getting to the head of the queue by greasing palms; some would say today's private medicine and education are the same sort of thing. But officials were advised to show restraint: the emperor Caracalla (AD 198–217) advised them not to take 'everything, nor every time, nor from every one'. Likewise, trying to win bribes by exaggerating one's influence could land one in hot water – or worse. When Severus Alexander (Roman emperor AD 222–35) heard that Verconius Turinus was making vast sums by claiming he had Severus' ear, the emperor set up a hoax petitioner to expose him. Verconius was caught red-handed and tied to a stake in the Forum; a fire of straw and wet logs was then constructed around him. There he was suffocated to death by the smoke, while the herald cried 'He who sold smoke is punished by smoke.'

POMPEIVS MAGNVS: POMPEY THE GREAT, 106–48 BC

The career of the young Pompey illustrates perfectly the political importance of having an army at your back and keeping it with you in a series of successful campaigns. In 89 BC, at the tender age of 17, Pompey had served in his father's army against rebel Italians in the Social War; in 81 BC, aged 25, after his first full triumph granted by Sulla, he modestly took the cognomen *Magnus*, 'the Great', in imitation of Alexander. Nobody had ever celebrated a full triumph at so absurdly young an age. It was a sign of things to come. After many other military successes Pompey was made consul for the first time in 70 BC – at the tender age of 36, never having been *aedile*, *quaestor* or *praetor*, and six years under age. A friend had to write him brief notes on senatorial procedure! That is what an army could do for you.

THE ROMAN TRIUMPH

Romans loved a good triumph: our sources inform us of some 320. The sight of captives, exotic foreign leaders, wagonfuls of booty and money, and soldiers on parade, marching through the streets, confirmed everything that Romans believed about the power of Rome and its right to conquer the world, bringing people and products back for them to enjoy (p. 306). Triumphs attracted crowds of thousands; we hear of Romans crushed to death in the excitement.

But it is very difficult to generalize about triumphs. Some descriptions mention a slave standing behind the victorious general, telling him to remember he is mortal; others depictions show the goddess Victory, and there are references to the triumphant general being dressed as Jupiter. However, in AD 118 when Trajan was celebrating his triumph over the Parthians, he was replaced by a dummy. He had to be. He was dead.

As for the route of these triumphs, all we can say for certain is that they started outside the city's sacred boundary and ended at the temple of Jupiter Optimus Maximus on the Capitoline Hill (p. 37). Things did not always go smoothly. At Pompey's first triumph in 81 BC he decided to hitch his chariot to elephants instead of horses. They could not squeeze through one of the gates. He reversed and tried again, without success. So he had to hang about until some horses were found.

Nevertheless, the top Romans yearned to be granted a triumph. In 51 BC a friend of Cicero, a governor of Cilicia (south-eastern Turkey), wrote to him:

> If only we could find exactly the sort of war that fitted the strength of our forces, and we did what was necessary for glory and a

triumph, without facing a really dangerous engagement – that would be the ideal situation!

Thinkers, however, used triumphs to muse on the dangers of power: a great man at the pinnacle of his success, likened to a god, surrounded by everything the world had to offer – what next? Seneca, the millionaire philosopher and tutor to Nero, put it this way: 'Petty sacrilege is punished, but sacrilege on a grand scale is the stuff of triumphs.'

THE FARMING SLAVE-GANGS

Throughout the third to second century BC, Rome was taking command of territory from Italy to Spain, North Africa, Greece and Asia Minor (West Turkey). The result was a massive increase in the slave population. Perhaps as many as 250,000 slaves came on to the market between 200 and 150 BC; we hear of 65,000 Sardinian slaves put up for sale in 177 BC. Many of these were sent to work on *latifundia* in Italy (*latus*, 'wide', 'broad'; *fundus*, 'land', 'farm'). These were large farms developed by the wealthy, who had been taking over vast tracts of technically 'public land' for years (p. 47). Conditions in such places were very different from those of household slaves – more akin, perhaps, to American slaves in chain gangs working the cotton, beet, rice, tea and tobacco plantations of the nineteenth century.

SPARTACUS

In 73 BC Spartacus – a slave being trained up for combat in a gladiatorial school in Capua – escaped with other gladiatorial slaves. The reason was the cruelty of their master, who kept them locked up. Only 78 of the planned 200 got away, and they took refuge on Mount Vesuvius. They were joined by other runaway slaves and peasants, many (presumably) from the local *latifundia* (p. 145). In this way they became the focus of a serious revolt.

The final size of Spartacus' army is disputed – somewhere between 70,000 and 120,000, according to the sources – but it was big enough and well enough led to deal with the, perhaps unfocussed, Roman forces sent against it. Spartacus' army fought its way north to the border with Gaul, where (presumably) it was supposed to disperse. But it chose to retrace its steps and continue ravaging Italy. Spartacus enjoyed further military success, until the Roman general Crassus finally trapped him (71 BC). He annihilated Spartacus' army and crucified the survivors, planting the crosses all along the Appian Way from Rome to Capua. That is a distance of 115 miles (185 km). With 6,000 survivors, there would have been a crucifixion about every 30 to 35 yards (27–32 m). Pompey, returning from Spain, mopped up the remainder of those who got away. Naturally, he claimed all the glory and got a second triumph.

SLAVERY: THE LAW

The Roman jurist Gaius (AD 160; see p. 347) said of slaves:

> The primary distinction in the law of persons is this: (i) all men are either free or slaves; (ii) free men are either born free or are freedmen; freedmen are those manumitted [legally released] from lawful slavery . . . slaves who are not disgraced [Gaius cites gladiators] become on release sometimes a Roman citizen and sometimes a Latin [i.e., a citizen, but with fewer rights].

SLAVERY: THE NUMBERS

The US State Department says that between 600,000 and 800,000 people are annually trafficked into the United States and are forced, defrauded or coerced into labour or sexual exploitation. In Roman eyes, they would have been getting off lightly. Roman slaves were 'chattel' slaves, i.e., they were the equivalent of property, over whom their master had *rights* of life and death. By the end of the Republic, maybe 25 per cent of the population of Italy were slaves; over the whole Empire perhaps 10 per cent. In Rome itself, perhaps they made up about a third of the inhabitants. The rich could own very many. Slaves made splendid status symbols. Pompey recruited 800 of his own slaves and shepherds to fight Julius Caesar. We never hear of slaves being in short supply.

SLAVE VALUE

Slaves were precious. To draw a modern parallel, no one would spend all day kicking the washing machine – unless it failed to do the job for which it was bought. So while they were classified as 'property', like a sofa, slaves were bought to do serious work. They came from all walks of life: some were born slaves (if a mother was a slave, the child was also a slave; the status of the father was irrelevant), others were taken as booty in war or by pirates or brigands; some were traded, others were sold into slavery by their parents, who were unable to support them (this was what happened to the Stoic philosopher Epictetus, see p. 307). This could make some slaves very expensive. Imagine the American businessman Bill Gates being captured at sea – he would be worth a penny or two on the slave market, unless his family decided to ransom him. When the emperor Augustus fell sick, he told the Senate that if they needed to know the state of the Empire – finances, provinces and army – they should apply to a certain slave in the imperial court who held all the information. He was clearly a superb civil servant. Such relationships also made slaves loyal. A slave attached to an influential political master depended on him and him alone; the politician never knew where the loyalty of his free friends might lie, but he could trust his slave.

SLAVE OCCUPATIONS

The unlucky slaves were those sent to work in mines or large agricultural estates (p. 99). Of these we hear little. Domestic slaves with an understanding master could have a reasonable existence, especially if they had skills or training (e.g., nurses, secretaries, doctors, librarians, architects, teachers, musicians, jewellers, goldsmiths, glaziers, masons, plumbers, and so on; see Crassus, p. 151 and cf. Cicero, p. 173). Job titles were important for inter-slave 'status'; we hear of a range of slave jobs in the imperial households, e.g., 'valet', 'cup-bearer', 'crystal steward', and so on.

If the master was a senator and therefore debarred from trade or finance, his slaves could act for him in those areas (p. 126). Slaves with a special expertise could work for free (e.g., on building projects), and a slave with a job (e.g., running a farm) could own slaves himself. Slaves could also make money from any paid work they were hired out to do. Strictly, this was the master's property, but it was often treated as if it were their own. As a result, some slaves could buy their freedom. A number of funerary monuments tell us that slaves and master were buried together – but that was the point. Household slaves were part of the *familia* – the whole household.

MANUMISSION

The technical term for freeing a slave was 'manumission'. Latin *manus* means 'hand', and by extension 'legal control/authority/power', especially of a father over his family or master over his slaves; *mitt-/miss-* means 'release/released'. So to manumit meant to release someone from someone's control.

Compared to the Greeks, Romans were liberal about manumitting slaves. Ex-slaves became citizens, though they could not hold political office. Their sons could, but it often took time to shake off the stigma of slavery. However, even if he was not quite 'one of us', he was still a Roman citizen. It was something to arrive from abroad a slave and emerge a Roman. Many such freedmen went on to do well for themselves in urban trade and crafts. There is a vast funerary monument in Rome put up by the freedman Eurysaces, who had made it big in bread in the city. The monument features a series of dough-kneading bins stacked on top of each other.

If they had been freed by the emperor and continued to serve in the imperial household, ex-slaves could have powerful influence over policy. All that said, manumission depended on the whim of the master, as did every other aspect of a slave's life, for good or ill, pleasure or pain. His or her body was at the master's disposal. The hope of manumission had the advantage for the master of (perhaps) keeping the slave obedient and helpful; certainly any slave could see how such an attitude might work to his advantage. Likewise, since freed slaves were regarded as their ex-owner's (now patron's) children, the patron could continue to use them to his advantage; and it could be greatly to the freedman's benefit to continue being part of a Roman family, especially if it was a powerful one. Incidentally, it is worth pointing out that freed slaves would not have suffered the racial discrimination of American black slaves. Most slaves were indistinguishable in skin colour from their free masters.

SLAVE THEORY

There was a strong general feeling in the ancient world that slavery was a natural state, i.e., some people were born to be slaves, and that was that. So no one ever suggested abolishing it, not even ex-slaves. The Stoic philosopher Seneca argued that slaves should be treated humanely because mankind was one, but that was about as good as it got. Christians did not inveigh against the institution either. St Paul told slaves to obey their masters 'with fear and trembling'. Christians sometimes used 'slavery' as an image of obedience to God, arguing that being a slave to God was a good thing. 'Slavery' in that sense bore no relation to the daily reality of the slave as property. Other Christians said that slavery was part of the natural order and therefore good for slaves and good for society. That was much more in accordance with the pagan view. Others said (as Stoics did) that it was the state of one's soul that mattered: being free or slave made no difference.

MARCUS LICINIUS CRASSUS, C. 115–53 BC

Pompey was not the only pro-Sullan to rise to the top of politics at this time: there was Crassus, too. In 87 BC Marius killed Crassus' father (consul 97 BC) and brother, but in 83–81 BC Crassus played an important part in Sulla's victory over Marian forces. He made a vast fortune out of Sulla's proscriptions (p. 133) and became an influential figure in Rome through his wealth, easy ability to make connections with the rich and poor, and the infinite care he put into the legal cases he took on. He did not take kindly to Pompey claiming the credit for the defeat of Spartacus. When he called himself 'Pompey the Great' Crassus asked 'As great as what?' But Pompey knew it would be wise to have Crassus on his side and helped him to become consul with him in 70 BC.

DECIMATION (LATIN, *DECIMUS*, 'TENTH')

When Crassus sent his lieutenant Mummius to follow the slave-leader Spartacus but not to confront him, Mummius disobeyed. He joined battle and was so badly beaten that many of his men dropped their weapons and ran for it. Plutarch takes up the story:

> Crassus split up the 500 men who had been first to run for it into 50 groups of ten. One from each of the 50 groups was selected by lot and put to death, reviving an ancient form of punishment last dealt out long ago. It is a disgrace to die in this way, a punishment with many hideous and revolting features attached. The whole army watches.

AS RICH AS CRASSUS

Plutarch tells us that Crassus made his enormous fortune through 'public disasters – war and fire'. First, he snapped up as much as he could, at bargain prices, of the houses and land that Sulla put up for sale from those he had proscribed (p. 133). Further, he took advantage of the daily occurrence of fires and collapse of buildings in Rome. Gathering a team of 500 slave architects and builders, he would persuade terrified owners of buildings on fire and others threatened by the flames to sell them to him cheap. 'In that way, most of Rome came into his possession.' But the sheer number of his slaves made the biggest impression – readers, secretaries, silversmiths, stewards, waiters and so on. He oversaw their education and taught them himself as well. He took the view that a master's chief task was to look after his slaves. 'The slaves do the work,' he said. 'I direct them.'

ATOMIC THEORY

In his magnificent six-book poem *On the Nature of Things* Lucretius (*c.* 94–51 BC) is a poet with a mission: to lay to rest, once and for all, the ghost of death.

> For we by Day, as Boys by Night, do fear
> Shadows, as vain and senseless as those are.
> Wherefore that Darkness that o'erspreads our Souls,
> What can disperse but those eternal Rules,
> Which from firm Premises, true REASON draws,
> And a deep Insight into NATURE'S Laws.
>
> (trans. Thomas Creech)

Lucretius argues that our soul is mortal. It dies with us. So there is nothing after death. All this derives from the atomic theories of his hero, the Greek philosopher Epicurus (341–270 BC), who said that the world consists of nothing but atoms; at death, our body and soul simply dissolve into their constituent atomic parts.

But what about the gods? Do they not exist and watch over us? Far from it: they live apart, have no hell and little interest in us:

The Gods, by right of Nature, must possess
An Everlasting Age, of perfect Peace:
Far off, remov'd from us and our Affairs:
Neither approached by Dangers or by Cares:
Rich in themselves, to whom we cannot add:
Not pleas'd by Good Deeds; nor provok'd by Bad.

(trans. Earl of Rochester)

Condemning religion as a major evil, Lucretius goes on to describe how atomic theory offers a complete description of the workings of the universe. It explains phenomena like the senses, thought and sex, how the world began and human civilization developed; and the great geological and celestial phenomena (earthquakes, lightning, etc.) which most of all make men believe in divine intervention in the world – and Lucretius does this in the most glorious poetry too (atoms falling to earth are likened to dust caught in a shaft of sunlight).

So Richard Dawkins need never have been invented. The ways of the Lord are mysterious indeed.

FROM LUCRETIUS TO THE ATOMIC BOMB

Lucretius' work on atomic theory had little influence, because Aristotle's theory of matter ruled the roost. He said that earth, air, fire, water and aether were the basic substances. Furthermore, after the collapse of the Roman Empire in the West, Lucretius' poem vanished entirely until its rediscovery in a monastery library in Italy in 1417 (though it was known about because of references to it in surviving authors). *On the Nature of*

Things was soon to take on enormous significance. The French Jesuit Pierre Gassendi (1592–1655) became fascinated by Lucretius' account (as was Francis Bacon (1561–1626) before him), and argued that atomic theory was the best way of investigating nature. His work came to the attention of Robert Boyle (1627–91) and others, and soon the idea that matter consisted of 'minute particles' became received wisdom. Translations of Lucretius were all the rage (the first by Thomas Creech, 1682 – see p. 152). As a direct result of this, John Dalton in 1803 founded modern atomic theory.

JULIUS CAESAR, 100–44 BC

Gaius Julius Caesar came from a very distinguished patrician family claiming descent from the goddess Venus, through Rome's founder Aeneas and his son Julus (whence 'Julius'). Although he had family connections with Marius, Caesar managed to escape execution at the hands of Sulla. However, his inheritance was confiscated – a serious blow for a rising politician. Sulla, prophetically, said that he saw 'many a Marius' in Caesar. Caesar then wisely spent time with the Roman army in Asia, taking on Mithradates (p. 117) and spending some time at the court of King Nicomedes in Bithynia, trying to persuade him to allow Rome the use of his fleet. In 78 BC, with Sulla dead, Caesar returned to Rome where his personal charm and brilliance as a political and legal orator attracted attention. He became known for prosecuting corrupt provincial governors, which went down very well with the people. He was apparently 1,300 talents in debt when he became *quaestor* in 69 BC, but borrowed and spent lavishly (a talent = 24,000 *ss*; it is in fact a weight of silver equal to approximately 71 lb (32 kg)). This further increased his popularity. When he became *aedile* in 65 BC, he paid for a show starring no fewer than 320 pairs of gladiators, together with public banquets, processions and theatrical shows – a true 'man of the people'.

STONING FRUIT

The Roman people had certain expectations of their magistrates and could turn nasty if they were not met. In 56 BC Vatinius was *aedile* and put on some very poor games, so the people began to throw stones at him. The jurist Cascellius persuaded the *aediles* to rule that only fruit should be thrown in the arena. When someone asked Cascellius if a pine-cone counted as fruit, he replied, 'No, unless it's going to be thrown at Vatinius.'

THE NAME OF CAESAR

Caesar was not himself born by Caesarean section. The name, we are told, was given to the *first* of the Caesar family, for any of four reasons: he was cut from the womb of his dead mother (Latin, *caedo, caes-*, 'I cut'); he had a 'thick head of hair' when he was born (Latin, *caesaries*); he had grey-blue (Latin, *caesius*) eyes; or that in battle he killed an elephant (*caesai* in Moorish). Take your pick.

QUEEN OF BITHYNIA

Caesar never shook off the rumour that in order to get his way with Nicomedes, king of Bithynia, he had agreed to be his catamite. For a male to be accused of being penetrated by another was a powerful slur (p. 118), suggesting corrupt Eastern decadence, and Caesar's political opponents used it against him frequently, as they did his many affairs with women. One politician referred to him as 'Every woman's husband and every man's wife.'

CAESAR SEIZED

We are told that, on his way back from Asia, Caesar was captured by pirates. When they put a ransom of 20 talents on his head, he laughed at them, saying he was worth 50. For 38 days he bossed them about, telling them to stop talking when he went to sleep, calling them illiterate savages when they did not admire the poems and speeches he proclaimed for them, and saying he would crucify the lot of them when he was freed. Which he did. As soon as the ransom was paid, he manned ships and found the pirates where he had left them. But he considerately had their throats slit first. True or not, it tells us a great deal about how people perceived the man.

MARCUS TULLIUS CICERO, 106–43 BC

Cicero's family from the small town of Arpinum was very wealthy (the non-senatorial 'equestrian' order, see p. 66), but they had never been political players in Rome. It required unusual talent to make it in Rome as a *novus homo* (p. 76) without aristocratic backing, and Cicero was not a military man, though he fought with Sulla in the Social War (91–89 BC). However, he was abundantly talented in the most important ability needed to advance into a high position in Rome: his brilliant oratory – powerful, elegant, witty, incisive, covering the full emotional range – won him legal cases of great *political* importance and brought him to public attention. How very different from our own MPs.

In 79 BC Cicero married Terentia (probably of noble family – a good move), honed his oratorical skills in Athens and in 75 BC was appointed *quaestor* in Sicily. There he won the respect of the Sicilians, who later asked him to prosecute their corrupt Roman governor Verres. It was dangerous for a young, untried politician to attack a man in such a position and with so many powerful friends, but Cicero's case was unanswerable; also he had Pompey behind him, who had many supporters in Sicily. Verres fled before the case was heard, and Cicero's name was on everyone's lips. He was now one of the leading advocates in Rome, a man you wanted on your side if you had a political cause to fight.

WHAT'S IN A NAME?

Cicer is Latin for 'chickpea', and Plutarch says the Cicero family (p. 81) got the name from a chickpea-shaped cleft in an ancestor's nose. That is possible. However, since families often chose agricultural names (e.g., *Fabius* 'bean', *Piso* 'pea' and *Lentulus* 'lentil') perhaps the Cicero family made their fortunes in agriculture. Other Roman names could be less complimentary: *Flaccus* 'Big Ears', *Naso* 'Big Nose', *Crassus* 'Fatso', *Strabo* 'Cross-eyed' and *Peditus* 'Farter'.

VERY VERRES

Roman governor of Sicily from 73 to 71 BC, Verres had a taste for fine art: he plundered temples for their statues and relieved citizens of their silverware. He also had an eye for the ladies. Women were procured for him wherever he went, including the virgin daughters of distinguished citizens. Many cities wanted to avoid contributing money for the defence of Sicily, so they simply bribed Verres to let them off. As a result, the navy was a shambles. Further, Verres put a man called Cleomenes in charge of the fleet so that he could spend more time with Cleomenes' attractive wife. The fleet was promptly routed and set on fire by a pirate ship, watched by the whole population. The pirates then took an unhindered leisure-tour of the harbour at Syracuse. Finally, Verres subjected even Roman citizens to torture and death without trial. One was even crucified – a punishment usually reserved for criminals.

THE MONEY-LAUNDERING SCAM

Cicero's successful prosecution of Verres was made possible by his intensive and detailed research, which took him to Sicily for nearly two months (p. 157). There he interviewed those whose inheritances had been seized, property removed or daughters violated, and he went scrupulously through all Verres' files. In one scam Verres had demanded his victims pay bribes to him by borrowing money at an extortionate rate of interest from his business ally, Carpinatius. On the very day the Sicilians handed over the bribe, however, Carpinatius' accounts revealed that precisely the same sum had been (re-)deposited with the company, under the name of Gaius Verrucius. When Cicero looked more closely, he found that in each case the *–ucius* ending had been added later to overwrite the *–es* ending of Verres! In this way Verres protected his identity and doubtless took a decent share of Carpinatius' profits too.

COINING IT

Though Cicero once thundered 'There is nothing by which those in charge of public affairs can more easily endear themselves to the masses than by incorruptible abstemiousness,' powerful Romans like

Verres could coin the stuff on a massive scale, especially by picking up a governorship or in dealings abroad (e.g., *publicani*, p. 122). When Caesar and Pompey took steps in 59 BC to ensure that Cleopatra's father Ptolemy XII became king of Egypt, they picked up a cool 140 million *ss* from him. Even someone as incorruptible as Cicero banked 2.2 million *ss* after his spell as governor in Cilicia (p. 173), though he lost the lot by giving it to Pompey to fight the civil war against Caesar (p. 175). It was often said that governors needed a lot of cash because they had to make three fortunes: (1) to recoup election expenses from climbing the greasy pole in Rome; (2) to bribe the jury on charges of provincial mismanagement; and (3) to live off.

THE PIRATE PROBLEM

In the ancient world the sea was the only way to transport heavy goods (including people) long distances because it was the cheapest option. It has been calculated that if the cost of travel by sea was 1 *ss*, then it was 5 *ss* by inland waterways and anything from 30 to 60 *ss* by land.

Pirates were a constant menace. The real money lay not in goods but humans, either in capturing the wealthy and holding them to ransom, or rounding up large numbers of people and selling them off on the lucrative slave market. The island of Naxos, for example, once suffered a pirate swoop that removed 280 of its inhabitants. Local hit-and-run pirates would identify targets in harbour and lie in wait for them in areas dotted with small islands, where a surprise attack was easy and escape routes at hand (e.g., off the Adriatic coast). Some small, inaccessible, coastal communities, living near rich maritime trade routes, established their own pirate fleets and demanded tariffs for safe passage. But it was the pirate armadas that caused the most damage. Highly organized and run out of Cilicia in southern Turkey, these fleets worked the major trade routes and offered their services to anyone willing to hire them. This skilled and experienced maritime mafia presented a permanent and serious threat to all shipping and therefore all trade.

POMPEY'S PATCH

In 67 BC Rome decided it was time to stop the big pirate cooperatives. Pompey was given a three-year command with almost unlimited powers to do what was necessary. His strategy was to isolate the pirate bands so that they could not help each other, then deal with them one by one. So he raised 120,000 men and 270 ships, divided the Mediterranean coastline into 13 areas and assigned each area its own commander. Once they were in place, Pompey headed up a mobile force of 60 ships, starting in the Western Mediterranean and sweeping the pirates into the waiting arms of each area commander. Cilicia in southern Turkey – the pirate centre with its rugged, mountainous coastline and numerous inlets – was simply patrolled to keep the pirates hemmed in. When the rest of the Mediterranean was cleared, and the pirates were completely isolated, Pompey dealt with them too. The international pirate ring had been broken, for the time being. It had taken a mere three months. It was yet another huge feather in Pompey's cap – the man of the moment.

POMPEY – TRIUMPH OF THE PEARLY KING?

Pompey celebrated his Eastern triumph against Mithradates on his forty-fifth birthday (September 61 BC). The triumphant march past featured a golden moon weighing 30 lb (13.6 kg); enough gold vessels inlaid with gems to fill nine display stands; three gold figures of Minerva, Mars and Apollo; 33 pearl crowns; and a square mountain of gold with deer, lions, various fruit, entwined with a golden vine. Such events could prompt intense attacks of moralizing in historians. As Pliny the Elder observed:

> Pompey's portrait was rendered in pearls – the conquest of austerity and the triumph of extravagance! Not one of the men of that age would have called him 'The Great' had he celebrated his first triumph like that. Your face, Great Pompey – made of pearls! Pearls, wasteful stuff, designed for women! The sort of thing no real man ought to wear! Is that how you wanted to seem valuable! ... This was a cruel portent of Heaven's wrath – that head, divorced from a body, in oriental splendour, carried an obvious significance even then.

The significance was that in 48 BC Pompey, in flight from Caesar, was beheaded when he landed in Egypt.

MITHRADATES' TREACLE

Mithradates was so fascinated by poisons that he almost invented the vaccine. We are told he took minute quantities of poison every day in order to 'inoculate' himself against its effects. He even experimented with the production of a universal antidote. So successful was he that, when he realized he could not defeat Pompey and decided to commit suicide by poison, it had no effect. He had to order a slave to kill him. Pompey brought the recipe of this universal antidote back to Rome. It was translated into Latin and stimulated much medical interest thereafter. It was given the Greek name *theriakê* 'to do with wild animals', i.e., as a remedy against their bites. This gives us 'theriac' and (via an assumed diminutive *theriaculum*) 'treacle'. In the seventeenth century it was made out of molasses and regarded as a 'sovereign remedy'!

PONS FABRICIUS

As an inscription on the bridge still informs us, Rome's road engineer Lucius Fabricius built it in 62 BC to connect an island in the Tiber to the left bank. The bridge is short, requiring one pier between island and bank, and an arch either side of it to span the river. The inscription tells us that if the bridge lasted 40 years the contractor would have his deposit returned. He certainly earned it – and more. The bridge still stands, the last working Roman bridge in Rome.

BUILDING BRIDGES

Romans inherited the superb *voussoir* (keystone) method of bridge-building from the Etruscans. Piers (basically piles of rocks) were laid in the river at an appropriate distance apart. On these were constructed abutments – secure bases – from which the arches could be built that spanned pier to pier. First, wooden frames were swung into position between piers and the arches built up over them, block by block. The *voussoir*, the stone at the top of the arch, placed in position last of all, held the whole arch together. Mortar was not used to bind together the blocks that made up the arches – each block was very carefully carved so that they all fitted perfectly – but iron clamps were use to tie them in. The semi-circular arches, extremely strong and very beautiful structures, completed, the roadway was laid on top.

FROM ARCHES TO CHURCHES

You could not possibly build something like the 'Colosseum' (AD 70) if your basic model was the Greek temple. Romans changed all that. The arch – like the dome and vault (the 'barrel' vault is simply an extended arch) – had been known around the Mediterranean for thousands of years. But it was the Romans who first started to exploit them seriously, and in so doing revolutionized building – for the arch can span a very wide space indeed and is immensely strong (think aqueducts, see p. 321). Basic materials were also readily available. The area being of volcanic origin, volcanic basalt (once lava) was used to pave the streets and roads; volcanic pozzuolana cement (p. 103) could be aggregated with rubble and used as fill-in, then faced with high-quality stone.

Stone such as tufa (a volcanic conglomerate) and limestone were widely available and relatively easy to carve; and, as time went by, high-quality stone like travertine and other marbles became available. Iron wedges and hammers split the rock into chunks; chisels and punches worked it into a basic shape. Put all that together with the usual brick, and the construction of very large, free-standing buildings suddenly became feasible, as well as far cheaper than those put together out of solid blocks of stone. Stucco, painting and mosaic completed the interiors. The technology survived in the Roman East after the fall of the Empire in the West, and resulted in vast churches like Hagia Sophia (Greek for 'Holy Wisdom', AD 537) in Constantinople. That still stands, though when Constantinople finally fell to the Turks on 29 May 1453 its interior was converted into a mosque.

POPULAR THEATRE

Romans adopted the theatre from the Greeks in the third century BC. But permanent structures were not erected because Romans feared they might become places where large crowds would gather, without warning, for whatever fell purpose. Pompey turned this argument on its head. Instead of regarding a permanent meeting place as a danger to order, he saw the considerable advantages in a fixed, luxury location, dedicated to himself, where loyal followers could be stage-managed into hysterical displays of support. So in 55 BC he funded Rome's first stone theatre (for about 20,000 people), a fabulous, hugely popular building complex with colonnades, streams, and fountains with spacious gardens; its porticos were filled with antique statuary and paintings; there was also a room for meetings of the Senate, plus a temple dedicated to Venus the Conqueror. This started the practice (eagerly embraced by the wealthy and powerful) of funding huge national monuments in their own name for all to enjoy, using the latest building techniques.

'CAESAR'S WIFE MUST BE ABOVE SUSPICION'

On 25 January 61 BC Cicero wrote to his old school chum Atticus about the scandalous *Bona Dea* affair. This was a secret, women-only festival in honour of the 'Good Goddess' (her exact name is uncertain), held at night in a magistrate's house 'for the security of the state'. The magistrate concerned that year was Julius Caesar, and his wife Pompeia conducted it. The 'man' Cicero refers to here was Clodius, a ruthless young aristocrat out to win popularity with the people, and rumoured to be having an affair with Pompeia. Cicero wrote:

I expect you have heard that, during the *Bona Dea* sacrifice in
Caesar's house a man dressed in women's clothes got in . . . it was
judged sacrilege and the consuls asked the Senate to set up a court
of inquiry. Meanwhile, Caesar divorced his wife.

Cicero wrote of the trial in June:

The challenging of the jurymen then took place. The prosecutor
rejected all the bad characters, while Clodius the defendant, like a
kind-hearted collector of gladiators, refused all the most respectable.
So people began to have misgivings as soon as the jury took their
seats – you would never see such a disreputable lot in a low-grade
gambling den.

[Everything goes against Clodius, and Cicero's evidence that Clodius
was in Rome that night, which Clodius had tried to deny, is applauded.
But]

Within a few days Crassus, using one slave (and a gladiator at
that) as a go-between, settled the whole business. He called the
jurors to his house, made promises, settled debts or paid down
cash.

And so Clodius was acquitted. Cicero was in despair at the corruption
of public life in Rome.

CAESAR – COMING OUT ON TOP

Plutarch tells us the following stories about Caesar when he was serving
in Spain in 67 BC:

We are told that, as he was crossing the Alps and passing through a native village which had very few inhabitants and was an altogether miserable-looking place, his laughing companions joked among themselves and said 'Can it be that here too one would find people pushing themselves forward to gain office, and here too there are struggles to get the first place, and jealous rivalries among the great men!' Caesar said to them in all seriousness 'I would rather be first man here than second in Rome.' We are also told that, in Spain, when he was at leisure and reading from the history of Alexander, he was lost in thought for a long time, and then burst into tears. His friends were surprised, and asked the reason. 'Do you not think,' said he, 'it is matter for sorrow that while Alexander, at my age, was already king of so many peoples, I have as yet achieved no brilliant success!'

Caesar was 33, the age at which Alexander died.

CAESAR: BANKING ON GAUL

Caesar knew that he would at some time have to clear his debts. The way to do that was foreign conquest. So when he, Pompey and Crassus buried their differences in 60 BC in order to impose their combined will on the Senate, Caesar got for himself a special command of the two Roman provinces in Gaul: Gaul 'This side of the Alps' (Cisalpine, i.e., north Italy) and Gaul 'That side of the Alps' (Transalpine, i.e., roughly modern Provence). Control of Cisalpine Gaul was vital: it gave Caesar easy access to Rome, if needed, and in those turbulent times one never knew what one's enemies back home might be plotting. Control of Transalpine Gaul gave him access to the rest of modern France, Belgium and part of Holland as far as the Rhine, and even Britain.

That is what Caesar was after: expanding the Roman Empire, with all the prestige, glory and (most important of all) rich pickings this would entail. It would also bring him, if he played his cards right, a devoted army that owed everything to him and would follow him wherever he went. The ghosts of his uncle-by-marriage Marius (p. 108) and of Sulla would have approved. In the event, the campaign brought him a million slaves for the market, the Treasury got none of his booty, and he won the backing of many young aristocrats who joined him to make their fortunes.

CATULLUS

Everybody loves a lover, and they did not come more love-struck than the poet Gaius Valerius Catullus (*c.* 84–54 BC). He thought about *relationships* in a new and interesting way. Here he reflects that his lover Lesbia is always on at him, but then, so is he at her:

> Lesbia for ever on me rails:
> To talk on me she never fails:
> But, hang me, but for all her Art,
> I find that I have gain'd her heart:
> The proof is thus: I plainly see
> The Case is just the same with me:
> I curse her evr'y hour sincerely;
> Yet, hang me, but I love her dearly.

(trans. Jonathan Swift)

This is not quite the way that the sex-obsessed Greek epigrammatists wrote about their feelings or their lovers. Nor did their poems try to define a relationship or deal in *uncertainty* as Catullus did:

> Dost thou, my life, a tender bond propose
> Of lasting truth and constant love's delights?
> Gods grant, that truly from thy heart it flows,
> And nerve that heart to keep the faith it plights!
> Thus let their sacred vows, their fond career
> Till both shall end, our lives and loves pursue;
> And coming time through each succeeding year
> Find me as fond as now, and her as true.

> (trans. G. Lamb)

Bonds? Sacred vows? No, bed will do fine for me, you can hear the Greeks saying, till the next one comes long. But Catullus was exploring and thinking about his feelings for Lesbia more deeply, and there was more than posing in his fears.

Catullus was one of a smart set of young poets on the make, well versed in Greek love poetry and seeing what they could do with this sort of poetry in Latin. They moved among arty, elegant, educated Romans in high society. Lesbia (the pet name Catullus used for her) was probably in real life Clodia, wife of Metellus (consul in 60 BC). That Catullus should be having an affair with the wife of the consul may be thought foolish, and to boast about it in poetry even more so. But this was Rome of the first century BC, when aristocratic women, observing the developing, fashionable demi-monde of high-class courtesans in Rome, began to see possibilities for themselves outside marriage. This was, perhaps, their form of liberation. The question was – how far to go? Not far enough, for Catullus anyway. The affair came to an end:

> None could ever say that she,
> Lesbia! was so loved by me.
> Never all the world around
> Faith so true as mine was found:
> If no longer it endures
> (Would it did!) the fault is yours.
> I can never think again
> Well of you: I try in vain:
> But – be false – do what you will –
> Lesbia! I must love you still.
>
> (trans. Walter Savage Landor)

This became condensed down to his famous *odi et amo*:

> odi et amo; quare id faciam, fortasse requiris.
>   nescio, sed fieri sentio, et excrucior.
>
> I hate and I love. 'Why do you do this?' perhaps you ask.
> I don't know, but I feel it happening, and I'm in torment.

Note the helpless antitheses: love/hate; do/happen; know/feel. Result? Torture.

In another poem Catullus tried and failed to look ahead to a Lesbia-free future, when she would want him and he could reject her. And finally it turned nasty: he described her as 'the woman Catullus once loved more than himself . . . peeling the skin off' Romans in the back alleys and doorways.

Catullus was a highly innovative poet, looking back to Greek love poetry but creating something fresh, original and wholly Roman out of it. He was beginning to push Latin poetry into corners it had not explored before, sexual and personal.

CICERO'S HOUSE: POLITICS AND RELIGION

Ancient religion was not a thing apart. It was bound up with correct ritual, to be performed at the right time on the right social, political or religious occasion. In 58 BC Cicero, fearful of being prosecuted for ordering the execution of some of Catiline's conspirators without trial, fled Italy and was declared an exile. As was the law, he lost all his property.

When he was recalled in 57 BC his property had to be restored to him. But his house had been destroyed, and part of the land turned into a temple to Freedom. So it was now the god's, no longer up for human ownership. Cicero did not dispute that principle, but argued that it had not been dedicated correctly and was therefore still his. The pontifexes and Senate pondered the matter and agreed. Next year there were some strange omens, and Cicero's enemies argued that the gods were angry at the Senate's decision. Further pondering ensued, but the Senate decided not to budge.

Such use of ritual for political purposes was commonplace. In 59 BC Bibulus, Caesar's colleague as consul, unable to stop Caesar's legislation, retired to his house and issued periodic statements that he was 'watching the skies' – that is, for signs that the omens were unfavourable. From then on there was always doubt about whether Caesar's laws were valid. The big problem was that there was no definitive work of reference on the topic, and the main religious authorities were nearly always senators anyway, so no decision could be even remotely 'objective', let alone 'final'. This made religion an extremely useful political tool, as it once used to be in Britain.

ABSENT PRESENCE

Caesar's *Gallic Wars* are his magnificent 'extended diary' from his campaign in Gaul, in effect a series of war reports. They revealed how in 57 BC he brought northern France and Belgium under control; in 56 BC he subdued tribes bordering the Atlantic; in 55 and 54 BC he campaigned in Britain and Germany; in 53 BC he dealt with rebellions in the north; and in 52 BC he met his most dangerous opponent in central France, Vercingetorix. Caesar's defeat of Vercingetorix and subjugation of other rebellions in 51 BC brought his Gallic campaign to a successful conclusion. These coolly dramatic, on-the-spot accounts, written in pacy, clear, elegant Latin (Caesar was acknowledged to be a superb stylist) and always referring to Caesar 'objectively' in the third person, were rushed to Rome and devoured by the reading and listening public. This was popular entertainment of the most gripping kind – and the most effective propaganda imaginable for a man absent from the bear pit that was Rome, but ever present in the minds of the people.

'USEFUL VIOLENCE'

The ancient world had no conception of human rights, let alone war crimes tribunals. Like today's drug gangs, the ancients took it for granted that violence would earn 'respect'. As Tacitus commented after the Romans slaughtered 10,000 in Uspe (Crimea): 'it instilled terror in the others'. So after one battle in Gaul, Caesar had the hands of all the surviving males of the town cut off. When Romans sacked a town, we are told, they even sliced the dogs in half. But that was not just the Romans: it was the ancient world in general. Mithradates and Boudicca were quite their equal (pp. 130, 246). When the poet Virgil talked of Romans imposing peace, sparing the defeated and warring down the proud (p. 205), he was anticipating Dr Johnson's comment on Cromwell: 'he introduced by useful violence the arts of peace'. It is not a sentiment with which we in the West feel quite so comfortable these days. But as the emperor Claudius later pointed out, the key to successful imperialism lay in a willingness to transform one's enemies instantly into allies: after the iron fist, the velvet glove.

INTELLECTUAL SOLDIERS

Rome's top men were highly educated and debated matters of language, literature and philosophy as keenly as politics. In between dictating his famous *Gallic Wars*, Caesar also wrote a book on word-formation while crossing the Alps. Cicero adapted and extended Greek philosophy, thereby inventing Roman philosophy, and wrote widely on language, rhetoric and ethics. As a result, Caesar said of him: 'You have won greater laurels than the triumphal wreath, for it is a finer achievement to have extended the frontiers of the Roman genius than those of the Roman Empire.'

We hear a fine story of Pompey preparing to consecrate his temple to Victory in 55 BC. He could not work out how to describe himself on the accompanying inscription: should he be consul *tertium* ('for the third time'), that is, consul *throughout* the whole of the year, or consul *tertio*, that is, consul *in* that year? He consulted leading grammarians, but there was no agreement, so he gave up and asked Cicero to adjudicate. Cicero suggested he miss out the ending *-ium* or *-io* and simply write the root of the word, *tert*, without any ending to indicate 'throughout' or 'in'.

CAESAR IN BRITAIN

As far as Romans were concerned, Britain was on the very edge of the known world. So though Romans were dimly aware of the place – indeed Roman goods had been traded there since the second century BC – it was very exciting for them to learn that Caesar had landed on the island, mainly in order to warn Britons to keep their noses out of Gaul. The Senate voted him a public thanksgiving for 20 days. Cicero was less entranced, commenting in a letter to his friend Atticus in July 54 BC:

> We are keenly awaiting the result of the war against Britain . . .
> but we now know this for certain, that there is not a sliver of
> silver in the place, and no hope of booty except slaves – and I can't
> imagine you will expect any of *them* to be over-endowed in the
> literary or musical departments.

This tells us a lot about what a cultured Roman might expect from some of his slaves.

THE MYSTERY OF THE LOST PANTHERS

Deeply disillusioned and largely marginalized by the stranglehold that Pompey, Caesar and Crassus held over the Senate, Cicero gave up on active politics in the 50s and consoled himself with writing about political philosophy. But in the summer of 51 BC he was sent to govern Cilicia in south-east Turkey. It was not a posting he relished, but a top Roman still had his obligations. So he made the best of it and maintained connections back in Rome as diligently as he could.

When he left Rome his young friend Caelius was standing as *aedile*. Wanting to impress the people, Caelius decided to put on a wild beast hunt and wrote to Cicero, asking him to send some panthers. Cicero unenthusiastically obliged. Then Caelius asked if Cicero would send some more for a chum. Cicero replied:

> About the panthers, the usual hunters are doing their best as per
> my orders. But there are strikingly few of the animals about, and
> those that do remain are said to be complaining loud and long
> that no other creatures in my province have such reason to fear for
> their safety. Consequently, it is reported that they have taken the
> decision to emigrate to Caria.

Witty fellow, Cicero. We have about 800 of his letters, and just under 100 letters to him – a historical goldmine.

MARC ANTONY

It was while Caesar was campaigning in Gaul that Marc Antony was persuaded to throw in his lot with him. Antony was a popular soldier and an attractive but inconsistent figure. Plutarch describes him as follows:

> It was, moreover, an ancient tradition, that the Antonys were
> descended from Hercules, by a son of his called Anton; and he
> thought it reasonable to believe this because of his similar stature

... what might seem to some offensive – his boasting, ribald language, drinking in public, sitting down by the men as they were taking their food, and standing up while he took his food at the mess tables – made him the delight and pleasure of the army. His love life, also, made him very attractive: he gained many friends by the assistance he gave them in theirs ... his generous ways, his open and lavish hand in gifts and favours to his friends and fellow-soldiers did a great deal for him in his first steps to power.

Caesar left Antony in charge of troops and administration in Italy when he set off after Pompey in 49 BC. When Caesar was assassinated in 44 BC the conspirators took care to ensure that Antony was not there to protect him. Cicero, who was not involved in the conspiracy, thought this was a mistake. In a letter he congratulated the assassins on their Ides of March 'feast', but said that he himself would have ensured there were 'no leftovers'.

CROSSING THE RUBICON

The Rubicon is the small river that separated Italy from the province of Cisalpine Gaul. In 50 BC Caesar's tenure of command in Gaul came to an end and by law he was required to lay down his commission once he re-entered Italy. But Caesar's enemies in Rome – now including Pompey – were waiting for him. If he entered as a private citizen they would prosecute him and almost certainly succeed in having him condemned and executed. But if he crossed the Rubicon with his army it meant civil war. After much thought he said, 'Let the die be cast,' and hurried his soldiers across the river. Pompey, knowing he stood no chance against

Caesar's veterans, left Italy to gather troops in the East, where he was well known from his campaign against Mithradates (p. 139). Little good it did him. Defeated at Pharsalus, he fled to Egypt where he met his end – beheaded on an Egyptian shore (p. 161).

CAESAR'S CALENDAR

According to the old Roman calendar Caesar crossed the Rubicon on 10 January 49 BC – in the middle of winter. Brrr! Hold on. It was actually mid-autumn, because the Roman calendar had got completely out of kilter with the solar calendar (see p. 25). When he became dictator Caesar got it sorted. He added 90 days to the year at the end of 46 BC to get the months back in line with the seasons, and made further adjustments by inventing the leap year, adding one day every four years to ensure the Roman calendar matched the solar calendar and the seasons came round at the right time. Cicero made a rather pointed joke about this: on 4 January 45 BC someone mentioned to him that the constellation of Lyre would rise the next day.

'It certainly will,' Cicero said. '*He* has instructed it to.'

Caesar the ruthless dictator could control even the stars!

NAMES OF THE MONTHS

January was named from Janus, the god of gates who looked both ways; February from *februa*, an act of purification (no one knows why); March from Mars, god of war (it was when the fighting season started); April's derivation is unknown; May, probably from the god Maius; June from Juno, wife of Jupiter; July (originally *quintilis*, 'fifth') from Julius Caesar; August (originally *sextilis*, 'sixth') from the emperor Augustus; and the rest from the Roman number system.

CICERO ON CLEOPATRA

Romans had mixed feelings about Queen Cleopatra. When she produced a son (Caesarean) for Caesar and he lodged them both in Rome in 46 BC, the great and good were fascinated and flocked to visit. But Cicero was not impressed by Cleopatra or her entourage. She had apparently been angling for some favours from him and he later said of her: 'I hate the queen . . . I get extremely angry when I remember her insolence, when she was living in Caesar's house in the gardens beyond the Tiber.'

CLEOPATRA: BEAUTY ICON?

A coin, datable to 32 BC, with a head of Cleopatra on one side and her lover Marc Antony on the other, was recently found. The world convulsed. She hardly looked like the pouting goddess of film legend. But why should she? We have hundreds of depictions of Cleopatra (statue heads and coins). Many show major differences. Nor does any ancient source call her beautiful. Indeed, Plutarch says, 'Her beauty was not in and for itself incomparable,' and he goes on to say that it was her speech and character that made her so spell-binding. That was the point: beauty is in the eye of the beholder and Cleopatra knew how to make herself seem beautiful – in her own and Egypt's political interests. Why do we assume powerful ancient women must have been stunners? We don't make that assumption about powerful modern women. In this respect, it is a delicious irony that the first surviving depiction of Cleopatra (dedicated 2 July 51 BC) is as a man – a statue of her father hastily re-dedicated to her at his death, without re-working.

A PROPER ROMAN DEATH

One of Caesar's most implacable political rivals had been Cato the Younger, great-grandson of the famously stern Cato the Elder (p. 106). Defeated by Caesar at Thapsus (North Africa) in April 46 BC, Cato rejected Caesar's offer of reconciliation. Vowing not to live under what he regarded as a tyranny, he provided a lasting model for Romans of a good death: suicide. He tried to kill himself, alone, with his sword, but a wound in his hand from battle made that impossible; the surgeon stitched up the wound, but Cato tore it open in front of his appalled friends and died in agony. Here was a Stoic bravely enduring a ghastly death in order to proclaim that liberty was more important than life.

And that was the point. Romans regarded dying as an active, not a passive, process, and one which revealed as much about a man's character as his life. Death was therefore regularly presented in the sources as a conscious performance, an act loaded with moral significance. A violent death – murder, execution, suicide – was a display of Roman virtue.

PREPARING FOR DEATH

It fell to philosophers to prepare Romans for death. The Roman philosopher-poet Lucretius argued that, since the world and its gods were all atoms (p. 152), then from atoms we came and to atoms we would return, and that was that. Seneca said that we should try to die as happily as we tried to live, which meant dying gladly, not pointlessly fighting the inevitable, for that would merely make the experience miserable: 'There is only one chain that binds us to life, and that is the love of life.' Cicero thought of death in old age in terms of a fruit reaching its ripeness and falling naturally from the tree, or like a man reaching land after a long voyage. The Stoic emperor Marcus Aurelius commented:

> How trivial life is: yesterday a drop of semen, today a mummy
> or ashes. Spend therefore these fleeting moments as Nature would
> have you spend them, and then go to your rest with a good grace,
> as an olive falls in season, with a blessing for the earth that bore it
> and a thanksgiving to the tree that gave it life.

THE AGE SPAN

Perhaps a third of infant Romans did not reach one month. About half
of Romans born would not reach the age of five; those who reached ten
could hope to live until nearly 50. Only about 5 per cent might make 60,
and just 1 per cent saw 80. Diet, genes, the avoidance of killer diseases
and penetrative battle wounds made the difference. The antiquarian
Varro judged boyhood to last until 15, then adolescence until 30; youth
lasted until 45; old age did not begin until 60. In contrast, the poet
Horace regarded the stages of age in term of their characteristics: after
dumb infancy, children needed control – youth was wild and excessive
– adults calmed down, looking for money and friends – then old age
was querulous, a time of gradual decay, physical and mental. Middle age
did not seem to be a concept the Romans understood. No mid-life crises
for them. One imagines they were just happy to be around in the first
place. So, though 'Senate' derives from *senex*, 'old man', Rome was not
a gerontocracy; besides, any senator who did make 60 was relieved of
attendance. In this light, each woman had to produce from five to seven
children to maintain a stable population. Giving birth, in other words,
was a serious business, a life-and-death matter for the mother and for
the whole civilization. If female roles were limited in ancient society

it was because of the demographic imperative to maintain population numbers, not misogyny.

THE JUST WAR

In his treatise *de officiis* ('On Obligations', 44 BC) Cicero discusses how justice should be applied in a range of cases, including war. He begins with the principle 'The only excuse for going to war is that one may live in peace, unharmed.' Various conditions follow. An official demand for satisfaction must be submitted or a warning given and formal declaration made. Wars fought for the sake of survival would be to the death, but wars fought for glory must be fought 'with less bitterness'. Provided the defeated had acted without cruelty or barbarism, the victors must treat them mercifully, especially those who laid down their arms. Only legally enlisted soldiers could fight. Finally, all promises must be strictly observed. All this formed some of the basis for Augustine's later theory of the 'just war', but the big questions remain: 'just' or 'justifiable' or 'ultimately justified'? And, crucially, in whose eyes?

THE IDES OF MARCH 44 BC

Caesar was assassinated because people feared his overweening ambition. Brutus (p. 43) led the conspiracy. Since all leaders held public consultations for people to come and make requests (p. 301), the conspirators decided to surround Caesar and strike, having first diverted Marc Antony. Suetonius, the author of the *Lives of the Twelve Caesars* and a member of the emperor Hadrian's administrative staff, wrote:

Cimber caught his toga by both shoulders; then, as Caesar cried 'Why, this is assault!', one of the Cascas stabbed him from one side just below the throat. Caesar caught Casca's arm and ran it through with his stylus, but as he tried to leap to his feet, he was stopped by another wound . . . he was stabbed twenty-three times, uttering not a word, but merely a single groan at the first blow, though some have written that when Marcus Brutus came at him, he said in Greek: 'You too, my child!' [*kai su, teknon*]

ET TU, BRUTE?

Caesar's last words were Greek, not Latin, as Shakespeare would have it. Some Romans did indeed think that Brutus was Caesar's illegitimate son, but though Caesar was a notorious ladies' man it seems unlikely. The words spoken by Caesar at his death were commonly used in greetings ('Good health!' 'You too!'). So one tempting interpretation is that the words are not a cry of astonishment or despair but rather an aggressive 'And the same to you, kiddo!' Caesar, in other words, remained defiant to the end. This is attractive. He was a man of iron determination, never one to be worsted – even in death. Hugely popular, he was promptly deified.

Incidentally, *Veni vidi vici* ('I came, I saw, I conquered') were the words written on a placard displayed by Caesar's soldiers as they marched through Rome in 46 BC to celebrate Caesar's conquest of Pompey's troops. The words commemorated the speed of Caesar's victory in 47 BC over a Pompeian ally Pharnaces, son of Mithridates (p. 130), in the city of Zela (modern Zile, northern central Turkey). It took him four hours!

VIII

44 BC – AD 14

TIMELINE

43 BC	'Triumvirate' of Antony, Octavian and Lepidus
	Murder of Cicero
42 BC	Brutus and Cassius defeated at Philippi
41 BC	Affair begins between Antony and Cleopatra
36 BC	Lepidus 'resigned' from triumvirate
	Roman world split between Octavian and Antony
31 BC	Octavian defeats Antony at Actium
30 BC	Deaths of Antony and Cleopatra
27 BC–AD 14	Augustus [Octavian], Rome's first emperor (Julio-Claudians)
27 BC	Octavian made *princeps* and titled 'Augustus'
c. 25 BC	The poet Horace in full flow
23 BC	Augustus made Tribune of the plebs
19 BC	Death of Virgil

18 BC   Augustus' moral legislation

2 BC   Julia banished

AD 6   Judaea comes under Roman control

        Augustus' fire service and veterans' pension fund

AD 8   The poet Ovid exiled

RISING FROM THE ASHES

The First Emperor — Augustus

If the conspirators thought the Republic would spring newborn from Caesar's corpse, they were sadly mistaken. Caesar had built up a huge following that was not going to go away. There was a riot at his funeral. The bewildered Senate ratified all Caesar's legislation and waited to see what would happen next. It turned out to be the emergence of three men: Aemilius Lepidus, in charge of Caesar's troops near Rome at the time; Marc Antony, consul in 44 BC and Caesar's most loyal ally; and Octavian, aged 18, Caesar's great-nephew, but also his adopted son and heir (as Caesar's will revealed). Caesar would not die. Brutus and Cassius accepted provinces abroad – virtual exile.

Cicero, fearful of a new tyrant in Antony and inspired to enter politics again, tried to win Octavian to the traditionalists' side. He failed. In 43 BC Lepidus, Antony and Octavian formed a coalition, carving up the Empire among themselves, killing rivals – including Cicero –

and seizing their property. In 42 BC at Philippi in Greece, Antony and Octavian defeated Brutus and Cassius, which meant virtually the end of the republican cause. Lepidus was 'retired' in 36 BC, leaving Antony and Octavian.

They now split the Empire between them: Octavian in control of the Western Empire, Antony of the Eastern and spending more and more of his time with Cleopatra, with whom he began an affair in 41 BC. It came, yet again, to civil war. On 2 September 31 BC Octavian defeated Antony and Cleopatra at the naval battle off Actium. Pursued by Octavian, the two lovers fled to Egypt where they committed suicide in 30 BC. Octavian, like Marius, Sulla and Pompey before him, could now claim to be master of the Roman world.

Were the Romans about to replay the bloodshed of the last hundred years?

Octavian – henceforth to be called by his imperial name Augustus – did three things to stabilize Rome. First, he persuaded the Senate, *magistratûs* and people that he had restored the Republic. Second, he created a professional standing army under state control, so that they spent their days fighting foreigners rather than screwing deals out of individual dynasts like Sulla, Caesar, Antony and Octavian/Augustus in order to fight each other; and he established the means to pay them by a new tax and by tightening up revenue collection from the provinces. Third, he broke the stranglehold that the old, discredited families had had on politics and opened up power in Rome to Italians, provincials and 'equestrian' families.

Meanwhile, he began to stamp himself on Rome: its architecture, rituals and laws. He found Rome brick and left it marble, said one admirer; temples were restored and others constructed; his trusty lieutenant Agrippa inaugurated new rituals and ceremonies, and new festivals were initiated; he made himself *pontifex maximus* (as did all subsequent emperors), the ultimate source of all religious (i.e., ritual) authority (see p. 24); and he put himself in charge of the law-making process, producing more laws than anyone before him. It was, after the utter disaster of the last years of the Republic, a complete makeover of the way Rome ran itself and projected itself over its burgeoning empire, and Augustus was at the heart of it. But Romans still continued to call it a *res publica* – Republic. It is only we who call it an empire.

The result of his success in this area was a lengthy period of much needed peace. Augustus regularly travelled round the provinces (only in 23, 18, 17 and 12 BC did he spend the whole year in Rome) and he carefully orchestrated diplomatic relations with those on the edge of the Empire. All this was designed to suggest that he had the whole wide world in his hands.

A spanner in the works, however, was this: what happened when Augustus died? In the event, he spent many years trying to establish and prepare the Roman people for a successor of his choice, but he was endlessly foiled by nominees ungratefully dropping dead. His successor in AD 14, ironically enough, was not only the last possible choice but also probably the one man who had no interest in being emperor at all – Tiberius, son of Augustus' wife Livia by her first husband. Many thought this was Livia's doing, and the death of earlier nominees no mere coincidence.

OCTAVIUS-OCTAVIANUS-AUGUSTUS

The young Octavius, born in 63 BC, was from a fairly obscure family, the son of C. Octavius, a very wealthy 'equestrian' and ex-*praetor*. However, his mother, Atia, was a daughter of Caesar's sister Julia. In the mafia world of Roman patronage politics that made all the difference. In 45 BC Caesar adopted him as his son. As a result he would become Gaius Julius Caesar Octavianus – Octavian – with all Caesar's men behind him. It is quite extraordinary to think that when Caesar was assassinated Octavian was immediately raising troops and politicking with veterans like Mark Antony and Cicero – aged 19. In 13 years he would be Rome's first emperor. Caesar could spot them.

ADULTS ONLY

For us, adoption is class-free and all about babies – caring for the unwanted and satisfying emotional needs. In the ancient world, adoption was largely an upper-class institution and far too serious a matter for babies to be involved. Its purpose was to ensure that the family inheritance was passed on to the most favourable person (sometimes at the expense of legitimate sons), so that the family would remain intact and flourish; and, since inheritance went only through the male line, only males, not females, were the targets. The father, as head of the family, made the decision. For an aristocrat in this position, adoption (if needed) was rather like marriage. He would survey the market of spare sons among his aristocratic and successful friends and relations, and hope to make a deal with the best available prospect. This man would then pass fully into the new family, adding –*anus* to his previous family name (thus *Octavius*, but on adoption by Caesar *Octavianus*). It was big business. From AD 14 to 200, for example, only three Roman emperors were survived by natural sons, so families battled it out to get their son adopted into the imperial household. Most famously, Agrippina persuaded her husband the emperor Claudius to adopt Nero, her son by a previous marriage. When Claudius died, Nero succeeded, murdering Claudius' natural son Britannicus for good measure, just in case (p. 241).

THE DEATH OF CICERO

When in 43 BC Octavian, Lepidus and Antony decided to form the coalition and carve up the Empire among them, they bargained between themselves to make a list of 300 rivals for proscription (p. 133): you can list my friend X if I can list your friend Y. Cicero, who regarded Antony as a second dictator, had launched ferocious political attacks against him in 14 speeches known as the *Philippics* (named after the Athenian statesman Demosthenes' attacks against king Philip of Macedon). At one stage Antony was even declared a public enemy. Antony demanded Cicero's head. Cicero heard the news and tried to flee, but was caught and his throat slit. Plutarch continues:

> Antony . . . ordered his head and hands to be fastened up over the public platform in the Forum. When these were brought to him, he gazed at them triumphantly, and burst into peals of delighted laughter. Then, after he had enjoyed the sight to the full, he had them nailed up.

Cicero was not party to the assassination of Caesar, but he once observed that if he had been involved 'there would have been no leftovers'. That is, Marc Antony (at least) would have been killed as well (p. 180). What if . . . ?

ANTONY AND CLEOPATRA

In 41 BC Mark Antony took up with Cleopatra where Caesar had left off. The relationship exploded in a vast sundae of schmaltz when the two met in Cleopatra's royal barge in southern Turkey, and for the same reasons: Antony needed the fabulous wealth of Egypt, while Cleopatra knew the advantages of having mighty Rome on her side. Shakespeare based his description of their encounter ('The barge she sat in, like a burnish'd throne', *Antony and Cleopatra*, II.2) on Sir Thomas North's translation of Plutarch:

> She disdained to set forward otherwise, but to take her barge in the river of Cydnus, the poope whereof was of gold, the sailes of purple, and the owers of silver, which kept stroke in rowing after the sounde of the musicke of flutes, howboyes, citherns, violls, and such other instruments as they played upon in the barge. And now for the person of her selfe: she was layed under a pavillion of cloth of gold of tissue, apparelled and attired like the goddesse Venus, commonly drawen in picture: and hard by her, on either hand of her, pretie faire boyes apparelled as painters doe set forth god Cupide, with litle fannes in their hands, with the which they fanned wind upon her . . .

And so on.

SLING SLANG

Soldiers are soldiers and their language is earthy. At a Gallic triumph Caesar's soldiers sang of him: 'Roman males! Lock up your wives! The bald adulterer's home! In Gaul he shagged away a fortune – borrowed here in Rome!' From the civil wars of the 40s BC we find lead slingshot with messages scrawled on them: 'Aimed at Octavian's arsehole', 'Octavian can't get it up', and so on. In 37 BC Octavian rounded on Antony for abandoning his wife (Octavian's sister Octavia) and settling in Egypt with Cleopatra. Antony replied:

> What's wrong with you? So I'm screwing the queen. But she's my wife. I've been doing it for years. And you just screw Livia, right? Well *done* if, by the time you've read this letter, you haven't also screwed Tertulla or Terentilla or Rufilla or Salvia or the whole lot. Does it matter where or with whom you get it in?

PROPAGANDA MACHINE

As it became clearer in the 30s BC that Octavian in the West and Antony in the East could settle their differences only by war, Octavian, an early and deadly master of the spinner's art, swung into action. Whatever Cleopatra looked like, Octavian's propaganda has controlled our image of her ever since: lubricious, irresistible, extravagant, luring men to disaster. The poet Horace talks of her as a 'mad queen, with her contaminated flocks of men diseased by vice . . . crazed with limitless ambition and drunk with sweet fortune'. When it came to conflict in 31 BC, Octavian declared war on her, not Antony. Octavian was spinning the idea that this was not a civil conflict, but rather a battle against a malign, corrosive foreign power.

HORACE

Quintus Horatius Flaccus – the Roman poet Horace to us – was born on 8 December 65 BC in Apulia (modern Venosa) at a time when the Roman Republic was about to implode. In 44 BC Horace was studying in Athens, the capital of ancient culture where aspiring Romans (Horace was of humble birth, he tells us) went to round off their education. Commissioned by Brutus against Julius Caesar in the post-Ides civil war (i.e., on the losing side), Horace counted himself lucky to find a position back in Rome in the Treasury – where he started writing poetry. Enter Gaius Maecenas, a millionaire confidant of Augustus and agent of his unofficial court. He drew to himself many like-minded Romans, including a number of poets – Virgil, in particular. It was through Virgil that in 38 BC Horace was introduced into the inner circle. Maecenas encouraged the young man and made him financially secure with an estate of half a dozen farms in the Sabine hills. Horace could now devote himself to poetry and pleasure. This was no propagandistic 'lolly for lyrics' deal. Monarchs love to schmooze with elites in the hope of getting a leg-up, and elites love being schmoozed (remember Tony Blair's 'Cool Britannia'?). So it was in Roman literary circles.

Left to their own devices, Maecenas reckoned, poets might be useful to the new regime. Virgil certainly was. As for Horace, his poems acknowledged his gratitude to Maecenas for his farms and acceptance into the cultural elite, and (like most Romans) to Augustus for restoring peace and prosperity. But he valued his independence from the imperial court. He even turned down Augustus' request to become his personal private secretary: not for this short, fat man the burdens of office ('little man, little books', said Augustus). A reputation as a poet was Horace's priority, together with peace of mind, if we can judge by his poetic subjects – pleasure, the country life, wine and friends, love and the passage of time, reflections on the folly of mankind, all underpinned by a sense of the importance of knowing oneself and what one can (and cannot) do. One can relax in Horace's company and enjoy his picture of himself as the convivial, humorous, humane man of the world, looking on the unchanging patterns of life – and smiling.

CLEOPATRA'S NOBLE DEATH

After Antony committed suicide, dying in Cleopatra's arms, Octavian tried to persuade her not to do the same. She tricked him into thinking he had succeeded, but went ahead anyway. Was it a poisonous asp brought to her in a basket of figs or a golden pitcher? Plutarch commented:

> Nobody knows the real truth, since there is another story that she carried poison with her in a hollow comb, which she kept hidden in her hair. Yet no inflammation or any other symptom of poison broke out over her body . . . Octavian was annoyed at Cleopatra's death, but could only admire the nobility of her spirit. He gave orders for her to be buried with royal splendour and magnificence, and her body to be laid beside Antony's.

DAMNATIO MEMORIAE

De mortuis nil nisi bonum was originally a sixth-century BC Greek saying: 'of the dead [speak] nothing but good'. The Romans had other ideas, however. After Antony's suicide the Senate decreed his birthday to be an unlucky day and ordered his name to be erased from every inscription and public monument, his statues to be hauled down and destroyed. Even the combination of the names *Marcus* and *Antonius* was henceforth forbidden. It makes one speculate: what if Antony had defeated Octavian at Actium in 31 BC? Octavian was rather a dour man, though of reptilian cunning. Antony was an altogether sunnier figure, a fine leader of men, all parties, girls and hangovers (he would never have exiled Ovid, p. 209). It would have been a close call whether the opposition, a heart attack or the drink got him first.

HAVING IT BOTH WAYS

When Octavian was returning after defeating Antony and Cleopatra at Actium, someone ran up to him holding a raven, which croaked: 'Hail, Caesar, victorious commander!' (*ave, Caesar, victor imperator*). Duly impressed, he bought it for 20,000 *ss*. The man's chum then revealed that he in fact had another bird. Octavian asked to be shown it, and it croaked: 'Hail, Antony, victorious commander!' Octavian suggested they share the spoils of the each-way bet. Others then arrived with a similarly trained parrot and magpie, which Octavian duly bought. A poor shoemaker saw an opportunity and bought a raven. But it was a very slow learner and the shoemaker kept on moaning at the waste of time and money. However, he eventually managed to get it to learn the words and duly offered it to Octavian, who replied, 'I've got enough of those at home already, thank you.' At which point the raven came up with the only other words it knew: 'What a waste of time and money.' Octavian laughed and bought it for more than any of the others.

FIRST AMONG EQUALS

Octavian needed to show who was boss, but did not want a public title smacking of royalty or grandeur. Likewise, he wanted to create the impression that the Republic was still in existence. So in 27 BC he was made *princeps Senatus* ('first man of the Senate', 'first among equals'; hence the term 'principate' for 'imperial rule') and firmly rejected titles like *dominus* ('lord', 'master'). Further, he reinstated orderly, legal succession to magistracies and other offices, annual elections, regular meetings of the Assemblies, and so on. So there were still consuls, *praetors*, etc., and they still went out to govern provinces after their term of office was over. After holding the consulship every year from 31 to 23 BC (in concert with his close associate Agrippa in 28 and 27 BC) Augustus felt able to relinquish it. A grateful Senate gave him the (religious) title Augustus, the Latin for the Greek *sebastos* ('awesome', 'revered', 'holy'). *Augustus* and *Caesar* were titles adopted by all subsequent emperors.

THE PEOPLE'S EMPEROR

In 23 BC the Senate granted Augustus the honorary power of the Tribune of the plebs. After everything that the Tribunes had done in the past 100 years (p. 115) this was a significant 'popular' power. They also gave him the *imperium* of the consul without having to be a consul (pp. 72, 103); further, it was *maius imperium* – 'greater *imperium*' than anyone else. So everyone else knew where they stood in relation to him: nowhere. But he could argue: was he not simply a senator? And had not the Senate given him all these powers? Since the Senate was the ultimate republican authority it was all entirely legitimate, simply the Senate's response to Rome's new needs after a century of bloodshed. Of *course* it was.

AUGUSTUS' NEW MODEL ARMY

In the first century BC the Roman army was still recruited on a largely
ad hoc basis and generals like Marius (p. 116) began enlisting anyone
on personal terms generous enough to win their loyalty. When Julius
Caesar was assassinated in 44 BC and civil war ensued, the price of a
soldier went through the roof as competing generals offered better and
better terms. After his victory at Actium in 31 BC Augustus wanted the
army loyal to the state and out of the hands of wealthy individuals. He
immediately disbanded the armies involved – about 500,000 soldiers –
and settled 300,000 in land in Italy and abroad (he used his newfound
wealth from Egypt to cover the costs). He decided that 28 legions would
be enough to control the Empire. At 5–6,000 men per legion, plus sailors,
auxiliaries and around 9,000 elite, very well-paid Praetorian Guard in
Rome (the emperor's personal army, used for everything from crowd
control to assassination, spying and fire-prevention), that made about
300,000 in all. The army was now turned into a professional body, with
fixed conditions of service, salaries and length of duty (12 to 16 years),
promotion prospects, a bonus at the end (cash or land) and other perks.
It offered the prospect of a secure and generally agreeable existence after
the chaos of the civil war years. This was central to Augustus' plans:
when asked how he was, he used to reply, 'I and the army are well.'
'Republic' or not, Rome was now a military state. The visible presence
of the emperor's elite Praetorian Guard, based *inside* the city, an area
previously forbidden to armed soldiers, could not have made a clearer
statement.

PAYING FOR THE ARMY

Rome's first professional standing army was not cheap. Since provincial revenues were an essential part of Rome's financial equation, Augustus introduced regular censuses and assessments of possible revenue streams. Further, though Romans did not pay tax on income, special taxes were raised, often for specific purposes (e.g., from the fourth century BC a 5 per cent tax on freeing slaves was used to buy gold ingots to go into Rome's emergency fund). So in AD 6 Augustus raised from *all* Roman citizens a 5 per cent tax on inheritances and bequests to pay for the veterans' pension fund. The army was now everyone's responsibility.

KEEPING PROVINCES LOYAL

Provincial governors were powerful people. They were in charge of the raising of provincial revenue and had troops at their disposal, but after the last hundred years of the Republic, everyone knew where *that* might lead. So Augustus took as his own *provincia* most of those provinces that contained Roman troops, which he ruled from Rome, through his own appointees. All provincial governors therefore came to be seen as his personal deputies. With governors loyal to him and not some other faction, an army would now move on *his* command and his alone. Furthermore, with Augustus breathing down their necks, governors had a strong incentive to keep the provincial revenues flowing.

AUGUSTUS' INNER CIRCLE

Aula – the Latin adaptation of the Greek word for 'monarch's court' – was the word used to describe the closed circle through which the emperor kept power. It was used once in republican literature, but became commonplace under the Empire. It described not a place, but the existence of an enclosed circle of courtiers around the emperor; they had access to him themselves and controlled access for others. Immediate family bulked large in the circle, as did slaves and freedmen, while the fear of being excluded kept the circle loyal. The philosopher Epictetus (p. 307) made this point: 'No one loves Caesar; but we do love riches, a tribunate, a praetorship, a consulship. Anyone who has these things at his disposal is our master.' The price was a high one, he went on: if you wanted office 'you must stay up at night, run back and forth, kiss hands, wait on other people's doors, and say and do many slavish things'. But even that was no guarantee of success, he continued: you can attach yourself to the emperor, but 'the emperor might die, or what if he became your enemy?' But so it was with all imperial courts. And modern political ones, too.

OUTSIDE IN

To maintain civilian control Augustus saw that he had to sideline the old guard – the powerful families who had caused such chaos in the past – and create a new elite, drawn from all over Italy and, later, the Mediterranean. These men would owe their position to him and nobody else, let alone to their families' *past* status and authority. So he opened positions as senators to Italians and provincials from, for example, Gaul, Spain, Africa and Greece. The wealthy non-senatorial class, the 'equestrians', were also given new, emperor-determined career paths in the service of the state – in the military and finance, in property management, provincial management, grain supply, praetorian command in Rome, etc. From now on, elites hitherto on the outside could find their way into the inner circle. The emperor's slaves and freedmen (p. 149) were also given important functions in the palace – advising on everything from finance to policy. So over the years Augustus completely restructured Roman society, releasing talent that would share his vision of what needed to be done and not keep harking back to the way it used to be. *Augustus* was now the way it used to be, and Romans had better remember it.

MONUMENTAL PROPAGANDA

Augustus understood the importance of public monuments, secular and religious, as an expression of the idea of Rome and 'Roman-ness', and their power to tie people into *his* vision of what Rome should be. So he built extensively and encouraged others to do the same. Augustus' faithful lieutenant Vipsanius Agrippa, a fine soldier who won Actium for him (p. 186), was one of the many people who spent their own money furthering Augustus' plans for the physical transformation of Rome. He renovated and built temples and aqueducts, piping water further across Rome, constructed public porticoes, gardens, a granary and a bridge, repaired streets and cleaned out and enlarged the Cloaca Maxima. Indeed, when it was completed, we are told, he sailed through it into the Tiber! He distributed free olive oil and salt to Romans, offered free baths for a year and free haircuts. This was an example of the way in which very rich, politically ambitious men saw it both as their duty and to their own advantage to spend lavishly on public projects for the benefit of the people.

FIRE BRIGADE

Rome was notorious for its fires. On average there seem to have been about 100 fires a day in the city, 20 large, 2 serious. As a wealthy Roman observed, the returns on urban properties were far higher than those on rural ones, and he would sell up all the latter and buy the former like a shot 'if some way could be found to stop houses in Rome catching fire all the time'. So in AD 6 Augustus put a 4 per cent tax on the sale of slaves to fund a new service. He set up a *praefectus* with its own headquarters and office staff in charge of seven cohorts of 500 firefighters (*vigiles*). Each cohort, housed in barracks, looked after two of the city's 14 administrative districts. Since, in the absence of matches, for example, fires were kept burning, they patrolled extensively at night when the danger was greatest.

House owners were required to keep a supply of water available and other material for fighting fires – vinegar, mats, poles, ladders, sponges, buckets and brooms. In the absence of hoses, manpower and buckets were essential; the brigades brought pumps, hooks, mattocks and axes, and *ballistae* to knock down nearby houses and create fire breaks. Four doctors were attached to each cohort. The secret was to get in early. Smell was very important.

Eventually, one Egnatius Rufus tried to set up an elementary fire-fighting force. The emperor had him executed. He would have gained too much political credibility from this highly beneficial scheme.

VITRUVIUS, MASTER ARCHITECT

Romans adored technical literature: books on farming, warfare, medicine, navigation and so on were wildly popular among most literate people. Around 25 BC Vitruvius wrote his ten books on architecture, taking classical Greek principles and showing how 'Roman' they really were. These books survive in full and are the most important work on the subject ever composed; they were especially influential during the fourteenth-century humanist renaissance. Vitruvius told his readers what to build and in what classical proportions, all with precise instructions appended: choice of site, use of material, styles, decorations and finishing as they related to temples, theatres, farms, houses, water supply, sundials, water clocks, cranes, pumps, catapults, siege engines and so on. But Vitruvius' influence was not limited to this. He also made the case for all responsible professionals to have a serious, broad grounding in the liberal, humanistic arts – history, geography, art, science, astronomy, technology, music, law, proportion, philosophy and so on were all considered important. The reason was simple: if one wanted to produce the best for humans, one had to understand the best of everything that humans had produced.

INESTIMABLE ESTIMATES

At the beginning of his Book 10 on architecture, Vitruvius launched an attack on inaccurate building estimates, proposing a Greek solution:

> In the famous and important Greek city of Ephesus, there is said to be an ancient law, the terms of which are severe, but its justice is not inequitable. When an architect accepts a commission for some public work, he has to promise what the cost will be. His estimate is handed to the official, and his assets are held as security by the state until the work is done. When it is finished, if the cost agrees

with his estimate, he is awarded special decrees and marks of
honour. If no more than a quarter has to be added to his estimate,
it is paid by the treasury, and no penalty is inflicted. But when
more than a quarter has had to be spent on the work, the money
required to finish it is taken from his assets. If only the immortal
gods had made it so that this law had also been adopted by the
Roman People, not only for public buildings but private ones too!

Not to mention modern governments, whose grotesque failure to
control expenditure on any projects, especially military ones, makes one
wonder why they bother with estimates at all. The Ministry of Defence,
we are told, recently spent a billion pounds to produce precisely no
armoured vehicles.

POETIC POWER

Nobody pays any serious attention to poets these days except other
poets. But in Rome they carried clout. The composition of the *Aeneid*
by Virgil – the story of Rome's first founder Aeneas, written to look
forward to Augustus as its re-founder – was eagerly followed by
Augustus. When he was away on his campaign in 26 BC he begged the
poet with a combination of entreaties and joking threats to send him
'either the first sketch or any specimen'. Much later, when the work
was essentially finished, Virgil recited three books to him – the second,
fourth and sixth.

Augustus also tried hard to befriend the lyric poet Horace. Augustus
wrote to him: 'Take advantage of any privilege in my house as if you
lived with me.' When Horace turned down a job, Augustus wrote, 'Even

if you disdainfully reject my friendship, I do not return your disdain.'
As for Ovid, perhaps Rome's most brilliant poet, Augustus thought his
love poetry so dangerous that he exiled him (see p. 209).

VIRGIL: *ECLOGUES* AND *GEORGICS*

Why does a culture suddenly start sprouting seriously high-class
poets? Lucretius and Catullus should have been quite enough for first-
century BC Rome, but they kept on coming. Enter Publius Vergilius
(the Roman spelling) Maro (70–19 BC) – Virgil, the most famous of
them all, living through a period of bloodshed and turmoil, but with
hope renewed in the emergence of Augustus. Virgil cut his poetic
teeth on what to us is a most unlikely poetic genre: pastoral, invented
by Theocritus, a Greek poet living in Sicily in the third century BC. In
Virgil's *Eclogues* (38 BC) assorted shepherds and goatherds tootle away
to each other on their pipes. They sing of their lives and loves and gently
explore the possibilities of comparing country life with political life, to
see what light the one might cast on the other – or whether they can
coexist at all. This poem was Virgil's passport into the literary circle
of the fabulously wealthy Maecenas, Rome's greatest patron of the
arts and friend and agent of Octavian/Augustus. Virgil's next work,
Georgics (c. 29 BC), took much further the theme of country and political
life. It ran to four books on the work of the farmer (I: crops; II: trees and
shrubs; III: livestock; IV: bees); and in it, Virgil combines agricultural
instruction with reflection on the nature of the world and man's place in
it. At the heart of this masterpiece is a call, in a period of total upheaval,
for a return to ancient values, in the shape of praise for the virtues of
country life in contrast with Rome as it was then:

Here right and wrong are reversed: so many wars in the
world, so many faces of evil: the plough not worthy of any
honour, our lands neglected, robbed of farmers, and the
curved pruning-hooks beaten into solid blades.
Here Germany, there Euphrates wages war:
neighbouring cities take up arms, breaking the laws
that bound them: impious Mars rages through the world:
just as when the chariots stream from the starting gates, add
to their speed each lap, and the charioteer, tugging vainly
at the bridles, is dragged on by the horses, the chariot not
responding to the reins.

(trans. A. S. Kline)

VIRGIL: *AENEID*

Virgil's *Aeneid* is an epic – the story of the founding of the Roman race.
The poem begins:

Arms and the man I sing, who forced by Fate
And haughty Juno's unrelenting hate,
Expelled and exiled, left the Trojan shore.
Long labours, both by sea and land he bore;
[and founded in Italy the Roman people] –
From whence the race of Alban fathers come,
And the long glories of majestic Rome.

(trans. John Dryden)

The 'man' is Aeneas, who fled the burning city of Troy as it was
being sacked by Greeks and with a band of Trojans set out on the high

seas for Italy. The pro-Greek goddess Juno hated them and harried them all the way. But their mission was divinely ordained. The Trojans finally landed in Italy and after fighting off local opposition settled in Alba Longa. It was Aeneas' descendant Romulus, some 300 years later (by myth-historical reckoning), who founded Rome in 753 BC (p. 3).

Virgil here has one eye firmly on Homer. In his first six 'Odyssean' books he tells us how Aeneas ('the man') travels the seas to reach his (new) home; in the following six 'Iliadic' books ('arms') we learn how he allies himself with the local king Latinus and fights off the opposition to their settling in Italy.

Virgil also had his eyes on the contemporary world. When Aeneas visits his father Anchises in the underworld he 'predicts' the Augustan age and Rome's mission. Leave all that fancy artistic stuff, says Anchises, to the Greeks –

> But, Rome, 't is thine alone, with awful sway,
> To rule mankind, and make the world obey,
> Disposing peace and war by thy own majestic way;
> To tame the proud, the fetter'd slave to free:
> These are imperial arts, and worthy thee.
>
> (trans. John Dryden)

Anchises also 'foresees' the death of Marcellus, the first of the young men Augustus hoped would succeed him (p. 214). Octavia, Marcellus' mother, fainted when Virgil finished reading this section aloud to her and her father Augustus. Aeneas' affair with Dido in Carthage, which ends in her curses and suicide when he leaves her to continue on his mission, 'explained' the later Punic Wars (p. 86). But overarching all this was Aeneas the *pius*, a man who respected the claims of family, gods and country: a true Roman.

Virgil knew that empire exerted a painful price in lives and happiness and he did not attempt to disguise the fact. But the question remained: 'Was it worth it all?' By locating his epic in the deep 'Homeric' past, gods and all, and both historicizing and Romanizing that mix, Virgil generated a sense of the historical and divine inevitability and therefore rightness about the founding of Rome. For Romans, the *Aeneid* was the ultimate statement of true *Romanitas*: what it meant to be a Roman and why they were winners. One cannot imagine a modern poet being invited to take on such a commission, let alone fulfilling it – not in England, anyway. Though the European Union might.

CARTHAGE RISES AGAIN

When the Romans destroyed Carthage in 146 BC (see p. 109) it was assumed that was the end of it. But it was far too important a strategic position, a harbour on an inhospitable coastline. Caesar started to refound it and Augustus finished the job. In so doing the Romans sliced off *the whole of the top of the hill* to form a flat base on which to begin the rebuilding (we know this because the hilltop is scattered down the hillsides). Romans did not do things by half. In time Carthage was to rise again as one of the most important cities of the Mediterranean.

THE CENSUS AT JESUS' BIRTH

Augustus kept a regular check on the population of his Empire for tax purposes. St Luke recorded one of these censuses as the background to his version of the nativity story. It went as follows: Joseph of Galilee was of King David's line and David was born in Bethlehem in Judaea. So Joseph had to travel to Bethlehem to be registered for the Roman census there. Wrong. Romans were taxed by property, not lineage; and Joseph owned property in Nazareth, not Bethlehem. Mary was irrelevant. But there are more problems. Matthew said that the Judaea of that day was ruled by King Herod, not a provincial governor. So Romans did *not* control it. How, then, could they take a census there? Luke is even more confused. He tells us that the Roman governor of Judaea, Quirinius, was in power at Jesus' birth. But Herod died in 4 BC and only in AD 6 did Judaea come under Roman control for census purposes. Finally, Joseph came from Galilee, and Galilee was *not* under Roman control at that time. So Joseph had no reason to pay Roman tax. What on earth is going on? Well, the Old Testament said the Messiah would be born in Bethlehem. So Luke, like Matthew, had to find some excuse for Jesus being born there. This was the best he could do. Alpha for invention, gamma-minus for accuracy.

THE GOSPEL'S GOOD NEWS FOR HISTORIANS

Whatever one's view of the Gospels as religious documents, they are invaluable as historical ones, for a very specific reason. All Roman literature that we possess was composed by educated authors for their peers from the upper reaches of society. So it is strongly Romano-centric: whatever the matter in hand – pursuing the woman you love or describing the habits and lifestyle of the Germans – the culture, values and outlook of the educated Roman underpinned every page. To read the Gospels, however, is to come into contact with a Jewish loaves-and-fishes peasant world in which Rome barely featured, until the climax of the story. Omit the crucifixion and one would hardly know the narrative was set in what was then a Roman province. It raises the question: what impact did the Empire have on the average peasant in the field? Very little indeed, would seem to be the answer from the Gospels. But then the Gospel writers had their own agendas, as did the Romans.

LEGISLATING MORALS

The first century BC in Rome had seen something of a sexual revolution. Catullus boasted in his poetry about his affair with a married woman whom he nicknamed Lesbia (p. 168); Ovid's poetry seemed openly to celebrate such liaisons. Augustus thought such behaviour was a threat to the political and social order. So in 18 BC he launched a back-to-basics campaign to stamp out adultery and force the upper classes to marry and have children. First, adultery became a public crime as well as a private offence. A wronged husband could prosecute both wife and lover, with punishments including exile. Then a marriage law was passed which placed liabilities on those who did not marry (men, between 25 and 60, women between 20 and 50); and further consequences if the married couple did not have any children. The first was that their property automatically reverted to the state; the second was that the more children a man had the earlier he could stand for office. The Romans deeply resented the whole fatuous scheme. It was a total failure. It always is.

LOW JINKS IN HIGH PLACES

Augustus' daughter Julia was a victim of her father's moral legislation. If the stories are true she was a practical joker, born to have fun, enjoying riotous parties and assignations with her many lovers in the very middle of the Forum. In 2 BC Augustus banished her to Pandateria (Ventotone), a tiny island west of Naples, and exiled her lover Gracchus to Cercina (an island east of Tunisia). In AD 8 the same treatment was meted out to the poet Ovid. His deliciously immoral poem *Ars Amatoria* (*Seduction Made Easy*), a witty, sexy treatise on how to get your woman (or man), did not find favour with the strait-laced Augustus, though it enjoyed great success after the Julia scandal. Augustus exiled Ovid to Tomis (Constanta) in Romania on the Black Sea, for (as Ovid said) 'a poem and a mistake'. The poem we know about. The mistake was perhaps some (sexual?) indiscretion involving Augustus' household.

OVID: POET OF LOVE

Every culture has its joker. In Augustan Rome this honour fell to Publius Ovidius Naso (43 BC–AD 17) – Ovid. Asked which line of his poetry he would consign to the flames, he said (from the Minotaur story), 'A half-bull man, a half-man bull'. And what line would he keep? 'A half-bull man, a half-man bull'. Very Oscar Wilde. Very Ovid.

Perhaps as early as the mid-20s BC Ovid had made his mark with his *Amores*, a selection of elegiac love poetry in three books. It was a stunning debut for one so young. Further slender volumes poured out, the most controversial being his light-hearted instruction manual *Ars Amatoria* (how to get your girl/boy), soon to be followed by his *Remedia Amoris* (how to get rid of your girl/boy). Very Ovid. All these books treat the subject matter lightly, wittily and ironically – Ovid's own escapades in love have at times an almost soap-opera quality about them – and parody and self-mockery are well to the fore. They also use 'heroic' myth extensively to illustrate the dilemmas of everyday young lovers, thereby increasing the fun.

When it came to love Ovid did not feel he always had to stir his soul to its depths with a pole. To give an example: in *Amores* 3.2 he imagines himself at the chariot races with a woman he wants to sleep with. After admitting he couldn't care less about the races but it's a great place to be with the woman he's after (various *doubles entendres* on 'riding'), he presses up close to her ('one advantage of the narrow seating'), picks up her dress ('it's trailing on the ground') to admire her legs (just like Atalanta's or Diana's, he comments) and admits he's feeling 'hot' ('let me fan you – unless it's just *me*'). 'Look! Some dust on your dress! Let me brush it off.' Then the race starts. Ovid urges on his girl's favourite, the crowd goes wild ('hide your head in my cloak in case your hair gets spoiled'), the right chariot wins and:

> She laughed. Her eyes sparkled and she promised –
> something.
> That'll do for me here and now. Do the rest for me . . .
> somewhere else.

Ovid's sexy, witty and indiscreet elegiacs, which made *pleasure* the purpose of love and poetry, were quite unique. No Roman had ever written love poetry like this, nor ever would again: the genre died out with Ovid.

OVID: POET OF TRANSFORMATION

Ovid's great masterpiece is his 15-book *Metamorphoses* (*Transformations*). The basic *mise-en-scène* is Olympus, where the gods are chatting among themselves. With fiendish narrative ingenuity (involving changes of scene and narrator, usually through 'Chinese box' stories within stories) Ovid uses this setting to string together almost every myth known to man involving a change of shape.

'What if these stories involved real people?' he asks. 'How might they work in real life? What would the characters be like and what would they do and say?' He then applied all his ingenuity to humanize them and bring them vividly to life in a way his readership would enjoy. Having a more powerful, inventive and sympathetic imagination than perhaps any other ancient poet, he was able to find the contemporary human angle in even the most fantastic of ancient myths; and as a master of pathos and humour, he had rich territory to work with as Narcissus falls in love with himself, Byblis falls in love with her brother, and Io finds herself turned into a cow. What would it be *like* to realize you are a cow? Ovid asked. He was the master of 'What if . . . ?'

If Ovid was an entertainer, the performing flea of Roman poetry, that should not be taken to mean he was lightweight. Go to any art gallery and it is Ovid's account of a myth that will often have caught the artist's eye. Read sixteenth- and seventeenth-century poetry and Ovid will be in the mix somewhere – he is possibly the West's most influential poet.

PUNISHMENT BY EXILE

Exile is not fashionable as a punishment these days, but is rather an escape route for those wishing to avoid paying taxes (hence 'tax exile'). In Roman times it was quite common. At its mildest it meant temporary expulsion from Roman territory; at its harshest it meant banishment in perpetuity to a specific location ('an island or oasis', as the saying went) with loss of property and citizenship, and certain death should you return. However, exile was also available *voluntarily* to any Roman threatened with the death penalty; even those on whom the death sentence had already been passed were usually given time to flee before it was carried out. This option, however, tended to be restricted to the upper classes.

FOOD FOR THOUGHT: POLLIO AND THE MORAY EELS

While the wealthy nowadays compete on the size of their helipads, swimming pools or desks – many so large they have their own postcode – the Romans did so in the first century BC with their fishponds, which Lucius Murena ('Eel') invented. Eels indeed were a favourite, including congers, morays and lampreys. They live in salt, brackish or fresh water, and at all temperatures. Moray eels are especially nasty. They have rear-hooked teeth, a very strong bite and can seriously wound humans; they sometimes bite off the fingers of those who feed them. One Vedius Pollio kept morays and on one occasion he was entertaining Augustus in his luxury villa when a slave accidentally smashed a glass. Pollio ordered him to be thrown into the moray pond. (The Christian writer Tertullian observed that when Pollio had slaves killed in this way, he would order the eels to be cooked immediately, so that he could taste his slaves' flesh.) However, Augustus wanted the slave to be spared and Pollio, naturally, yielded. The emperor then asked to see Pollio's crystal glass collection. It was produced and Augustus smashed the lot. When Pollio died he left his villa *Pausilupon* (Greek for 'Duncarin' or *Sans Souci*) in his will to

Augustus. Augustus destroyed it. But the name survives in the modern name of the town Posilippo.

MOSAIC LORE

We automatically associate mosaics with the Romans, but as with so much that is deemed Roman the art was learned from the Greeks after Rome provincialized Greece in the second century BC. Corinth boasted the first surviving Greek decorated (pebble) mosaic – a circular shape, bordered with triangles, meanders and a wave band, featuring an ithyphallic donkey, a centaur pursuing a leopard and dated *c*. 420 BC. Such work required trained craftsmen and the training became even more intense when, from the third century BC, Greek mosaics began to be made from stone of a wide range of colours, precisely cut into cubes (*tesserae*) and soon of such fineness (less than one millimetre square) that from no great distance they looked like paintings.

MOSAICS FIT FOR PURPOSE

A mosaic is not simply a picture made of pebble, stone or glass set in clay, plaster or mortar. It is also an architectural and social form. Elaborate, multi-coloured mosaics were luxury items, designed to impress and found almost exclusively in wealthy private houses rather than public places. Laid in dining rooms they reflected the layout of the couches, the area which the couches cover being less finely worked. Mosaics established a room 'hierarchy', the cheaper black-and-white mosaics ushering visitors through to the multi-colour designs defining the main reception areas (in the baths at Roman Ostia, a sequence of marine figures 'greets' the visitor and 'guides' him round). When the floor mosaic was designed as a picture, however, it could be seen the 'proper' way up from only one side of the room. So a common compromise was to orient it in such a way that at least everyone entering the room saw it the right way up. A mosaic's subject matter could also indicate room usage – food and drink in the dining area, love scenes in bedrooms, masseurs in bathrooms (one mosaic contains their names, so that they can be summoned).

Some exhibited a fine sense of humour. Pliny the Elder describes a *trompe l'œil* mosaic by Sosus from Pergamum depicting an unswept floor, littered with the debris of a meal. Frequently floor mosaics, wall paintings and ceiling designs were integrated, suggesting a high degree of advanced planning. From the first century AD mosaics flooded the Empire from Italy to Britain, from Spain to North Africa, from Sicily to Syria; and their placement on walls and vaults began a tradition that was to be dramatically extended in Christian churches from the fourth century AD. We know little about individual mosaicists, though a few of them left us their signatures. Mere artisans, they were paid in the same range as bakers, carpenters and blacksmiths (but less than painters). Only one contract survives for laying a mosaic. It instructs 'for the flower, follow the design provided by the royal palace'. So were there copybooks illustrating the repertoire? And did the same man design and lay the mosaics? Many questions remain.

LINE OF SUCCESSION

Augustus had a terrible job trying to line up the next emperor, without whom he could not establish the principle of imperial succession. One by one his choices died or were killed in battle. Eventually only Livia's son by her first marriage, Tiberius, was left, as well as the uncongenial

Agrippa Postumus, Augustus' last grandchild by Julia. Which gave Livia great satisfaction, according to the rumour-mongers. However, another rumour spread that Augustus on his deathbed was thinking of making Agrippa Postumus his successor after all! Livia moved like lightning. She recalled Tiberius from Rhodes and (the historian Tacitus hints) 'saw to' Augustus. Silence descended on the palace. Then the sudden announcement: Augustus was dead and Tiberius was emperor. Done and dusted. And Agrippa Postumus? Well, stuff happens. He was promptly done away with. That was the tabloid world of hints and rumours about what went on in the imperial palace – and how women were typically thought to play their cards. It is not unknown today.

WOMEN IN ROMAN HISTORY

Thanks to Freud and others we possess a psychological language of character and personality – traumas, inhibitions, repression and so forth – that encourages biographers to probe deeply into their subjects' lives, seeking that intimate understanding that makes them unique and therefore interesting. Ancient historians knew nothing of such individual subjectivity. It was the celebration of great men and their achievements that counted, especially their ethical stances – were they just, courageous, patriotic, loyal, virtuous, prudent, wise and so on? – and the extent to which they met norms of acceptable communal behaviour. Plenty of moralizing rammed the lesson home.

Women did not count. They were individually valued, but great public achievements were the preserve of men, who held political office and led armies into battle. Any woman who aspired to that sort of thing was regarded as a dangerous pervert. So the life of a Roman woman remains something of a mystery, even a long-lived, famous and influential woman like Livia, wife of Augustus.

LIVIA, WIFE OF AUGUSTUS: TRUTH AND FICTION

Livia's story emerges only around the edges of Augustus's – and there is precious little of that. The first two certain events to which the record gives us access are her birth (probably in 58 BC) and her first marriage (probably in 43 BC). But because Tiberius, her son by her first marriage, survived all the disasters of succession that beset Augustus, Roman historians grew suspicious. Surely the real reason for Tiberius' success was that Livia got rid of his rivals one by one, using that old female standby, poison, so that her boy could succeed (and was she not a keen herbal gardener? See p. 55). But that is what Romans *would* say of an influential, determined woman who exemplified the virtues of the traditional, self-disciplined, home-loving, hard-working Roman wife and mother. She also achieved an unexampled position of respect and authority in the male political world. When someone asked her what she did to maintain her grip over Augustus, she replied that 'she remained scrupulously chaste, gladly did everything he wanted, did not meddle in any of his business, and pretended not to hear about or be aware of any of his love affairs'. Augustus set great store by such a wife at a time when he was trying to restore Rome's 'traditional' probity after the bloody nightmares of civil war. On his deathbed, his last words to his wife were reported to be: 'Farewell, Livia; always live mindful of our marriage.'

AUGUSTUS' MEMORIAL

You can think globally, as the advertisement says, but you must act locally – or the locals will act for you. Augustus' memorial offers a good example. His *Res Gestae* ('My Achievements') was inscribed on two bronze plaques and placed outside his mausoleum in Rome and all around the Empire. This document of approximately 350 lines is a stupendous list of achievements and honours ('I restored these buildings, built these temples, put on these shows, conquered these lands, took these offices') interspersed with occasional comment emphasizing his conservatism (e.g., 'I did not accept office contrary to our ancestors' customs'). Its main purpose was to show how Augustus 'brought the world under the Empire of the Roman people'. But local communities tinkered with the text. Whereas the Latin plaques tended to stress the greatness of Roman power, Greek versions rather played down that aspect. Greeks still had their pride.

AUGUSTUS' BENEVOLENCE

Augustus was proud of 'the private money which he devoted to the state and the people' and on his memorial record he listed in detail his various benefactions. He recorded handouts to every single Roman of 300 *ss* in 44 BC (under Julius Caesar's will) and 400 *ss* in 29, then 24 and 11 BC. He bought land for troops in Italy and the provinces to a sum of 860 million *ss*; and gave another 400 million *ss* in 'rewards' to soldiers later on. He transferred private funds of 320 million *ss* to the Treasury; he paid for grain distribution among the people when Treasury funds ran short, and so on. It seems unlikely any modern politician could match such a record.

IX

AD 14–96

TIMELINE

AD 14–37   Tiberius emperor

AD 26   Tiberius retires to Capri

AD 31   Sejanus' conspiracy uncovered

AD 37   Pontius Pilate relieved of control of Judaea

AD 37–41   Caligula emperor

AD 41–54   Claudius emperor

AD 43   Invasion of Britain

AD 48   Introduces Gauls into Senate

Claudius has his wife Messalina murdered

AD 49   Claudius marries Agrippina

AD 50   Claudius adopts Nero

AD 54–68   Nero emperor

AD 54   Murder of Britannicus

AD 56   The historian Tacitus born

AD 58   St Paul arrested

AD 59   Murder of Agrippina

         Gladiator riot in Pompeii

AD 60   Boudicca's revolt

AD 64   Great Fire of Rome

AD 66   Jewish rebellion

AD 68   Death of Nero; end of Julio-Claudians

AD 69   Year of Four Emperors

AD 70–79   Vespasian emperor (Flavian emperors)

AD 70   Jerusalem captured

AD 73–7   Frontinus governor of Britain

AD 77–84   Agricola governor of Britain

AD 79–81   Titus emperor

AD 79   Pompeii buried under explosion of Vesuvius

AD 80   'Colosseum' completed

AD 81–92   Domitian emperor (last Flavian emperor)

AD 82–92   Rhine and Balkan campaigns

AD 83   Battle of Mons Graupius

AD 89   Stoic thinker Epictetus sets up in Nicopolis

AD 90   The poet Martial in full flow

BEDDING DOWN TOGETHER

Emperor and People

Note: surveys will be a little longer now because every emperor was different and there were so many of them. Yet there are continuities – the transition to the new man; his authority; relations with the elite, people and army; and the finances, stability and extent of the Empire. Economic planning, so familiar to us, barely featured in the emperor's thoughts.

Augustus' successor Tiberius (AD 14–37) was in a difficult position taking over from someone like Augustus. Like all the early emperors he had to reconcile the elite, and those with memories of the free debate of the Republic, to one-man rule. Indeed, the armies on the Rhine and Danube immediately mutinied – potentially disastrous for Augustus' imperial, military-backed 'Republic' – but they were brought to heel, and Tiberius secured the basis of the Empire's northern frontier along the Rhine–Danube. But the real problem was twofold: he did not want the job, likening running the Empire to 'holding a wolf by the ears', and felt that the Senate should play a more active part in government, not simply kowtow to the emperor's every whim. The historian Tacitus recorded that, whenever Tiberius left the Senate house, he muttered in Greek, 'Men trained for servitude!' Indeed, Tiberius seemed much happier with intellectual problems, quizzing academics on obscure horological and mythical matters.

Thoroughly fed up with the whole business, in AD 26 Tiberius retired to his villas on Capri, never to return, leaving a sidekick in charge in Rome. Sejanus, prefect (commander) of the imperial Praetorian Guard, had never held public office, but he was a non-senatorial 'equestrian' appointment (p. 198), and duly given *imperium*, a consulship and so on. This did not go down well with the plebs, who expected the emperor to be there looking after them – that's what Augustus had done, wasn't it? When Tiberius learned Sejanus was plotting to overthrow him, he had him and many senators killed, which caused tremors across the Empire. One of the people he dismissed was Pontius Pilate, governor of Judaea, in AD 37. That said, Tiberius did maintain Augustus' policy of not attempting to expand the Empire.

Tiberius' successor was Gaius Caligula (AD 37–41). He was a great hit with the people because he looked to them for support rather than to the Senate, lavishing shows on them. But the money soon ran out, and with it, his popularity. He adopted Eastern styles of behaviour. Lurid tales sprang up about his private life, not disproved by his public performances (he set off a riot in Jerusalem by trying to get his image set up in the Temple). He became more and more erratic – he was so hairy no one was allowed to mention goats in his presence – and relations with the Senate deteriorated because no senator knew where he stood. Attempts were made on his life, finally successful in AD 41.

With no successor lined up, the Praetorian Guard stepped in and hauled out Claudius (AD 41–54), Caligula's uncle. He had taken refuge behind a curtain in the palace, in fear of an anti-imperial coup. So the military-backed 'Republic' continued. Since he was no soldier and crippled as well, Claudius was never accepted by the Senate, and repaid it in kind with more executions than any first-century emperor (around 200 'equestrians' and 35 senators). The problem was that the Senate was still reluctant to play its part in government, not knowing where it stood any more, but the burden of administration grew. So Claudius relied more and more on his own household, slaves, freedmen and (four) wives to get it all done. This did nothing to endear him to the aristocracy and made accusations of corruption possible. That said, Claudius, who had a love of history and Roman antiquities, seems to have been a good administrator; he sorted out the imperial finances and kept the show on the road. He tried to make up for his lack of military achievement – always an important part of an emperor's image – by invading Britain in AD 43 and turning it into a province (it was to cause endless trouble to the Romans) and he extended the Empire in the East. Claudius was not helped by his marriages. His third wife Messalina was said to have won a shagging competition against prostitutes; his last wife, the strong-minded Agrippina (his niece), managed to persuade Claudius to adopt her son by a previous marriage, Nero, into the line of succession, while (it was said) bumping off Claudius' son Britannicus. In AD 54 Claudius died. Some said Agrippina poisoned him.

❀

Nero (AD 54–68) became emperor at 16. In his early years he was guided by Seneca (the Younger), his millionaire philosopher-tutor, as well as the bureaucrat Burrus, both the choice of his mother Agrippina. This left Nero time to indulge his passion for acting, singing and charioteering, not the sort of thing an emperor did, but popular with the plebs. When he wanted to divorce his wife Octavia for one Poppaea, Agrippina tried to stop him. In AD 59 he had Agrippina murdered, his wife executed and married Poppaea. This drew protests and changed everything. Seneca and Burrus were sidelined and Nero turned to his inner circle of advisers, mostly freedmen. A revolt in Britain in AD 60, led by Boudicca, was finally put down. A devastating fire in Rome in AD 64 was ascribed to Christians and enabled Nero to build a huge folly – his 'Golden House' – on the ruins, wrecking Rome's finances. In AD 66 Nero caused a rebellion in Jerusalem with his tax demands. Conspiracies formed against him, senatorial bloodbaths ensued, but Nero survived and to demonstrate his domination of affairs he went on a tour of Greece, the home of culture, to show off his charioteering skills. It was all becoming too much for the usually loyal Roman elite. In AD 68 a number of provincial governors mutinied, including Galba in Spain. On 9 June the Praetorian Guard declared for Galba. A friendless Nero fled and committed suicide.

There was no obvious successor and AD 69 became known as the 'Year of the Four Emperors'. Galba, the first to claim the throne, was quickly murdered and replaced by a disillusioned supporter Otho. But the Roman army on the Rhone had its own candidate in Vitellius. Otho's army was defeated, but the armies in the East had *their* own candidate

Vespasian, who was busy suppressing the Jewish revolt started by Nero. Vespasian marched on Rome, Vitellius was defeated and killed and Vespasian became emperor. Clearly emperors could be made outside Rome, 'anointed' by their armies and put in place by force. So was it back to civil wars and the final bloody years of the Republic? This time at least the armies in question were regular ones (not the *ad hoc* personal armies gathered by Marius and Sulla), and the new emperors were all properly ratified by the Senate and the people. Further, it did not look as if there was any demand for the Republic to be restored: the military-backed, imperial 'Republic' was secure.

So ended the 'Julio-Claudian' emperors, i.e., emperors descended from the Julius and Claudius families (the Claudian element entered through Livia's first marriage to a Claudius and her son Tiberius Claudius, the second emperor). Vespasian was of the Flavius family and succeeded by his two sons, the elder Titus and Domitian – the Flavian emperors.

Vespasian (emperor AD 70–79) had served in many military campaigns – including Britain in AD 43 – and had accompanied Nero to Greece; he was then sent to deal with rebellion in Judaea, whence he emerged to become emperor. He was of humble origins, simple tastes and hard-working. When he became emperor his first job was to restore the finances, wrecked by Nero and civil war, and regroup and impose discipline on the army. He also mended bridges with the Senate. In Britain the Romans moved into Wales, the north and Scotland; Vespasian made Agricola (the historian Tacitus' father-in-law) governor of Britain (AD 77–84) and began building what we (but not the Romans) call the

'Colosseum' on the ruins of Nero's Golden House. *Pax* ('Peace') was the symbol most commonly found on his coins.

His son Titus (AD 79–81) had finished off his father's work in Judaea by capturing Jerusalem in AD 70. His love of the stage made some see in him a potential second Nero, but the transition to emperor in AD 79 went well. He put on lavish shows for the people, maintained friendly relations with the Senate, finished off the 'Colosseum' and tried to deal with the consequences of the eruption of Vesuvius (AD 79), plus a nasty fire and plague in Rome (AD 80). Titus' reign was generally agreed to have been a success.

Domitian (AD 81–96), Titus' brother, was a strict moralist, ran a tight ship at home and abroad, put up many buildings religious and secular, and kept the public well entertained. He built himself a huge new palace on the Palatine. He led military campaigns on the Rhine (AD 82), the Danube (Moesia, AD 85–6) and Pannonia (AD 92). But he was a solitary, remote man, kept a few friends close, never got on with the Senate, liked to parade his power as emperor (he made himself consul ten times), and he was ruthless in doing away with opponents. Plots were formed against him and he was murdered on 18 September AD 96. His memory was expunged from the records. Rome offers perhaps the bloodthirstiest example of the 'monarchic' succession in history (p. 327).

SHOCKING DOCS

Since Romans seemed enthusiastically to embrace all things Greek, one might have thought Greek medicine would be included. Far from it, if

Pliny the Elder is to be believed. 'Medicine alone of the Greek arts we Romans have not practised,' he proclaimed. It was, in his view, a very dodgy profession, the territory of almost exclusively Greek doctors. To his way of thinking they were nearly all charlatans who could get away with any crime in the name of their 'art', and charge monumental sums for so doing. After that rant, Pliny then went on to give a long list of remedies for illness, beginning with the use of wool and eggs, and most of them Greek! But this was not a contradiction. Pliny was highlighting what a good Roman could safely and properly take over from the vast store of potentially dangerous and corrupting Greek medical lore. Incidentally, Scribonius Largus (who accompanied Claudius to Britain) was the first to use electrification for medical purposes: he recommended torpedo fish (an electric ray) to cure headaches and gout.

DOCTORAL DISSERTATION

One of the most important treatises on medicine was written by Cornelius Celsus, probably during the reign of Tiberius. After giving a brief history of medicine down to his day, Celsus dealt with preserving good health; healthy and unhealthy constitutions and times of the year; diseases and how to spot and treat them; the internal organs (the first ever description in Latin); specific ailments in a head-to-toe sequence; prescriptions; wounds, bites, skin disorders (very sound on swellings); surgery; the human skeleton; and surgical techniques, especially concerning bones (dealing with fractures, etc.). What is so interesting about Celsus is not just the elegance of his Latin, but the cautious distance he kept between describing medical procedures and any suggestion that he was himself a practising doctor! He probably was, but it was not the sort of thing an educated, upper-class Roman wanted to admit. So he reads like an encyclopedist rather than a practitioner. At the heart of Celsus' work is a very Roman ethical approach to the subject: Greek medicine was invented only because the world had become corrupt and decadent. We should therefore rely on regular Roman virtues like 'moderation' and a 'sense of decency' to see us through.

Incidentally, Celsus gave us the word 'cancer'. The great Greek physician Hippocrates had given the name *karkinos*, Greek for 'crab', to malignant tumours, and Celsus turned that into the Latin for a crab, *cancer*. As accurate as any account could be from the Graeco-Roman world, Celsus' was the first medical book to enjoy the Gutenberg revolution and be printed (in Florence in 1478).

TACITUS

Publius Cornelius Tacitus (AD 56–*c*. 120) wrote history covering the period AD 14 to 96 – the early emperors of Rome (though not all of his work survives). And he knew what he was talking about. He served in various capacities under the emperors Vespasian, Titus and Domitian (AD 69–96) and he was proconsul in Asia AD 112–13. But he did not like what he saw. Here is Tacitus the debunker, wondering whether the two armies fighting it out for supremacy in the civil war between Otho and Vitellius (AD 69) might have laid down their arms and let the Senate take over, as one Paulinus had suggested:

> Though I would allow that there were some few who, in their
> secret wishes, prayed for peace in place of disorder, and for a
> worthy and blameless emperor instead of men utterly worthless

and wicked, yet I cannot suppose that Paulinus, wise as he was, could have hoped, in an age thoroughly depraved, to find such moderation in the common herd that men, who in their passion for war, had trampled peace under foot, should now, in their affection for peace, renounce the charms of war; nor can I think that . . . lieutenants and generals, who were for the most part burdened by the consciousness of profligacy, of poverty, and of crime, could have endured any emperor who was not himself stained by vice, as well as bound by obligation to themselves.

(trans. Church and Brodribb)

There is real passion in Tacitus' writing. History, for him as for all ancient historians, had a high moral purpose. He wanted to set the record straight. Here he analyses when the autocratic rot set in. It was, he reckoned, with Augustus (first emperor, 31 BC–AD 14), who came to sole power after years of civil war. Read it carefully. This is typical Tacitus:

Augustus won over the soldiers with gifts, the populace with cheap corn, and all men with the sweets of repose, and so grew greater by degrees, while he concentrated in himself the functions of the Senate, the magistrates, and the laws. He was wholly unopposed, for the boldest spirits had fallen in battle, or in the proscription.

(trans. Church and Brodribb)

Nothing in this brief analysis is historically inaccurate, but the tone is relentlessly negative. Is this just? What one must do is observe how

Tacitus frames the argument:

- good points are buried under bad. Augustus' restoration of peace after the terrible years of civil war is lost in accusations of bribery and of autocratic designs on the constitution;

- innocent actions are given the worst possible gloss. Augustus' cheap food policy was standard Roman practice and there is no evidence to suggest that he was any more lavish than anyone else;

- damaging innuendo is allowed to stand. Observe the innuendo that all the war and murder were Augustus' sole responsibility.

Tacitus claims to have written 'without anger and prejudice'. Nothing could be further from the truth. But he remains almost unmatched as the wielder of a poisoned pen and a historian who understood and analysed the darker side of men and politics.

COWBOY BUILDERS

In AD 27 Atilius, an ex-slave, built an amphitheatre at Fidenae for a gladiatorial show. However, he neglected to put in firm foundations or a solid superstructure. Tacitus comments: 'he had taken on the project not because of his wealth or to further his local ambitions but only for sordid profit'. Because Tiberius laid on virtually no entertainment of this sort, people flocked to it. The structure collapsed, mutilating or killing 50,000. The Senate decreed that henceforth anyone putting on a gladiatorial show would require capital of at least 400,000 ss, and amphitheatres should be safety checked.

DOMPEROR

When Tiberius retired to his villas on Capri, rumours spread about what he was getting up to (tabloid gossip existed even then). Suetonius says that Tiberius was so fond of wine he was called not Tiberius Claudius Nero but Biberius Caldius Mero, 'Bibulous Warm Neat' (wine was usually served with hot water). The emperor spent days and nights drinking with chums, held dinners with naked serving girls and gave a man a quaestorship for draining a six-gallon (*c.* 28 litres) amphora of wine at dinner! Straight and gay men and women performed before him in threesomes; his library was full of books illustrating coital positions; and he set up 'haunts of Venus' in groves all over the island, where boys and girls dressed as Pan and nymphs offered their services. He trained small boys to swim between his thighs, licking and biting him playfully. Or so we are told. His death was not an occasion for mourning.

CALIGULA: HATRED AND FEAR

Tiberius had his doubts about Caligula, calling him a 'viper for the Roman people and a Phaethon for the world' (in myth Phaethon tried to drive the chariot of the sun, lost control and scorched vast tracks of land, creating the Sahara Desert, for example). And indeed, when Caligula went to the bad he did so in no small measure. He had statues of gods brought from Greece, their heads removed and replaced with copies of his; he became the cruel, capricious and autocratic tyrant beloved by film and TV producers – sleeping at will with his sister and other men's wives, playing vicious jokes on the innocent, which often ended in their deaths, building extravagant villas all over the place and generally rejoicing in the hatred of the people. *Oderint dum metuant*, he said contemptuously of them – 'let them hate me, as long as they fear me' – when he was not expressing the wish that the Roman people had a single neck. In one year he worked through the whole 2,700 million *ss* that Tiberius had built up, reducing the state to penury.

NODDING ACQUAINTANCE

Having exhausted Rome's coffers Caligula turned to auctions, taxes and false accusations to make them up. On one famous occasion he was flogging off everything left over from some games he had put on. He told the auctioneer to keep an eye on the *praetor* Aponius Saturninus, who had fallen sleep and kept nodding his head. The bidding finally came to an end and Aponius woke up to find he had bought 13 gladiators for 9 million *ss* (the going rate for a gladiator was *c.* 1,000–15,000 *ss*, depending on quality).

THE HORSE-FANCIER

Like Nero, Caligula was very keen on the performing arts, especially on performing himself. He was mad about the races (he was said to sleep in the stables with his favourite racing team, the 'Greens'). His most prized horse was called Incitatus ('Speedy'). Its stable was of marble, the manger ebony, its blankets purple and its collar gem-studded. Incitatus also had a house, with slaves and furniture. The day before a race Caligula would command soldiers to ensure silence in the area where the horse was sleeping. It was said Caligula wanted to make it consul.

CHARIOT-RACING: THE HIGH LIFE

Circus is Latin for 'circle' or 'circuit' and the 'circus' refers not to big tents, clowns and seals playing trumpets but to chariot-racing. Racing with chariots was originally the privilege of aristocrats, but the Romans turned it into a mass entertainment. And that was the point. If you were a Roman only the best was good enough: from time to time, you too could taste the high life, courtesy of the state. For all its historical inaccuracies, the film *Ben Hur* captures the essence of the event.

THE ARENA

The Circus Maximus was twelve times bigger in surface area than the Colosseum, and could hold about 150,000 people (against the Colosseum's 50,000). It was 600 yards long and 90 yards wide (548 x 82 m). Down the middle ran a *spina* ('spine') 365 yards long and 9 yards wide (333 x 8 m). The chariots raced anti-clockwise round the *spina*. It has been calculated that a chariot would cover the seven laps (about 3.2 miles or 5 km) in about nine minutes. Such arenas did not reach their fully developed state until the second century AD, and, being very expensive to build, they were rare in this form across the Roman Empire.

THE RACING CLUBS

There were only four chariot-racing clubs in Rome: the Blues, Greens, Whites and Reds. Their headquarters and stables were in the Campus Martius where the races were held. Each club would put forward one, two or three teams for any race. The teams were usually four-horse or two-horse (we have discovered one depiction of a 20-horse team!).

THE HORSES, DRIVERS AND PRIZES

Chariot-racing was a very serious business. The horses (Spanish and African being the most coveted) were adored: 'Win or lose, we love you, Polidoxus' run the words on a mosaic from North Africa. The drivers, though usually slaves or freedmen, were career-professionals, who could be transferred between the colours. For example, slave-born Polyneices, who died aged 29 in a race, won 655 races for the Reds, 55 for the Greens, 12 for the Blues and 17 for the Whites. For protection racers wore leather crash-hats, and leather strapping around their torsos and legs. They wrapped the reins around their bodies, using the left hand to guide the horses, and wielding a whip in the right. They carried a knife to cut themselves free if they fell. Blocking and cutting-in were common tactics. A crash was called a *naufragium*, 'shipwreck'. Vast prize money was at stake: according to one inscription a man called Diocles took part in 4,257 races, won 1,462 of them and made over 35 million *ss* (a soldier's annual pay was 900 *ss*) before retiring aged 42. *Miliarius* ('thousander') was the title given to a driver who won more than a thousand races.

THE CHARIOTS

Unlike the large, decorated chariots in *Ben Hur*, Roman chariots were lightweight affairs, basically a wooden framework. Leather or cloth covered the sides; straps of interlaced leather formed the floor. The chariot base was about 2 feet by 1 foot 9 inches (60 x 57 cm), the six- or eight-spoked wheels were 2 feet 6 inches (65 cm) in diameter. In all it probably weighed no more than 55–66 lb (25–30 kg). On the assumption that drivers would be small and wiry, the horses would have to pull no more than 220 lb (100 kg) – not a lot for two or four horses.

THE ORGANIZATION

With 24 races a day, each with the full complement of 12 four-horse teams, 1,152 horses had to be handled. Add 200 or 300 more horses for staff and the accompanying acrobatic troupes (entertaining the crowds between races by galloping round the arena, leaping from horse to horse); hundreds of stable lads and grooms, cartwrights and saddlers, vets and doctors; staff to work the starting-boxes, tidy up between races and remove the wrecks; boys called *sparsores* who stood inside the arena to refresh the teams with water (they are often depicted fallen under the wheels of the chariots); referees, officials and trumpeters – the sheer logistics take the breath away.

THE FANS

Racegoers were as fanatical about their favourite club as any football fan today. We have a fan's curse-tablet, invoking demons to smash the Reds and Blues:

> Bind the charioteers' hands, remove their victory, their exit, their sight . . . snatch them from their chariots, twist them to the ground so they fall and are dragged all over the racecourse, especially at the turn, with damage to their bodies, with the horses they drive. Now, at once.

Pliny the Younger points out that (just as for today's fans) it is the club that counts:

> If fans were attracted by the speed of the horses or the drivers' skill one could account for it, but in fact it is only the racing-colours

they support and care about. If the colours were to be changed
in mid-course during a race, they would transfer their favour
and enthusiasm and rapidly desert the famous drivers and horses
whose names they shout as they recognize them from afar. Such
are the popularity and importance of a worthless coloured shirt.

One race-horse owner was so keen to let his home town know who
had won that he relayed the result via a carrier-swallow with the winner's
colour painted on its legs.

CURSE TABLETS

Ancients turned to magic when they had to deal with people they
considered were threats to their well-being: they laid an official curse
on them. These were often written on thin lead tablets, rolled up and
dropped in a shrine, where the god would act on them, or in the grave
of someone who had died early. The theory was that their spirit, waiting
until the 'right' death-date came, would roam the earth, carrying out
any such requests.

Curses were regularly aimed at rivals in love, business, sport or law.
They called up underworld gods and an assortment of fabulously exotic
demons, then launched a long series of requests that their rival should
suffer hideous injuries. Another common type of curse took the form of
a plea for justice, citing wrongs done by someone and asking for redress.
These named the curser. We have one from Britain:

> To the divine [native god] Nodens: Silvianus has lost his ring and
> given half what it is worth to Nodens. Among those who bear

the name Senicianus, let none enjoy health until he brings it to the temple of Nodens.

However, clearly the Seniciani remained annoyingly healthy, because a second word has been added to the curse: *rediviva*, 'renewed'. It's always worth reminding a god of his responsibilities: Nodens had been promised half the cost of the ring, so it was time to deliver on his side of the bargain. That is how ancient gods were thought to work.

CLAUDIUS: NOT BORN TO THE PURPLE

Stricken with cerebral palsy from a young age, limping and hoarse of speech, Claudius (Tiberius' nephew) was described by his mother Antonia as 'a monstrosity of a human being, one that Nature began and never finished' (see p. 242). When he assumed the toga of manhood at the age of 14, usually an event of some importance, it was done secretly, at night. When Claudius was seen in public, he was dressed as an invalid. The first emperor Augustus took a policy decision never to give Claudius proper public office, and his successor Tiberius maintained it. So Claudius turned to scholarship, writing 28 books of Etruscan and Carthaginian history, 43 of Roman history from Julius Caesar's assassination, and a monograph on the introduction of new letters and spellings into the Roman alphabet, some of which could be seen on official inscriptions (he favoured 'Caisar' over 'Caesar'). The result of all this was that Claudius was not involved in the hurly-burly of the imperial succession after Augustus and Tiberius. His first taste of real office did not come until AD 37 when his nephew Caligula came to power. But even then he was still treated as a joke, and never felt accepted.

FOOLS RULE

Claudius was quite open about the secret of his success – pretending to be an idiot; though some wag soon published a book entitled *The Idiot's Rise to Power*, arguing that only a real idiot would pretend to be an idiot. One thing Claudius did understand, though he did not remain constant to the principle: it is more effective to provide benefits to people rather than wage war against them.

THE INVASION OF BRITAIN

An emperor had to demonstrate that he was the man for the job, and this meant successful military campaigns. Hardly a soldier, but realizing he must live up to his calling, Claudius went for military glory in AD 43 by ordering the invasion of Britain. The aim was probably to subdue the fertile south of the country first of all, then extend west and north, turning it into a secure Roman base in the far west. Aulus Plautius led the assault with a force of 40,000 (see also Caesar's 27,000 in the mid-50s BC, p. 171). When a bridgehead had been securely established, Claudius arrived. Wisely, he brought with him many of the most powerful men in Rome to share the glory – better that than leaving them behind to plot against him. Once the capital, Colchester, had been taken Claudius entered in state with his court and soldiers on parade, topped off with elephants and mahouts. That showed the Brits what the Romans could do!

Having spent 16 days in Britain, Claudius returned to Rome, celebrating his triumph in AD 44 – the man who had outdone Caesar! The glorious news spread all over the Empire. A relief in Aphrodisias (central Turkey) shows a handsome, youthful, beefy Claudius holding down a female Britannia (p. 309) with his right knee and left hand.

But the province was not a success. Britain could never be left without legions on the ground, and, as the geographer Strabo foresaw, the wealth it contributed to Rome in tax, tribute and material (e.g., lead and silver) never matched the outlay. The British king Caratacus, a captive in Rome, made the point as he surveyed the magnificent city: 'With the countless treasures you possess, why on earth did you covet our pathetic little huts?'

CONVICTS ON STRIKE

One of the most dramatic projects Claudius undertook was draining Lake Fucinus in central Italy, an area of some 77 square miles (nearly 20,000 hectares, an area equal to the size of the local authority of Windsor and Maidenhead or Darlington). Claudius decided to commemorate the start of the operation with a grand farewell display – a sea battle involving 19,000 convicts, buckets of blood guaranteed – watched by a huge crowd as if at the theatre. The convicts due to fight lined up in front of him.

'Hail, emperor!' they shouted. 'Those who are about to die salute you!'

'Or not,' Claudius replied.

At this they all dropped their weapons and refused to fight, on the grounds that Claudius had spared them.

With threats and encouragement the furious emperor finally persuaded them to do their duty. Their words to Claudius are thought by some to echo what gladiators said before combat in the arena. It's possible, though they occur nowhere else in Roman literature.

GAULING FOR SENATORS

In AD 48 Claudius tried to introduce Gallic chieftains into the Senate. The senators were outraged, arguing that they had never welcomed foreigners before – what was wrong with good honest Romans? The great offices of state must not be cheapened. Claudius, a keen historian, gave them a history lesson: Rome's strength was its ability to welcome foreign elements into the citizen body and adjust the constitution to each new change (p. 12). The result, he said, was that newcomers had now proved their worth by 'assimilating our customs and culture and marrying into our families', and bringing their wealth with them too. Claudius' proposal was agreed.

MESSALINA

In AD 40, a year before becoming emperor, Claudius contracted a marriage with a great-grand-niece of the first emperor Augustus (an Augustan connection was always a useful card for an emperor to play). Her name was Messalina and she was 14. Though she bore two children, including a male heir Britannicus, the marriage was not a success. Messalina was, we are told, a sex maniac. In a wild rant against women, the satirist Juvenal (c. AD 100) gives the following account of her:

> As soon as she saw her husband was asleep, she would creep
> away, taking a single maid with her. Disguising her raven hair
> with a yellow wig, she made her way to a whorehouse, beds
> reeking with use, and went into one of the cells. She stripped and
> stood there, nipples gilded, calling herself 'She Wolf', spreading

wide the womb that gave Britannicus birth. When the pimp let
all the other girls go home, she stayed as long as she could
before shutting up shop, sad to leave and still on heat, clitoris
rigid. Finally she got back to the palace, exhausted but still
unsatisfied, and, cheeks filthy with grease, stinking of smoky
lamps, she transferred the steaming fumes of the brothel into
the emperor's bed.

Claudius was unaware of (or ignored) the rumours that gathered
around his wife. In AD 48 Messalina left him and went through the
formalities of marriage to Gaius Silius. Not long afterwards, she and
Silius were murdered.

AGRIPPINA: THE CUCKOO IN THE NEST

Agrippina, Claudius' second wife, was given the full 'wicked
stepmother' treatment by Roman historians (see Livia, p. 216). She was
a widow, but had a son by a previous marriage – Nero. She persuaded
Claudius to adopt him (AD 50) and give him priority over Britannicus
(Claudius' son by Messalina). Determined to ensure Nero's succession,
it was rumoured, Agrippina sprinkled poison on a particularly delicious
mushroom for Claudius to eat. He did so, but promptly evacuated it.
However, Claudius' Greek doctor Xenophon knew what was going on;
pretending to help Claudius vomit, he put a feather with a quick-acting
poison down his throat (p. 55).

Nero now became emperor and Agrippina's triumph was almost
complete. To crown it (so rumour has it) she arranged to do away with
Britannicus. The story was that over-heated mulled wine was served to

him at dinner. The wine got past the taster, but (as planned) Britannicus found it too hot. Water was brought to cool it – and that was where the poison was.

GOURD BLIMEY

Seneca – the billionaire orator and philosopher exiled by Claudius in AD 41 – was recalled in AD 49 and made tutor to the young Nero, and later adviser to him as emperor (see p. 244). Shortly after Claudius' death and Nero's accession in AD 54 Seneca composed a devastating prose-and-verse satire on Claudius, *Apocolocyntosis* ('Gourdification'). The title suggests that Claudius was turned not into a god at death but a gourd or pumpkin, a vegetable known for the speed with which the internal pulp decomposed, leaving nothing but pips and hard rind. Of his death, Seneca wrote:

> The following was his last utterance heard among men, after he had let out a louder noise from that part by which he found it easier to speak: 'Whoops! I think I shat myself.' I do not know whether he did so, but he certainly shat up everything else.

In Seneca's cruel text, when Claudius dies Jupiter sends the tough guy Hercules (he of the Twelve Labours) to find out who has arrived among the gods, because the messenger says the visitor is acting rather threateningly, wagging his head, dragging his right foot and speaking an unintelligible language:

> Hercules was shocked at the sight, as if he had come across a new sort of monster to be afraid of – the strange shape, the odd walk,

the voice unlike that of any terrestrial creature but more typical of
sea monsters, hoarse and inarticulate. He thought his thirteenth
labour had arrived.

Nero was quite happy to see Claudius mocked as a fool. It made him
seem such a great improvement, and it did no harm to Seneca to flatter
the new man by insulting the previous incumbent.

THE POWER OF RUMOUR

Two of our major sources for this period, Tacitus and Suetonius,
regularly quote rumours. This does not sound very praiseworthy in
historians, but the problem was that the imperial palace was a closed
shop. No one but the emperor's inner circle knew what was going on
(p. 197). At any rate rumour is still history, in the sense that it is a
record of the word on the street at any time. Whether it bears any
relation to the truth is another matter, but it certainly coloured the
ordinary citizen's image of the imperial palace. Modern journalism
grasps just as keenly at such titbits, shaping our own sense of what is
'really' going on behind the scenes. In ancient Rome, as nowadays, it
was all about perceptions.

KOWTOWING

Elite Romans needed all the self-defence mechanisms they could muster
against the insecurities of imperial life. Marcus Terentius was a close
friend of the treacherous Sejanus (p. 222). When Sejanus was executed
on Tiberius' orders, Terentius did not deny his friendship and won an
imperial reprieve for his honesty.

'It is not for us to judge the man you have elevated above others, and for what reason,' he said to Tiberius. 'The gods gave you supreme power; the only glory left to us is to obey.'

Too true. Seneca reports an old courtier, asked how he lasted so long in imperial service, replied: 'by accepting insults and expressing gratitude for them' (p. 198).

NERO THE ARTIST

Nero thought of himself as a great artist. He took up the lyre so that he could accompany himself on it, and kept his voice in trim by diet and slimming. He controlled his weight with enemas and emetics. He kept a voice-trainer by his side to advise him on looking after his precious vocal chords. In a competition he once sang the complete opera *Niobe* without a break so that no one else could compete. When he performed, no one was allowed to leave. Women gave birth during his shows; men shammed death in order to be carried out (we are told).

Feeling unappreciated in Rome, he went to Greece where he thought they would understand true art. Wisely, they gave him a rapturous welcome. In return he remitted Greek taxes. Polite society was shocked by this degrading behaviour, though (as with Caligula) the general populace thought him rather fun.

MOTHER-KILLER

For the first five years of his reign Nero was advised by two wise heads: Burrus and Seneca, put in place by his mother Agrippina. But Nero tired of this, so in AD 59 he decided the only way out was to kill his mother, then dismiss the two advisers. He invited Agrippina to his villa near Naples for an evening meal, and sent her back home across the bay by boat. But the boat was booby-trapped and, by some mechanism involving weights, was holed and sank. Everyone swam for it. When a maidservant cried out, 'Help! Save me, the queen!', and was promptly bludgeoned to death, Agrippina put two and two together and made for the shore, where a boat took her safely home. There she pretended ignorance of the plot and sent a message to Nero to say she was safe. Nero sent his men to finish the job. One of them clubbed her down and, as the other drew his sword, she cried, 'Strike the womb!' and died under a hail of blows.

DRUID THREAT

In Britain, Romans were greatly worried by the influence of the Druids whose name was connected with Celtic words for 'prophet' or 'magician'. They carried out human sacrifice to cure the sick or protect warriors (Julius Caesar mentions their practice of creating colossal images made of wickerwork and burning people alive in them: the 'Wicker Man'). But they were very highly regarded, regulating all religious practices and acting as judges. Since Druids were also exempt from tax and military service, the young flocked to them to be educated in matters physical and metaphysical, with the hope of one day graduating as Druids themselves. Many top Gauls sent their children to board in Britain on courses that lasted up to 20 years. The problem for the Romans was that these religious leaders, influential across Gaul and Britain, seemed to exert considerable political power at a supra-tribal level. In other words, they had the potential to unite tribes against Roman rule. Labelling them 'fanatics', Romans had exterminated them by the second century AD.

ST PAUL: IDENTITY AND CITIZENSHIP

About AD 58 St Paul, a Greek-speaking Jew from Tarsus (south-east Turkey), caused a riot in Jerusalem. So the Roman authorities arrested him. The garrison commandant Claudius Lysias ordered him to be flogged. Paul had been tied up for the punishment when he said to the centurion, 'Can you legally flog a man who is a Roman citizen and has not been found guilty?' The centurion immediately reported it to the commandant, who came and asked Paul if he was a Roman citizen. 'Yes,' he said. The commandant replied, 'It cost me a lot to acquire my citizenship.' Paul said, 'It was mine by birth' (*Acts* 22:25–30).

How so? Tarsus had been incorporated into the Roman Empire more than a century earlier. So Paul had inherited his status as a citizen of Rome from his father. Claudius Lysias was probably Greek ('Lysias'). He had been a slave in the service of the emperor Claudius and had bought his freedom. This automatically made him a Roman citizen. It is fashionable these days to wonder in what sense Paul or the Greek ex-slave Claudius Lysias *felt* themselves to be Roman.

ARMS AND THE WOMAN

In AD 60 Prasutagus, the tribal leader of the Iceni in East Anglia, died. A 'client king' of the Romans, he left his daughters and Nero as co-heirs to his kingdom. The Romans had other ideas: they decided to grab the territory outright. Without further ado, minor officials seized the land, flogged Prasutagus' wife Boudicca, raped her daughters and treated the king's relatives like slaves – hardly the way to win hearts and minds.

There was a massive revolt, masterminded by the original Essex girl Boudicca. We are told that 70–80,000 Romans and provincials were killed in the sack of three towns: Colchester, St Albans and London. Rome, finally understanding that it had 'a serious disaster' (Tacitus) on its hands, ruthlessly suppressed the rebellion. Suetonius Paulinus, the governor of Britain, put down the rebels, but (almost uniquely) was relieved of his position because his revenge was deemed too bloody even by Roman standards and thereby hindered efforts to restore peace. A statue depicting Boudicca and her daughters stands in front of the House of Commons by Westminster Bridge. After her defeat by the Romans, she killed herself or died of illness, and is said to be buried under Platform 10 of King's Cross Station.

THE GREAT FIRE OF ROME

In AD 64 a huge fire swept through Rome. Nero was said to have started it in order to create the space for his vast new palace the *Domus Aurea* ('Golden House'). But according to Tacitus, Nero blamed the 'notoriously depraved Christians, whose originator Christ had been executed in Tiberius' reign by the governor of Judaea, Pontius Pilate'.

The fire lasted ten days and destroyed virtually all existing monuments of historical importance. Afterwards, Nero set about rebuilding Rome with a Fire Relief Fund. Many sensible measures were put in place: wider streets, restricted height of tenements, no party walls, severe punishments for lighting a fire in the house, fire-fighting equipment to be at hand, and so on (p. 200).

THE GOLDEN HOUSE

To build his *Domus Aurea* Nero took advantage of the devastation wrought by Rome's great fire to confiscate vast tracts of land in the middle of Rome, much of it belonging to senators. The partly two-level palace, an innovatory architectural masterpiece, covered 125 acres (50 hectares) and was set in a park featuring ornamental ponds, fountains and wild animals, fronted by a 120-foot (36 m) statue of Nero himself – a Colossus. When it was finished, he proclaimed, 'Now I can live like a man!' Romans had little time for this megalomaniac folly. One graffito urged: 'Flee to Veii, Romans! The whole city's turning into one house!' The gigantic project almost broke Rome and was one of the many reasons Nero was finally done away with.

ON THE FIDDLE?

Nero certainly did not fiddle while Rome burned. If anything, as Suetonius tells us, he sang. Enraptured by the beauty of the flames, he put on his tragedian's clothes (Suetonius wrote) and worked his way through 'The Fall of Troy' from beginning to end. Another source tells us that he was in fact out of Rome when the fire started, but hurried back to deal with it.

PETRONIUS' *SATYRICON*: SATIRE AND THE CITY

The title of Petronius' novel *Satyricon* comes from the Greek word *saturikos*, 'to do with satyrs'. Satyrs were wild, naked, half-man, half-animal figures, lusting for sex and drink and sporting grotesque erections. So the title might almost be *The Lechers' Tale*. A Roman would also have heard *satura* in it, the Latin from which our 'satire' comes. So *Satyricon* is a lecherous, satirical comic novel, with a good deal of parody thrown in too. The whole story may have stretched to 20 books and 400,000 words, but we have only fragments from Books Fourteen and Sixteen, and most of Fifteen. Book Fifteen is taken up with the famous feast of Trimalchio, a freedman-made-very-good ('Buy well and sell well is my motto'), surrounded by parasites and no-hopers; a man of the worst possible taste, who imagines himself to be both the envy and epitome of polite society: the sort of man who, in mid-ball game,

> clicked his fingers and his eunuch gave him the chamber pot. He did not stop playing as he urinated into it, then demanded water for his hands, and after perfunctorily washing his fingers, wiped them on the slave's hair.

In the course of the feast Trimalchio describes how he was a sex-slave of his master and mistress, and eventually was named in their will as co-heir with the emperor. He spent the money on a shipping business, promptly lost 30 million *ss*, tried again, made 10 million *ss* and bought real estate. This was so successful that on his property, on one day alone, Trimalchio boasts, 70 slaves were born, 300 tons (304 tonnes) of wheat stored in the barn, 500 oxen broken in and 10 million *ss* returned to the safe, because they could not be invested! By the end of the feast he is completely plastered and insists on reading out his will: he describes the giant monument he wants put up, complete with pet dog, gladiator fight, ship under sail, a freedman guarding it so no one shits on it, and himself 'sitting, purple-togaed, in a magistrate's seat, scattering coins to the people out of a bag'. The epitaph reads:

> Here lies Gaius Pompeius Trimalchio Maecenatianus, made priest of Augustus while abroad on a mission [i.e., such a busy and

important fellow] . . . God-fearing, brave, loyal, he started out with little but left 30 million *ss*, without ever listening to a single lecture from a philosopher [i.e., completely uneducated].

At that he bursts into tears.

MR COOL IN LIFE – AND DEATH

Petronius (almost certainly the same man described by Tacitus as 'sleeping by day, working by night and enjoying himself') composed *Satyricon* in the time of Nero. He had had a political career in Nero's court – governor of Bithynia and consul – but earned notoriety as (in Tacitus' words) Rome's *elegantiae arbiter*: 'the master of cool', the authority on all things amusing, fashionable and up-to-date. It got too much for Nero's enforcer Tigellinus, who disliked competition in the hedonism stakes. He trumped up a false charge against Petronius, who decided to commit suicide – at leisure. He severed his veins, then bound them up whenever he felt like it; chatted with friends, who read out frivolous poems to him rather than sermonizing about life, death, the universe and everything (p. 178); dozed off at dinner, and died.

FOOD FUN

Romans could be tremendous jokers when it came to food. Lamb did not have to taste of lamb – any fool could make it do that. Instead, Romans often preferred to swamp food in powerful sauces to produce a melange of flavours. Likewise they loved to disguise plain food to make it look like some delicacy. You want anchovies? Cut fresh turnips into anchovy shapes, blanch, oil and salt them and add black peppercorns. You want

Greek wine? Take Italian wine and adulterate it. The vulgar Trimalchio in *Satyricon* (p. 248) boasts that his cook can make 'a fish out of a pig's womb, a wood pigeon from bacon, a turtle-dove from ham'.

There is one thing Romans were spared: celebrity chefs. Cooks in Rome were simple technicians, like car mechanics or dentists. They did not hold court or appear on the Roman equivalent of TV shows. Indeed, cooks were largely figures of fun. The Romans got some things right.

A MAN, A PLAN, A CANAL – ALMOST

The geographer Strabo tells us that in 304–303 BC a Greek warlord Demetrius 'the Besieger' decided to cut a canal through the isthmus at Corinth. He was prevented by engineers who took measurements at either end and concluded that the sea at the west end was higher than at the east. Their conclusion was that if the canal was cut a gigantic surge would flood the islands to the east of the canal. Amazingly, the engineers were right. Because of wind and tidal effects the sea on the western side is 20 inches (51 cm) higher than on the east. Today a current up to 3 mph (4.8 kph) runs from west to east.

Nero did actually start it. Near the waterline on the south side at the Corinthian Gulf end there is still a memorial to his attempt: a niche with a small statue of Hercules in it, Hercules being the sort of strong man who would have dug it himself in a day or so. However, revolts across the Empire ended the attempt. It was finally built and opened in 1893 and, as Thomas Cook's tourist handbook breathlessly explained, was 'fitted with Electric Light so that the canal is navigable both by day and night'.

NERO LIVES ON

Revolts in the provinces and senatorial opposition forced Nero to flee Rome. He ended up in the villa of one of his freedmen Phaon, where news came that he had been declared a public enemy. He ordered a grave to be dug, declaring 'What an artist dies in me' as it was made ready (though 'artist' could also mean 'artisan', an ironic comment on his 'artistic' life in contrast with his death, digging a grave). After much self-dramatizing he finally managed to commit suicide.

Astonishingly, many believed he was still alive. Sightings were reported in the East. A hotchpotch of poems composed between the second and seventh centuries AD called the 'Sibylline Oracles' (p. 28) depict Nero as a champion of the East and of the oppressed against the tyranny of Rome. Nero, then, became in the eyes of eastern provincials a sort of Elvis figure – a hero of popular culture (all that acting, singing and charioteering) who had not died but was waiting to return to 'save' his people.

THE PETER PRINCIPLE

Tacitus' brilliant, stabbing four-word judgement on Galba, the first of the four emperors of AD 69, has rung down the ages, as relevant today as it was 2,000 years ago: *capax imperii, nisi imperasset*, 'capable of being emperor, had he not actually *been* emperor' – a sentiment applicable to many a modern politician and business leader. Tacitus here foreshadows the Peter Principle: 'In a hierarchy every employee tends to rise to his level of incompetence.'

LEAKING CASH

Vespasian had to deal with the legacy of Nero's spending. One tactic was to pinpoint provincial governors known for their greed. He promoted them (to encourage them to become even greedier) and then hit them with charges for extortion. His 'sponges', they were called: 'he put them in to soak, then squeezed them dry later'. His most striking revenue-raising ploy was to tax urine from the city urinals. This was used by fullers (wool-makers) for its ammonia content, to bleach and clean the grease off woollens. When his son Titus complained at this rather undignified scheme, Vespasian handed him a coin from the day's proceeds and said, 'Does this smell bad, son?'

'No, Father,' said Titus.

'Strange,' said Vespasian, 'it comes straight from the urinal!'

This gave rise to the later saying *pecunia non olet*: 'Money does not smell'.

There were eventually 144 public latrines in Rome, most in the public baths. Vespasian did manage to restore the finances and sensibly started paying teachers of Greek and Latin rhetoric (university teachers) 100,000 *ss* a year.

NOT THE 'COLOSSEUM'

No Roman called Vespasian's huge gladiatorial ring the Colosseum. The Roman name was the Flavian amphitheatre, because Vespasian was of the Flavius family and his son Titus finished it. 'Colosseum' is in fact the medieval name, used from *c.* AD 1000. It probably derives from the Colossus, the gigantic 120-foot (36 m) statue of himself that Nero commissioned (p.248). Vespasian replaced Nero's head with that of the Sun-god. Only the base survives today, located near the modern entrance.

BUILDING THE 'COLOSSEUM'

Vespasian built the 50,000-seater 'Colosseum' with money taken from the sack of Jerusalem, as part of a project to obliterate the self-indulgent folly that was Nero's Golden House complex and to restore the area to the use of the Roman people. It covered six acres and was about 160 feet (48 m) tall (15 modern storeys high). Recent investigation has shown it was decorated with highly coloured frescoes and littered with graffiti. It needed a very secure base, so was constructed on the site of Nero's 20-foot (6 m) deep lake. This was drained and more than 30,000 tons of soil removed to create a foundation 40 feet (12 m) deep in all, into which concrete was poured, further strengthened with brick. Observe that, since it was not built in Nero's time, the common idea that Nero had Christians slaughtered in it cannot be true; indeed, there is no hard evidence that Christians were slaughtered there at all.

ALTARED STATES

In the East it was common to associate kings with gods. Alexander the Great openly touted himself as a son of Zeus. Romans gradually took over this practice. When the people of Tarragona in Spain told Augustus that a miracle had occurred on his altar there – a palm-tree had sprouted! – he commented sourly that it just showed how infrequently they sacrificed to him. As a result, emperors and sometimes their wives were deified at their death. Livia begged her son Tiberius to deify her, but he vetoed the idea; Claudius eventually obliged. Vespasian's death was unexpected. In the grip of a violent spasm, he said, 'An emperor ought to die standing' and, as he struggled to his feet to do just that, quipped, 'Good heavens! I do believe I am turning into a god.'

ROME'S GREATEST INVENTION: THE BOOK

The poet Martial is the first person we hear of to publish his work in a *codex*, that is, the form of our book (p. 25). The codex probably had its origins in the Roman writing tablet: a pair of small wooden frames linked like two pages of a book, each frame filled with a thin coating of wax. In the wax a message was written with a stylus (metal pen). The two frames/'pages' were then folded together, tied around the outside with cord, the knot secured with a wax seal and sent to the recipient. He or she would break the seal, untie the cord, open the 'book', read the message, smooth over the wax and reply (or not). But a two-'page' tablet could easily be extended to a three or four 'page' one – just like a codex.

CHRISTIAN ROLL-OVER

The codex did not catch on for a long time. This is surprising. One could not fit many books (typically, not more than a 1,000-line play) on to one roll. A roll required unrolling from the right hand into the left as you read, so when finished it had to be rolled back again for further use; and finding a place near the end would require unrolling it all. Further, all that rolling frayed it. Of surviving literature, codices made up 2 per cent in the second century AD, 4.5 per cent in the third, 48 per cent in the fourth, 90 per cent in the fifth – and in the early centuries, almost all of them were Christian texts. Christians were prime movers in the spread of the codex, perhaps because rolls had pagan associations, but more likely because books were far less bulky (one can write on both sides of the page, unlike the roll) and so more portable, easier to conceal and, of course, much simpler to refer to.

COLOSSAL CEREMONY

The poet Martial wrote a sequence of poems describing the 100-day inauguration of the 'Colosseum'. Gladiators he mentions just once: they were the obvious entertainment. It was the novelty and inventiveness of the other combats that amazed him. He describes women fighting in the arena; criminals executed there, enacting parts in mythical stories (e.g., one criminal, playing the part of Prometheus having his liver pecked out, was gored to death by a boar; sex took place between a woman and a bull, evidently, re-enacting the Cretan queen Pasiphae's love for a bull); the animals joined in exotic battles – lions, rhinos, bears, sows, bulls, elephants, tigers; the sea battles (which cannot have taken place in the 'Colosseum'), and so on. Apparently 9,000 animals were killed in all.

ANIMAL FIGHTS

Whatever we may think of man's cruelty to animals, Romans were more interested in animals being cruel to men. To match a rhino against a lion, for example, was to do nothing that nature might not do anyway, at the same time removing two animals from nature that might do men serious harm. The same theory applied to the criminals who as gladiators fought men and animals in the ring. It was also agreed to be splendid entertainment. Social benefits all round, therefore. There was another point. The people could congratulate themselves on belonging to a mighty machine like the Roman Empire which could summon exotic animals of all species from all over the known world for their pleasure – though there was one recorded occasion when the crowd was sickened by the slaughter of some elephants.

COLOSSAL FALL

In the eighth century the Venerable Bede opined:

> quandiu stat Coliseaus, stat et Roma; quando cadet Colisaeus, cadet et Roma; quando cadet Roma, cadet et mundus

> 'While the Colossus stands, Rome too stands; when the Colossus falls, Rome too will fall; when Rome falls, the world too will fall.'

Note that the statue in medieval times was called *Colisaeus* (whence our 'Coliseum') to distinguish it from 'Colosseum'.

GLADIATORIAL ORIGINS

Gladiatorial combat seems to have been absorbed into Roman culture either from the Etruscans or the Samnites. In Rome gladiatorial contests were originally fought in the open, in the Forum, as some sort of ceremonial display 'owed' to the dead (the Romans use the word *munus* to describe them: 'duty, obligation of honour'). The first we hear of took place in 264 BC. It was staged by the Brutus family to commemorate their father. Eventually permanent buildings were put up to house them – the amphitheatre (Greek, *amphi-theatron*, 'all-round viewing-place'), the only type of building the Romans could claim as their own. We know of approximately 200 stone-built amphitheatres across the Empire, alongside roughly 200 others that were adapted from existing buildings, such as regular theatres. Gladiatorial combats were not part of Rome's state festivals, but were sponsored privately by emperors and budding politicians as a benefit for the people.

TRAINING SCHOOLS

Slaves, prisoners of war and criminals formed the bulk of the gladiatorial population – the lowest of the low – though anyone could join up if they so chose. They were trained in 'schools' under a *lanista*. Under the Empire four official schools were established in Rome, paid for by the state – another benefit bestowed by the emperor – and no private schools were permitted to compete there. The emperor himself appointed a non-senatorial 'equestrian' to run each school, each of which had a full complement of trainers, doctors and weapon-makers. The heavy bones found in a gladiator graveyard excavated in Ephesus in 1993 indicate powerful muscle development; broken bones had healed well (there were doctors who specialized in gladiators, including the very famous Greek doctor Galen, who claimed to have reduced mortality considerably). Gladiator diet was rich in beans and barley, good for growing protective layers of fat.

PRICING A GLADIATOR

Many Romans saw gladiators as a good private investment: Julius Caesar set up a school in Capua in 49 BC, and Cicero's friend Atticus did the same in 56 BC, getting his money back after just two shows. A number of gladiatorial schools had accountants on the staff. It was big business. The care bestowed on the fighters (see above) indicates that economic interests were at stake. But in AD 177, we are told, the shows were becoming too expensive to put on. Indeed, one had to get imperial permission to arm gladiators with sharp weapons or for fights to the death. So Marcus Aurelius abolished the tax on gladiator sales and fixed the maximum price. We have the figures: second-rank gladiators were priced at 1,000–2,000 *ss*, while first-rankers could be bought at anything from 3,000 to 15,000 *ss*. The amount that could be spent on putting on a show was also controlled: between 30,000 *ss* and 200,000 *ss*, though this did not apply to imperial shows (we are told that Hadrian once spent 2 million *ss* on one show).

ARMS AND THE MEN

Gladiator means 'swordsman' (Latin, *gladius*, 'sword'), but gladiators in fact fought with a range of different types of weapon and armour, usually one style of fighter against another style. Twenty types in all are mentioned, but the exact details of even the most common are not precisely known. Swords, spears, shields, knives and helmets of different shape, size and decoration, with armour protecting different parts of the body, were the main armoury components, except for the *retiarius* ('net-man'), armed with a net and trident, but no helmet; there was also the *eques*, fighting from horseback. Their names – many derived from Rome's enemies – indicate the martial origins of the institution: 'Samnite', 'Gaul', 'Thracian'. The gear they wore was so exotically different from that of a regular Roman soldier it must have heightened the sheer theatricality of the spectacle.

ARMS AND THE WOMEN

Female gladiators, *gladiatrices* (singular: *gladiatrix*) were rare, though the state became so worried about the number of upper-class women who wanted to take part that it legislated against them. If depictions are anything to go by, the women fought with one breast bare like Amazons. Male poets mocked their muscles and manly shape. Women were commonly believed to fantasize sexually about male gladiators – no surprise in a society that respected brute force – especially as women were popularly seen as sex-crazy anyway. So the satirist Juvenal laughed at the aristocratic Eppia, the wife of a senator, for eloping with a gladiator, commenting that women just *longed* for the sword (*double entendre* intentional). Incidentally, a wealthy, bejewelled woman was discovered among the dead in the gladiator barracks at Pompeii; but since children were there too, with the equivalent of suitcases full of stuff, she was probably seeking refuge from the explosion of Vesuvius rather than visiting her lover.

PUTTING ON THE SHOW

Advertisements for gladiatorial shows were written up on walls. Here are three examples. Note the reference to 'awnings' – a luxury extra in the amphitheatre to keep punters in the shade:

> Twenty pairs of gladiators supplied by Quintus Monnius Rufus will fight at Nola on 1–3 May. There will also be a hunt [i.e., animal fights].

> Twenty pairs of gladiators supplied by Decimus Lucretius Satrius Valens, lifetime priest of Nero, the emperor's son, and ten pairs

of gladiators supplied by his son Decimus Lucretius Valens, will fight at Pompeii on 8–12 April inclusive. There will be a hunt, and awnings. Aemilius Celer wrote this by moonlight.

Thirty pairs of gladiators and their substitutes, supplied by Gnaeus Alleius Nigidus Maius, the mayor, will fight at Pompeii on 24–6 November. There will also be a hunt. Good for mayor Maius!

IN THE RING

Graffiti of gladiator fights appear in Pompeii. They picture the two fighters, give their names, label one V (*vicit*, 'he won') and the other, if pardoned, M (*missus*, 'released'). Each has his number of fights and victories shown, for example XIV) XII means 14 fights, 12 victories. The defeated man is shown on his knees, without sword or helmet. The Greek letter *th* (θ, theta) indicates that the fighter died of wounds later (Greek, *thanatos*, 'death'). Since gladiators were expensive items and a gladiator who had fought a good fight would be worth seeing in action again, deaths were probably the exception rather than the rule. One graffito in Pompeii mentions 23 fights involving 46 fighters: 21 won, 17 were pardoned and 8 were killed or died from wounds, i.e., 1 in 6 met their end in the ring. Star gladiators – some of whom won between 60 and 150 victories – were very much the exception.

RULE OF THUMB

Referees controlled the contests, intervening if, for example, a piece of armour fell off accidentally, and using whips or red-hot brands to encourage poor fighters to get on with it. There were no time limits, though in a long fight the referee could apparently call a time out for a drinks-and-massage break. The fight went on until one man surrendered, though draws were allowed if the crowd agreed. The referee then stopped the contest and asked the stager of the games to give his verdict. He probably followed the inclinations of the crowd. There is a slight balance in favour of the belief that 'thumbs up' actually meant 'kill' (i.e., drive the sword into him) and 'thumbs down' meant 'let be' (i.e., turn the sword away). The dead man was dragged out, his throat cut (just to make certain), and prepared for burial.

LIFE-SPAN

A famous inscription from Venusia in southern Italy lists the names of (at least) 28 deceased gladiators from the training school of one Gaius Salvius Capito. (Nine of them appear to have been free Roman citizens.) Ten of these gladiators were described as *tirones*, trainees: they died of illness or accidents before they had ever displayed themselves in the arena. Sixteen of them died during or after fighting between one and seven contests, and the other three after twelve. Other inscriptions talk of gladiators dying aged 23 after 8 fights; aged 27 after 11; and aged 34 after 21. From Pompeii, a quarter of the fighters we hear of had more than ten years' experience, and the remaining three-quarters less. The record is skewed, of course, to those whose families could afford to put up monuments, but taken all in all the median age of death was 22.5 years. In the Ephesus graveyard (see p. 258), of the 68 identified bodies, all but two were males aged between 20 and 30. By contrast, for the normal male population, those who survived to mid-teens were on average likely to reach around 50 (see p. 179).

HOW MANY GLADIATORS?

Taking all the records that survive from all over the Empire it has been calculated that there was a through-put of about 16,000 gladiators a year (three legions), working in the 400 venues over the Empire. That would allow for an average for each location of two shows a year, featuring 30 gladiators, each fighting twice a year (12,000 gladiators), with 2,000 dying in the first and 2,000 in the second show. If this is right it suggests that the great arenas like the 'Colosseum' were empty for virtually the whole year! Perhaps spectators got their thrills from watching the practice sessions.

HEROIC ENDS?

In a Roman legion expertise at single combat was the highest virtue, and gladiators exemplified that *virtus* in a particularly uncompromising way. They had no other *virtus* to offer. Cicero conceded that 'there could be no better schooling against pain and death' than gladiatorial contests. Pliny the Younger argued that such contests inspired people to 'face honourable wounds and look scornfully on death by demonstrating a love of glory and desire for victory even in the persons of criminals and slaves'. If inferiors could set such an example, how much better would free citizens?

Such violence revolts us. We call it 'gratuitous' or 'pathological'. 'Nonsense,' Romans would have said. Romulus and Remus, the founders of Rome, had been fathered by Mars, god of war, then suckled by that lonely, dangerous predator the wolf: Rome was born from violence (p. 5). For Romans it both provided intense pleasure and served a deep, almost ideological purpose. No wonder prospective politicians so eagerly funded bloodshed in the arena. As the Empire spread, so did local enthusiasm to stage games and to prove that local communities were tough enough to be Romans.

PROTESTS

Seneca (first century AD) was the first to protest against gladiatorial combat, but not on humanitarian grounds. He argued against it in terms of the brutalization of the spectator. In the morning they throw men to the animals, he said, but in the afternoon they throw them to the spectators. Seneca granted that the gladiators deserved death, but goes on to say: 'What crime have you committed that you should deserve to sit and watch?' He concluded, after watching such a spectacle, 'I come home more greedy, ambitious, voluptuous, cruel and inhuman'. Few objected that these contests were cruel to the gladiators. These people, it was felt, deserved what they inflicted on each other.

GLADIATOR HOOLIGANS

In AD 59 there was a riot after a gladiatorial match between teams from Pompeii and Nuceria (a graffito survives in Pompeii illustrating the fight). It is here reported by the historian Tacitus:

> Trivial beginnings led to dreadful bloodshed between the inhabitants of Nuceria and Pompeii. It all began at a gladiatorial show put on by Livineius Regulus, a man who had been expelled from the Senate. Demonstrating the hooligan behaviour typical of people from country towns, they began hurling abuse at each other, then stones and finally weapons. The advantage lay with the home crowd where the show was taking place, Pompeii, and as a result many

wounded Nucerians were brought to Rome, while others mourned the deaths of children or parents. The emperor handed the judicial hearing over to the Senate, which passed it to the consuls. When the case returned to the Senate, all public gatherings in Pompeii were banned for ten years; all illegal associations were dissolved; and Livineius and those who had started the riot were exiled.

Our pusillanimous FA authorities might take notice.

UNROMAN POMPEII

It is easy to think of Pompeii as a typical 'Roman' town. But it took 400 years to become one. Of sixth-century BC foundation, its people fought with the Samnites against Rome in the fourth century BC (p. 56), becoming Roman allies only in the third century BC, and they spoke Oscan until the first century BC. The town sided against Rome in the Social War (p. 129), after which it was granted Roman citizenship. It became a Roman colony in 80 BC, when Sulla gave land to 2,000 of his soldiers in Pompeii, causing some friction. This was typical of many Italian towns: Rome may have been their master, but 'Romanizing' them was a slow process.

BROTHELS

It has been claimed that Pompeii had 35 brothels to serve a population of 20,000. This sounds mildly excessive. The problem is that both inns and bars (of which around 150 have been identified) feature erotic graffiti and explicit drawings, while legal texts classed inn-keeping with running a brothel, and it was assumed the women who worked there were prostitutes. In fact only one building can be safely identified as a brothel, complete with nearly 150 erotic graffiti, explicit pictures of lovemaking and five small cubicles, each with a stone bed.

ELECTION POSTERS

Parties today try to win elections with on-the-hoof policies which they hope will forge a polling-day bond with an electorate ignored for five years; election posters boast of the miraculous advances they will painlessly effect. There are 2,500 election notices from Pompeii, hand-painted in red or black on house walls by commissioned signwriters (who sometimes signed them). None of them talks of parties; none seems to have been composed by a candidate; none announces a new, cutting-edge policy or makes any sort of political case. Instead, clustered along main streets and around candidates' homes, they simply expressed various individuals' support for the candidate: 'I ask you to support A', 'B urges you to support C for office', 'D is worthy of office', 'Please vote for E'. Only very rarely did they add a justifying reason ('excellent young man', 'won't waste our money'). Sometimes women (who did not have the vote) also expressed their support, including four barmaids from a tavern. The name of one of them (Zmyrina) was whitewashed over – perhaps she was a little too close to the candidate for comfort? Another oddity is that unlikely-sounding groups sometimes announced their intentions: 'The pickpockets/runaway slaves/idlers ask you to support X'. Was this subtle negative campaigning or just a joke? The overall conclusion, however, is that mafia-like networks of bonds and obligations between powerful families and friends held the key to the annual election of officials.

VESUVIUS

Vesuvius is the only active volcano on the European mainland. The name may derive from the Oscan dialect *fesf*, 'smoke', or perhaps from Veiovis, a mysterious early Roman god. The volcano's base is 30 miles (48 km) in circumference and it is 4,000 feet (1,219 m) high. Before it obliterated Pompeii in AD 79 it was perhaps twice as high as it is now. Its volcanic soil was very fertile and therefore thickly inhabited (today, volcanic soil covers 1 per cent of the world and is inhabited by 10 per cent of the population).

AD 79: THE BIG ONE

On 24 August AD 79 Vesuvius exploded. It buried Pompeii in ash, pumice, sand, stones and mud, Herculaneum in pyroclastic surges, and Stabiae in ashes. The details are staggering. One possible account goes as follows (based on Pliny's description, the current state of Vesuvius, our understanding of volcanic activity and the pattern of the fallout):

1 p.m.:Vesuvius ejects molten ash, gases and pumice at some 600 mph (960 kph), about 10,000 tons (10,160 tonnes) every second, as if blown out by a repeating nuclear bomb; minutes later the column has climbed 9 miles (over 14 km) in the air. In force the initial explosion is 500 times greater than the bomb that destroyed Hiroshima.

2.30 p.m.: by now, Pompeii is 20 inches (50 cm) deep in pumice and ash, accumulating at 5 inches (12 cm) an hour. Buildings start collapsing.

6 p.m.: the volcano is now throwing out 40,000 tons (40,640 tonnes) every second, by 7.30 p.m. 100,000 tons (101,600 tonnes). This material is no longer crust, but coming from the centre of the volcano and becoming hotter, heavier and richer in gas.

1 a.m.: about this time on 25 August the soaring column of ejected material, hanging in the air, becomes too heavy for the upthrust from the volcano to contain. It collapses in swirling clouds of hot gas and fine ash ('pyroclastic surge') at 900°F (*c.* 500°C), hugging the ground and racing across it at 125 mph (200 kph). This surges down the mountainside towards Herculaneum. In four minutes this 'pyroclastic surge' buries the town. Other, less super-heated surges, hit Pompeii.

Sunrise: Herculaneum disappears under 82 feet (25 m) of fine ash, now set solid as a rock.

8 a.m.: Vesuvius' final blast, a surge which goes right across the bay of Naples, reaching as far as Stabiae and Misenum. The volcano has ejected about 10 billion tons of material (10.165 billion tonnes).

THE DEATH OF PLINY THE ELDER

When Vesuvius erupted Pliny the Elder, the famous encyclopedist (p. 6), was in charge of the Roman navy at Misenum, just to the north of the Bay of Naples. He had never seen a volcano in action before and was keen to inspect it. He asked the Younger Pliny, his 17-year-old nephew, who was staying with him, whether he wanted to come too, but he was busy with his homework, the weed. It soon became clear that a major disaster was at hand, and Pliny decided to respond to an urgent message for help from a villa owner. He tried to land his boat on the shore, but could do so only a long way from the site. There he was overcome by fumes from the volcano and met his end. Some years later, the Younger Pliny gave a vivid account of the explosion in a letter to the historian Tacitus, saying that when his uncle's body was found 'it looked more like sleep than death'.

THE LIBRARY OF PHILODEMUS

Herculaneum was buried under the pyroclastic surge, soon to set rock hard, a firestorm smashing down walls and tearing off roofs and penetrating everywhere under the terrifying force of its surge, even into the sewers. It relocated the shore 440 yards (400 m) further back – about one cubic mile (4 cubic km) of material in all.

With it was also buried the library of one Philodemus, a Greek intellectual-in-residence at a lavish villa almost certainly the property of Calpurnius Piso, father-in-law of Julius Caesar. A little hotter and the papyrus rolls in the library would have been destroyed; a little cooler and they would not have been carbonized and therefore preserved. The library contained 1,800 book rolls, most of them still waiting to be read. Unrolling and reading carbonized papyrus is a nightmare job, but modern computerized laser technology is coming to the rescue to scan the content of the rolls without needing to interfere physically with them.

ALL-BLACK TIE DINNER

Suetonius tells us that at the beginning of his reign as emperor Domitian would spend hours in his study, on his own, catching flies and impaling them. There was something of the night about Domitian. He put on dinners for the people during the night, and even animal fights and gladiatorial combats, which had to be lit by torches. The historian Cassius Dio (*c.* AD 150–235) reports that Domitian presided over a funeral dinner immediately after he had crushed a revolt, no doubt to remind Rome's top men who was in charge. He had a room painted pitch black on every side, furnishing it with bare couches of the same colour for his guests to recline on. They came at night, without any attendants. Beside each of them was set a slab shaped like a gravestone with a small lamp of the sort that hung in tombs. The food was served by beautiful boys, quite naked and painted black. They entered like phantoms, encircled the guests in a terrifying dance, and then took up their positions by their feet. Here they served the guests with black food from black dishes – the food consisting of things that were commonly offered at sacrifices to departed spirits. The meal was conducted in total silence, as if the participants were already in the realms of the dead, with the exception of Domitian, who talked about topics relating to death and slaughter.

HAIR TODAY

Domitian wrote a treatise *On Hair Care*. It was a topic of considerable interest. Rome was awash with barbers, and hair-dyeing, perfuming and skincare were all part of the service. While the top barbers took their time (the satirist Martial said of one that a second beard grew in the time he spent on the first) the average barber hacked away with crude instruments and could inflict painful injuries. Pliny recommended spiders' webs soaked in oil and vinegar to staunch these wounds. It was so common for barbers to hurt their customers that Roman jurists tried (in vain) to establish damages in advance.

Julius Caesar, a notorious dandy, was always carefully trimmed and shaved, but he worried about his baldness. So nothing pleased him more than when the Senate granted him the right to wear a laurel wreath at all times. Augustus, equally scrupulous about shaving, paid little attention to hair styling, and simple haircuts (bar Nero's) reigned during the first century AD. But Hadrian favoured the waved look, produced either with the comb or curling irons, heated in coals. Martial mocked the attempts of the bald to ape this style: the wind would soon blow back the curls artfully arranged on top, leaving the dome bald as ever, but now fringed with ringlets. What, he concluded, could be more repellent than a bald man covered in hair?

TAMING BRITAIN

The father-in-law of the historian Tacitus was Agricola, who was governor of Britain from AD 77 to 84 before Domitian recalled him. In his biography of Agricola Tacitus describes how the province was slowly brought to heel. Romanization was the key, through urbanization, public building projects and education. Togas began to be worn, Latin spoken, arcades and baths sprang up, and luxurious dining came into fashion. All this, says Tacitus, was greeted with delight by the Britons, who, ignorant as they were, reckoned it added up to civilization (*humanitas*). In fact, Tacitus continues, 'it was nothing but a hallmark of their slavery' – a remarkable comment from a man one would have thought to be in favour of the Roman Way.

A FREEDOM-FIGHTER SPEAKS

Agricola led a push into Scotland, but in AD 83 Calgacus, a Caledonian freedom-fighter, fought Agricola's army at Mons Graupius somewhere in the mountains of Aberdeenshire. Tacitus invented a powerful anti-Roman speech for Calgacus:

> Plunderers of the world, they have exhausted the land and now ransack the sea. Enemy wealth excites their greed, enemy poverty their lust for power – as is obvious, since neither East nor West has yet glutted them . . . Perverting language, they call robbery, butchery and extortion 'government'. They create a desert and call it 'peace'.

What a sentiment for a Roman to express about his own people! And not irrelevant to our times either.

BUILDING A LEGIONARY FORTRESS: INCHTUTHIL

A chartered surveyor has gone into the hard practicalities of what it took to construct the legionary fortress at Inchtuthil in Scotland. It was built for legion XX, *Valeria Victrix*, in the early AD 80s as advance headquarters for Agricola's brief venture into Scotland. This is the only fortress anywhere in the Empire whose complete ground plan is preserved (66 survive in all, 10 in Britain). It is a 53-acre (21 hectare) site, and would have housed about 5,000 troops (a full legion was supposed to number 5,400). It was constructed initially in timber for speed and ease of local supply, then would presumably have been rebuilt in masonry, but it looks as if it was abandoned after three years. The unexpectedly small proportions of some of the buildings add to the impression of a temporary structure.

Some of the summary statistics for the timber phase of the fortress make toe-curling reading: main timbers 16,900 tons (17,170 tonnes); external cladding 1,150 (1,170); defence timbers 780 (790); roof tiles 3,140 (3,190; 741,000 tiles in all); wall and other stone 24,840 (25,200); sand and gravel 24,500 (24,800); and then there are the lime, daub, wattles and nails. Total construction time is calculated at 2.44 million man-hours, with additional labour and provision and transport of materials, food and fodder at 4.6 million man-hours. Rebuilding in masonry would have added another 3.6 million man-hours in construction and 5.9 million in on-site support. More than 700,000 nails and 10 tons of other iron objects were discovered at the site, all very carefully buried. Presumably this was to deny them to the natives when the site was dismantled. Imagine what the stone-built, 160-foot-high Colosseum, holding 50,000 would have entailed, and (like Inchtuthil) all built by hand, without engine power, everything brought by cart into the middle of Rome!

REIGN OF TERROR

The historian Tacitus had an extraordinary capacity to analyse corruption and power. Here, in full Big Brother mode, he describes what it was like to live under Domitian:

> Rome of old explored the limits of freedom, but we the depths of slavery, robbed even of the exchange of ideas because of informers. We would have lost memory itself as well as our tongues, had it been as easy to forget as it was to remain silent.

George Orwell would have understood.

ROMAN POETRY BUT NO ROMAN POETS

It is one of those odd coincidences that there is no Latin poet we know of who was born in Rome. But that was where any poet had to go who wanted to succeed in the literary world. Rome was where the wealthy patrons were available to back you, if you were any good; Rome was where the literary mafia hung out. So there, clutching their styluses, came the budding young writers, from all over Italy and the Roman Empire, looking for patrons and glory. The brilliant epigrammatist Marcus Valerius Martialis (*c.* AD 40–104) or Martial, born in Spain, was one such. His dazzlingly witty epigrams (twelve books of them) show Rome in the raw – his Rome.

MARTIAL AND HIS CRITICS

Poets are always sensitive to criticism:

> Only the poets of old you admire,
> The living get no accolade.
> Please spare *me* your praises, Vacerra:
> That's too high a price to be paid.

MARTIAL AND OTHER POETS

Poets know each other far too well. Here Martial describes how his chum Gallicus wants to be told the truth about his performances:

> 'Please tell me plainly what you think of it',
>   You always say, 'I love a frank report'.
> Thus when you read the products of your wit,

> Thus when you plead a client's case in court,
>
> You pester me, a verdict to extort.
>
> And since refusal would not satisfy,
>
> Here is the truth you ask for, plain and short:
>
> The truth is that you'd rather have me lie.
>
> (trans. Pott and Wright, adapted)

LOOKING FOR PATRONS

Poets needed their backers, but it was not much fun trying to find them:

> Now you're home from your travels in lands far away,
>
> For a week I've been wanting to bid you 'good-day'.
>
> 'He's engaged', 'he's asleep' – that has been the reply.
>
> That's enough; if you won't have 'good-day', here's 'good-bye'
>
> (trans. Pott and Wright)

FLATTERING THE GREAT AND GOOD

Here Martial praises the emperor Domitian's gripping road-widening policy:

> Those brazen shops all had expanded, until
>
> They were sprawling all over the street.
>
> Domitian! You ordered cramped paths to be widened
>
> And turned into roads fit for feet.
>
> Now wine-shops don't chain up their flagons of wine
>
> To the doorposts, and block up the place;
>
> No *praetor* is forced to struggle through mud,

> No barber's blade threatens your face;
> No dirt-begrimed cook-shop now blockades the road;
> And vintner, cook, butcher, refrain
> From spreading their wares all over the streets.
> This shopping mall's Rome once again!

If you are going to be nice to your patron, street-widening seems as good a topic as any to wax lyrical about. We may find this cringe-making, but many Roman poets did exactly the same. You do not become a good or bad poet simply because you choose to keep your benefactors sweet.

MARTIAL ON DOCTORS

Martial gives doctors a hard time:

> Doc Diaulus changed his trade:
> He runs a mortuary.
> Result? The same as when he made
> A living in surgery.

MARTIAL AND SEX

Martial is a master of the sexual joke:

> Marulla carefully weighs in hand
> The penis erected at full stand,
> And tells the poundage of the gland.
> Its work done, she grabs hold the male
> Member, weighs it, rag-like, frail,
> And tells the difference, in detail.
> That's no hand: it's a weighing-scale.

MARTIAL'S ABUSE

A master of abuse, too, here is Martial mocking a woman called Galla:

> When Galla for her health goeth to the Bathe,
> She carefully doth hide, as is most meete,
> With aprons of fine linnen, or a sheete,
> Those parts, that modesty concealèd hath;
> Nor onely those, but e'en the brest and necke,
> That might be seene, or showne, without all checke.
> But yet one foule, and unbeseeming place
> She leaves uncovered still: What's that? Her face.
>
> (trans. Sir John Harington)

MARTIAL'S CHARM

This is one of Martial's most affecting poems, on the death of a little slave girl:

> Dear parents, to your charge down in the grave
> I hand Erotion, my little slave,
> My pet, my darling. Let her feel no fright,
> Poor tiny thing, at Hades' gloomy night,
> Or Cerberus' great maws, or river Styx –
> My birthday girl, just six days short of six.
> With her grandparents let her frolic and game,
> And chattering, as she used to, lisp my name.
> Oh earth, lie lightly on her! It's her due;
> The little girl so lightly lay on you.

X

AD 96–192

TIMELINE

AD 96–8   Nerva emperor

AD 98–117   Trajan emperor

c. AD 100   Date of Vindolanda tablets

AD 101   Campaigns in Dacia

AD 106   Trajan annexes Arabia

AD 111   Pliny–Trajan correspondence

AD 113   Trajan's column built

AD 114   Takes Armenia

AD 117–38   Hadrian emperor

AD 120   The poet Juvenal in full flow

AD 121–5   Hadrian on tour

AD 121   German *limes* built

AD 122   Hadrian's Wall begun

c. AD 125?   Hadrian's Villa started

AD 126   Rebuilding of the Pantheon

AD 128–34   Hadrian on tour again

AD 130   Antinous drowns in Nile

AD 132–5   Judaean revolt put down; Jewish diaspora

AD 138–61   Antoninus Pius emperor

AD 150   Roman Empire at maximum size
(*c.* 60 million?)

AD 161–80   Marcus Aurelius emperor

AD 166   Eastern plague kills millions

AD 170   Roman defeats on Danube

AD 180–92   Commodus emperor

BREAD AND CIRCUSES

Empire without End?

E dward Gibbon, author of *The Decline and Fall of the Roman Empire* (1776–88), said of this time: 'If a man were called to fix the period in the history of the world during which the condition of the human race was most happy and prosperous, he would, without hesitation, name that which elapsed from the death of Domitian to the accession of Commodus.' From Gibbons' eighteenth-century perspective perhaps it was true – provided one was a member of the ruling elite.

Domitian died without an heir, so the Flavian family dynasty ended. It was necessary, therefore, to appoint a successor. The conspirators chose the elderly Nerva (AD 96–8), who had been in imperial politics a long time and was not party to Domitian's murder. Nerva immediately started to repair relations with the elite. But the army had liked Domitian and some praetorians wanted the conspirators executed. A worried Nerva agreed. He then appointed as his successor Trajan, the governor of Upper Germany. It was a choice acceptable to all. So, no more family dynasties?

On Nerva's death Trajan (emperor AD 98–117) dealt with the rebellious praetorians, maintained friendly relations with the Senate and initiated major building schemes, including baths and a new harbour at Ostia. In AD 101 he campaigned in Dacia (northern Romania, AD 101–8), celebrated by his famous column in Rome; in AD 106 he annexed Arabia and in AD 114 took control of Armenia. He had some success, creating one, perhaps two, new provinces in the region, but Trajan was an ill man and in AD 117 he retreated, dying suddenly en route, but (apparently) ensuring his ward Hadrian became emperor (AD 117–38).

Hadrian immediately abandoned all Trajan's new eastern provinces and dealt with further trouble in the northern part of the Empire, including Britain. He appointed Suetonius (the future historian of the lives of the emperors) to his administrative staff. In AD 121 he adopted a policy of non-expansion and protected frontiers, with the *limes* (a defensive palisade) across Germany, and in AD 122 Hadrian's Wall. He continued this tour into Spain, North Africa, Asia Minor and Athens, and was back in Rome in AD 125. This was all part of Hadrian's wide-ranging cultural and intellectual interests, especially in all things Greek.

In AD 128–34 Hadrian was off again, this time with his young lover Antinous, who drowned in the Nile. In AD 132–5 the Jewish leader Bar Kokhba stirred Judaea to revolt; Hadrian had it ruthlessly suppressed and the Jews were expelled from Jerusalem – the start of the Jewish *diaspora* (Greek, 'dispersion'). Hadrian was back in Rome in AD 134, a sick man, spending most of his time in his massive villa in Tibur (Tivoli). He died in AD 138 and was buried in a huge mausoleum, now the Castel Sant' Angelo, after appointing Antoninus Pius as his successor, and after him Marcus Aurelius, sharing with Lucius Verus.

Antoninus (AD 138–61), nicknamed Pius, was a popular choice of successor with the Senate, and he initiated a reign of which our sources strongly approved: he remained in Italy and led a model family life. There was little military activity, though he did (briefly) plant his 'Antonine' wall further north than Hadrian's, and built an outer *limes* in Germany. By the time of his death his peaceful policies had built up a huge reserve (675 million denarii).

This reserve was soon needed. Marcus Aurelius (emperor AD 161–80) had been educated to a high standard by his tutor Fronto (many of their letters survive) and he became fascinated by philosophy at an early age. On Antoninus' orders he was kept from military service. Appointed emperor, Marcus insisted Lucius Verus be made co-emperor, as Hadrian had wanted.

In AD 162 King Vologaeses in Parthia was preparing to invade the Roman East. Marcus sent Verus to deal with it, but in AD 166 the army was struck down by a plague, which it spread further as it marched home. Up to 7 million people (nearly 10 per cent of the Empire) may have died.

If that was not bad enough, there was also trouble on the Danube frontier. The inexperienced Marcus suffered severe defeats from spring AD 170, with Germanic tribes flooding into the Balkans, Greece and northern Italy. This continued on and off, and Marcus died on campaign in AD 180. He left as his monument his so-called *Meditations*, deeply influential reflections on life. Less successful was the choice of his son Commodus as his successor.

Commodus (AD 180–92) became emperor at 19, backed up by a full advisory staff. But the 'kingdom of gold' now yielded to the age of 'rust and iron' (as the historian Cassius Dio commented). Like Hadrian, Commodus at once abandoned all new territories, dealt with trouble in Britain and the Danube, and on the whole maintained the peace. But he too easily handed day-to-day control to his advisers and friends in order to pursue his own interests, which were mostly gladiatorial. Things fell apart, and on the last day of AD 192 he was murdered.

Afer an unsuccessful interregnum, provincial governors decided to fight it out. Septimius Severus, a native of the North African colony of Lepcis Magna, leading the Balkan and Rhine armies, made the swoop and by June he was in Rome, its first North African emperor. Not since AD 69 had an army commander marched on Rome to seize power. It would not be the last time.

AN EMPEROR'S DAY

We are fortunate to possess correspondence between the emperor Trajan and Pliny the Younger when he was governor of Bithynia-Pontus (northern Turkey) *c.* AD 111. There are 61 letters in all. They illustrate what a laissez-faire concept the Empire was at this time: governors just got on with it, with a steer from the centre when required. Most of the letters raise problems for the emperor to solve, e.g., should I use slaves as prison guards? (Yes); can the people of Prusa build a public bath? (Yes, as long as no new tax is imposed to pay for it); what shall I do about two slaves who have enrolled in the army [it was illegal for slaves to serve]? (Execute them if they did so voluntarily, knowing they were slaves); after a nasty fire in Nicomedia may I set up a fire service there? (No, provide equipment for the property owners to deal with it; see p. 200); can permits to use the imperial road system be used when they have expired? (No); should the people of Amastris cover over a filthy open sewer running the length of an especially lovely street? (Yes) – and so on. The famous letters about how to treat Christians can be found on p. 361. Sometimes Trajan's irritation came through. Pliny once asked him if people who got promoted or married should be allowed to invite thousands of people and distribute money among them. 'No,' said Trajan, adding, 'I chose you to use your discretion in restraining excess in the population and to decide for yourself what will best serve peace and security.' One can well understand the tone. At this time there were 44 provinces, all with governors.

THE IMPERIAL POST

All countries, and especially empires, need good communications and a fast, reliable postal service. The Romans began to develop one under Augustus. Posting stations were established all over the Empire, which by the fourth century AD had the use of more than 53,000 miles (85,000 km) of roads. Administered locally, this network provided priority transport for all urgent military and government needs: mail, personnel, imperial freight, payment for troops, sick soldiers, etc. It was a tremendous financial burden. Three types of much-coveted official permit (*diploma*) were issued to allow holders to use animals, wagons and rest houses. To prevent officials using the service illegally for private tours they were not allowed to deviate more than half a mile (0.8 km) from the agreed route. There were changing stations for horses every 8 to 12 miles (13–19 km), and overnight rest houses every 20 to 30 miles (32–49 km; about 5,000 stations in all, each with at least 40 horses, as well as pack animals and oxen). A fit rider with frequent changes of horse could cover 240 miles in a day (380 km; Buffalo Bill once managed 384 miles (615 km)); the average day's journey seems to have been 24 miles (38 km). But there was no mail service for personal use as we know it. Long-distance letters could be delivered only by friends going that way. Local deliveries were made by slaves, who waited to take back the reply.

FRONTINUS ON WATER SUPPLY

Pliny tells us that Julius Frontinus was one of the 'most admired' men of his day. Frontinus was consul in AD 73, governor of Britain (AD 73–7: he built the *via Julia* in Wales) and appointed *curator aquarum* (Water Czar) by Nerva in AD 97. In that position he wrote an extremely important treatise on Rome's water supply, and it makes fascinating reading. He pulled no punches about its importance:

> Perhaps you may care to compare the idle Pyramids or other useless, though unquestionably famous, works of the Greeks, with these magnificent structures, so numerous, so irreplaceable, and carrying so many waters.

Frontinus gives a general history of Roman water supply and of each of the aqueducts (raised and channelled), the legal position, standard of maintenance and details of discharge rates and water quality. He was keen to ensure trees were not growing nearby the channel sections where roots could break into the pipes. He took steps to ensure that water quality was clearly distinguished – drinking, bathing and irrigation/cleaning – and not mixed up together. He was hot on fraud. Too many people were leading pipes off the channels and not paying for it (flow rates told him where this was happening). Leaks also greatly worried him. *Plus ça change* . . .

TAKING A BATH

Rome was eventually supplied by 11 aqueducts, totalling in length about 300 miles (480 km). These delivered more than 250 million gallons (1,136,500 kl) of water a day to its one million inhabitants. Clearly no one needed all that water for drinking purposes. But that is the point. The purpose of aqueducts was not to supply drinking water – you could not found a city without it anyway – but to fill the Romans' *public baths*. These were the equivalent of today's pub/club/gym/sports/shopping/leisure complex all in one. Wherever Romans went, the soldiery demanded that baths – the hub of their social life – go with them. On Hadrian's Wall, for example, all the forts had them as standard.

As soon as all that water was available, of course, it could serve other purposes, e.g., watering gardens. In Pompeii the arrival of the aqueduct changed garden layout and the flowers grown there: pre-aqueduct, trees were planted, post-aqueduct, flowers appeared, with fountains and ornamental water features.

Also, since the supply could not be stopped, it overflowed from the various fountains around the city, cleaning the streets and cooling the air. Hence the raised pavements and stepping stones across the streets in Pompeii to deal with the water from its numerous fountains.

BATHS

The baths were genuinely public and the entry fee minimal. Emperor, toffs, struggling workers and slaves alike, all naked, frequented them, women included (mixed and separate bathing was available, depending on local tastes). But there was never any question of social levelling or integration: people knew their place and mingled with their own kind. The wealthy came with slaves, to be oiled with the finest unguents, dried with thick woollen towels, to drink wine from superb goblets, sport expensive jewellery and have it protected from thieves, with a range of clothes to choose from, and they departed well perfumed; the poor man came with a thin towel and a prayer that his clothes were not stolen. Hadrian found a man rubbing himself down against a wall because he did not even have a towel!

KEEPING FIT

Physical fitness being an important 'lifestyle' priority (p. 373), Romans worked out before bathing: first in the sweating room, then the hot bath, the medium and the cold. Services offered included libraries, brothels, gyms and so on. Seneca the Younger complained about the noise they generated when he was lodging over a bath:

When the muscle-men work out with their lead weights and start to strain, you can hear their grunts . . . if someone wants a cheap massage, you can hear the thwack of hands on shoulders, one sort of noise from the flat hand, one from the cupped. Then a ballplayer arrives and starts counting his shots. At this point I give up. Add the hooligans looking for a fight, the thieves caught in the act and those who sing at the top of their voices in the baths . . . then there is the hair-removal expert screeching out his services, shutting up only when he's depilating an armpit and someone else is doing the screeching, the people selling drinks . . .

Add a supermarket and it is the sort of complex that any modern football club would surely dream of.

HYGIENE

It is easy for today's shower-crazed westerners to be impressed by Rome's drainage systems and bathing habits. But hygienic it was not. The emperor Marcus Aurelius commented that bathing was all 'oil, sweat, filth and greasy water'. The point is that germs were not discovered until the late nineteenth century (by Louis Pasteur). In the absence of that knowledge, hygiene as we understand it played little part in Roman life.

MUCK-SPREADING

The average Roman generated about one and half pounds (0.7 kg) of body waste a day. Rome's population of one million inhabitants would therefore produce 670 tons (680 tonnes) of sewage daily. Rome's Cloaca Maxima could deal both with this and flood-, rain- and aqueduct water. We hear of sewer-cleaners and the risk they ran of choking to death if the drains were underground. But few Romans were connected up to the system since, in the absence of the s-bend, stench and vermin could find their way from sewer into house and, if the Tiber flooded, sewage too. We even hear of one house entered nightly by an octopus via the drain to eat the owner's supply of pickled fish. But where there's muck, there's brass, and sewage was used to supplement animal manure. It was the job of the *stercorarius* (or 'night-soil man', as he was known well into the 1950s in Britain) to empty the household cesspits and sell on the contents to farmers on city outskirts. A graffito from Herculaneum records a payment of just under three *ss* for the removal of ordure.

VINDOLANDA PANTS

In 1973 more than 1,600 inscribed wooden tablets emerged from the ground in Vindolanda, a Roman fort on the Stanegate road running just south of Hadrian's Wall.

The first of these turned out to be a fragment of a letter written *c.* AD 100 announcing the dispatch from 'Sattua' of two pairs of sandals, twenty of socks and two of underpants. It's grim up north.

At Vindolanda two types of wooden tablet were excavated. The first was the traditional sort (p. 255). The wax in these Vindolanda tablets had long disappeared, but often the stylus scratched words in the wooden frame below the wax, and these can be read. About 180 were excavated. The second type of tablet was much more interesting and far more copious: thin slivers of wood, 1–3mm thick, about the size of a postcard. These were often folded so that the writing was on the inside and therefore protected. Nowhere else have these 'leaf tablets' been preserved in such vast quantities. Imaging technology makes the tablets easier to read and the results can be startling. Where before all we could decipher was *c..loinmaturaadmeta*, a meaningless string of letters, we can now read *Lepidinam tuam a me saluta*, 'greet your Lepidina from me'.

FROM BRITS TO BIRTHDAYS

The letters from Vindolanda reveal the lives of soldiers and families from the commander to the ranks, not to mention slaves, artisans, freedmen and traders:

> Octavius to his brother Candidus, greetings. I have written to you several times now pointing out that I have bought about 5,000 *modii* of grain (31 tons), and therefore need some cash. If you don't send it – at least 2,000*ss* – I shall lose the 1,200*ss* deposit I have paid and be thoroughly embarrassed . . .

There are military reports, accounts (how many chickens have been consumed over a two-year period by the garrison commander), petitions, prescriptions, leave applications and literary texts (writing exercises from Virgil for children, beside one of which the tutor has written *seg[niter]*, 'lazy work'). The tablets themselves tell us about strategies of occupation (considerable decentralization of decision-making), the Roman army (endless paperwork covering pay, duty-rosters, leave permissions – what's new?), and the social and economic life of a frontier town. They reveal a huge investment by the Romans in northern Britain, the place crawling with Tungrian (Gallic) and Batavian (Germanic) troops, all of whom, as these tablets show, are well acquainted with the Roman Way (indeed, provincial Romans from Gaul, rather than blue-blooded Romans, were the people who, for the most part, ran Britain; see Carausius at p. 334). There is a reference to the Britons, called *Brittunculi* ('miserable little Brits'). The most famous letter, dated 11 September, invites Sulpicia Lepidina, wife of the garrison commander Flavius Cerealis, to Claudia Severa's birthday party – 'Please do come! It'll be so much more fun if you're here.'

GOD OF CHANCE

In *c.* AD 106 Trajan put up in Rome a temple to Fortuna as the all-pervading power of the universe. So important was she that, even when the Roman Empire officially adopted Christianity under Constantine in the fourth century AD, Fortuna was one of the few pagan deities to stay put. Gradually she was assimilated into a Christian framework and became the god of Providence, a symbol of the transitory nature of human success. She was usually depicted with a cornucopia (a horn of plenty bursting with good things), a rudder with which to steer the course of men's lives, and, to show her variability, wings or a wheel – sometimes even (perhaps anticipating today's lottery) a ball. She was frequently shown blind. Most cities put up a statue to her crowned with towers to symbolize her role as guardian of the city and its prosperity. Incidentally, there was a home-grown god of chance of British-Celtic origin, Rosmerta ('Great Provider'), often shown with a bulging purse. A statue of her in Corbridge features what looks suspiciously like a bran-tub.

RICH AND POOR

The gap between rich and poor in the Roman world was huge. One calculation puts the maximum population of the Empire in AD 150 at

60 million. Of these, perhaps there were 5,000 super-elite adult males with the wealth to qualify as Roman senators. Outside Rome, across the established urbanized areas in the Empire, there might be 30–35,000 very rich elite males. Those two groupings between them might have held 80 per cent of the total wealth. That leaves 99.5 per cent of the population to account for. Perhaps 25 per cent of these could make a broadly sustainable living. They would mostly be city-dwellers: merchants and artisans, with soldiers and peasant farmers who had done well, and those who lived off the elites – teachers, doctors, architects and so on. But the rest of the labour force had to be flexible and lived on the edge most of the time. A graffito makes the point: 'You've had any number of different job opportunities – barman, baker, farmer, at the mint, now you're selling pots. Lick **** and you'll have done the lot.'

SERVING THE CITY

'No people on earth love their cities as the Romans do,' wrote the ancient historian Procopius. The Empire was in fact a network of cities. Probably about one-sixth of the population was urban. Rome itself with its one million habitants was easily the largest, far larger than any western city until Victorian London; the average was under 10,000 people. The purpose of the countryside was simply to serve the cities. In times of hardship, as the doctor Galen recorded, country-dwellers would be reduced to starvation: their wheat, barley, beans and lentils would be commandeered, leaving them a few pulses and leguminous fruits. When those gave out it was a diet of twigs, tree-shoots, bulbs and roots. Country-dwellers were in the majority and were the driving force behind the whole economy, but the city was no respecter of persons.

That said, Italy could not support a huge city like Rome on its own. Hence the vast range of imports from all over the Empire.

JUVENAL

Romans invented satire (poetry driven by anger), and the greatest of Roman satirists was Juvenal (c. AD 60–130). He whipped himself into a rage more often than most. Here, in the first of 16 satires which have come down to us, he gives a taste of his feelings about contemporary Rome:

> No Age can go beyond us: Future Times
> Can add no farther to the present Crimes.
> Our sons but the same things can wish and do,
> Vice is at stand, and at the highest flow.
> Then Satire, spread thy Sails: take all the winds can blow.

> (trans. John Dryden)

Juvenal was here staking a claim to the high moral ground. He had to make it look as if he was a man of decency forced into writing, not out of spite but virtuous necessity. Buoyed, then, by indignant self-righteousness, Juvenal launched out to flay the city of Rome, the court of the emperors, women, the upper classes, sexual deviants, the rich, the greedy, everyone who had, in his view, betrayed what it meant to be a true Roman, i.e., not like him.

In Satire 3 he pictured a true-blue Roman complaining about the city – full of corrupt foreigners (Greeks) and Flash Harrys with more money than sense, and impossible to live in for the traffic, noise, crowds, tottering tenements and thugs. Here he pictured the street bully carefully avoiding the aristocrat with a bodyguard, but

But me, who must by moonlight homeward bend,
Or lighted only with a candle's end,
Poor me he fights, if that be fighting, where
He only cudgels, and I only bear.
He stands, and bids me stand; I must abide,
For he's the stronger, and is drunk beside.
'Where did you whet your knife to-night?' he cries,
'And shred the leeks that in your stomach rise?
Whose windy beans have stuft your guts, and where
Have your black thumbs been dipt in vinegar?
With what companion-cobbler have you fed,
On old ox-cheeks, or he-goat's tougher head?
What, are you dumb? Quick, with your answer, quick,
Before my foot salutes you with a kick.
Say, in what nasty cellar, under ground,
Or what synagogue, your rogueship may be found?' —
Answer, or answer not, 'tis all the same,
He lays me on, and makes me bear the blame.
Before the bar [i.e. to court] for beating him you come;
This is a poor man's liberty in Rome.
You beg his pardon; happy to retreat
With some remaining teeth, to chew your meat.

                                        (trans. John Dryden)

Note the absence of street lighting.

Women also attracted Juvenal's scorn. In Satire 6, the longest satire in Roman literature, Juvenal advised a friend who was about to marry: don't – you're better off committing suicide or finding yourself a pretty boy. He then went on to list the vices of upper-class married women. It is a familiar Roman litany: they're sex-mad, faithless, spendthrift, loud-mouthed, vain, trivial, blue-stockings, murderous, too keen to assume men's roles, not interested in babies, and so on (see Claudius' wife Messalina, p. 240). The point is this: a satirist is not interested in balance or fairness, let alone political correctness (as if there were such a thing in Rome). He identifies a target, trains his weaponry on it and lets fly. What a magnificent newspaper columnist he would have made!

But if one aspect of the satirist is the attack on folly, the other is the defence of righteousness. A satirist must appear to be a man of positive principle or his authority disappears. It is in Juvenal's more ironic and cynical later satires, where he did not lay into individuals so much as reflect on human situations and characteristics, that this moralizing tendency came to the fore.

In Satire 10 – nicknamed 'The Vanity of Human Wishes' by Dr Johnson, who imitated it in 1749 – Juvenal reflects on how futile human aspirations are. Even prayer is a waste of time. Juvenal continues:

> Yet not to rob the priests of pious gain,
> That altars be not wholly built in vain;
> Forgive the gods the rest, and stand confin'd
> To health of body, and content of mind:
> A soul, that can securely death defy,
> And count it nature's privilege, to die;
> Serene and manly, harden'd to sustain
> The load of life, and exercis'd in pain:
> Guiltless of hate, and proof against desire;

That all things weighs, and nothing can admire:
That dares prefer the toils of Hercules
To dalliance, banquet, and ignoble ease.
The path to peace is virtue: what I show,
Thyself may freely on thyself bestow:
Fortune was never worshipp'd by the wise;
But, set aloft by fools, usurps the skies.

(trans. John Dryden)

Byron thought this should be read to all the dying, in preference to any religious rites.

POOR LAW

In AD 101 Trajan had established a system of *alimenta* (food subsidies) to help poor children. It worked by offering state loans to farmers, against a proportion of their land. The loans did not have to be repaid, but interest was charged. This money, however, did not revert to the state. It was used to support the poor of the community. An inscription in Veleia, a small town near Genoa, tells us that enough money was raised by this method to provide 263 boys, 35 girls and 2 illegitimate children with a working man's wage for about a week every month for a year. This cunning scheme created an admirable community of interests and responsibilities between wealthier farmers and the poor, and was widely rolled out. Ingenious, Holmes, very ingenious. Alimentary, my dear Watson.

TRAJAN'S COLUMN

Currently topped by a statue of St Peter, Trajan's column (124 feet (38 m) high) was constructed in AD 113 out of 29 vast blocks of Italian marble. It has an inner spiral staircase winding all the way to the top, carved out of this solid stone, lit by 40 slit windows. The superb external helical frieze is 650 feet (200 m) long and between 2 feet and 4 feet high. One scene of Roman military practice follows another – sieges, battles, taking prisoners, building walls, even a soldier dropping his shield in flight and so on – but there is no obvious story. It is an ideological representation of Trajan's successful wars in Dacia, perhaps based on his (lost) account. Its message is: Rejoice! Rejoice! This is Roman imperial power at work! Possibly the scenes were carved only after Trajan's sudden death in AD 117 (when the base became his tomb).

SOCIAL INSECURITY

The rich were contemptuous of workers, regarding them as little better than slaves. But work was the only means for people to keep body and soul together. The workers in Pompeii who supported political candidates saw themselves as 'cooperatives' (p. 266). Graffiti record requests from groups like the fruit-sellers, mule-drivers, goldsmiths, carpenters, cloth-dyers, innkeepers, bakers, porters and removers, chicken-sellers, mat-makers and grape-pickers to vote for this or that candidate for office. But self-help was still the rule. Antoninus Pius was once approached to settle a dispute between an ill workman and his father. His reply:

If you approach the relevant authorities, they will give orders that
you should receive upkeep from your father, provided that, since
you say you are a workman, you are in such ill health that you
cannot sustain your work.

The gamble that was life in the ancient world is reflected in an epitaph
popular enough for it to be known in two versions:

All a person needs. Bones reposing sweetly, I've no worries about
suddenly being short of food. I don't suffer from arthritis and I'm
not in debt because I'm behind with the rent. In fact my lodgings
are permanent and free!

Here are the average Roman's concerns: food, health, paying the
rent. The Latin for 'rent collector' is *extractor*.

MAKING GOOD

Here is part of an inscription composed at the end of his life by a local
Berber peasant who had made good in Numidia in Roman North Africa
(Tunisia) *c.* AD 200:

I was born of poor parents; my father had neither an income
nor his own house. From the day of my birth I always cultivated
our fields; neither my land nor I ever had any rest . . . I left my
neighbourhood for twelve years and reaped the harvest for another
man, under a fiery sun; for eleven years, I was then chief of the
harvest gang, gathering the corn in the fields of Numidia. Thanks
to my labours, and being content with very little, I finally became
master of a house and a property: today I live at ease. I have even

achieved honours: I was called on to sit in the Senate of my city, and, though once a hayseed (*rusticulus*), I became censor. I have watched my children and grandchildren grow up around me; my life has been occupied, peaceful, and honoured by all.

DEVOLVING AN EMPIRE

All empires run themselves or they don't run at all. That, in practice, means they rely on the local bigwigs to do what local bigwigs have always done, but under the direction of their new masters. What their new masters have to do is ensure the bigwigs feel it is worth their while. It is the ultimate devolved system. So it was with Rome. Until Diocletian's reforms (p. 331) only about 160 central government officials went out every year to administer the *c.* 40 provinces. By comparison, the British in India required nearly 1,000; the EU requires, by its count, 32,000 (by others' count, 170,000). Provided their governors were efficient and trustworthy, the taxes came in (p. 123) and the armies were paid and properly run, all the central administration had to do was respond to crises. The elites of the big cities were the key to making this happen, running cities from half a million (Alexandria) to the average city in the low tens of thousands.

WINNING THE LOCALS

Rome had no imperializing mission, driven by burning-eyed governors with a passion for bringing Latin to the masses. It simply wanted to be in control. It made it easier to do this when the locals saw advantage in taking what Rome had to offer (p. 346). And they did. Roman villas sprang up across much of the West. Bread replaced porridge and wine replaced beer. Elaborately mould-cast, glossy Roman 'Arretine' pottery (from modern Arezzo) became all the rage, though it was actually manufactured outside Italy, then stamped with Latin potters' names for 'authenticity'. The Latin language began to dominate. It was not quite the same in the Greek-dominated East, where local pride in their famous ancient culture and language was never seriously shaken.

HADRIAN'S NAME

Some assume the Adriatic was named after Hadrian, but the reverse is true. Publius Aelius Hadrianus (Roman emperor AD 117–38) took his personal name from the Adriatic, i.e., from Hadria, the port in the Po delta after which the sea was named. His family originated from that area, but they moved to Spain, which Hadrian's ancestors had helped to conquer. They settled near modern Seville in territory proudly renamed *Italica*, rich in agricultural produce (especially olives) and minerals from nearby Rio Tinto.

NO TIME FOR ORGIES

We have much evidence giving the lie to the idea that the emperor idled away his day in orgies. Like provincial governors, he too maintained a relatively small bureaucracy. When provincials wrote to him or petitioners approached him (and they swarmed round him when he was in public view, p. 180), they expected replies, and got them. Seneca wrote of the secretarial effort this entailed:

> So many thousands of people have to be given audience, so many *libelli* (petitions) to be dealt with; such a crush of matters coming

together from the whole world has to be sorted out, so that it
can be submitted in due order to the mind of the most eminent
emperor.

On one occasion Hadrian was on his travels abroad when a woman
came up to him, took hold of his toga and demanded to be heard.
Hadrian shook her off, saying he was too busy. She shouted, 'In that
case, don't be emperor!' Hadrian stopped and listened. *Caveat emperor*.

THE POWER OF THE IMPERIAL PRESENCE

Hadrian saw more clearly than most that the Empire was the sum of its
parts, and that one effective way of helping to keep those parts together
was to provide the political, social and communal glue of his own
physical presence. As a result he spent more than half of his reign on
tour, networking among governors and local elites, initiating building
programmes and cultural events, reforming military training, lecturing,
debating and indulging his ceaseless curiosity about ideas, people and
places. No fewer than 122 cities benefitted. Queen Elizabeth I (reigned
1558–1603) was of the same persuasion: every spring and summer for 44
years she toured the realm, ensuring her subjects had the chance to see
her in person. Queen Elizabeth II takes much the same view.

FROM ENGINEERS TO PILLOW SUPPLIERS

It is easy to think of the Roman soldiers as nothing but fighters. In
fact they had a huge range of activities to cover. They were also
administrators, industrialists, builders, a protective occupying force and
provincial policemen. We hear of many complaints of their behaviour

in that last role, whose main purpose was to preserve the interests of the state and its elites. As industrialists they ran quarries, mines and potteries, including bricks and tiles, and manufactured weapons and military equipment. Under specialist engineers they built bridges, roads, siege-works, walls, amphitheatres and aqueducts as well as military bases, from temporary, overnight camps to stone forts.

Pliny the Younger, governor of Bithynia-Pontus, kept on asking the emperor Trajan to send him army engineers to carry out peace-time work. Trajan always refused. But one can see why Pliny thought they were the best. When the emperor gave a city an amphitheatre, street or a square, for example, his soldiers built it. But freelance activity was also undertaken. We hear of army commanders in Germany being reprimanded for sending their men on goose-hunting expeditions to collect down for selling to luxury pillow merchants!

HADRIAN'S WALL

Ever since its provincialization in AD 43 (p. 238) Britain had meant trouble, and trouble on the edges of empire was not to be taken lightly. The purpose of Hadrian's famous wall was to do in the West what he had earlier done in the East, when he gave up large tracts of the Empire there – Armenia, Mesopotamia and Assyria – and also in Germany, where he constructed a 350-mile (563 km) *limes*, a continuous oak palisade perhaps ten feet high. The aim was not so much to separate barbarians and Romans as to mark the limits of Rome's expansion and to be able to guarantee that within those limits, civilization ruled, OK. It has been calculated that the wall's construction required 1,700,000 cubic yards (1,300,000 cubic metres) of masonry, each yard involving the movement of a ton of material. Ten thousand men would have taken 240 days to build the wall and dig the ditches alone; double that for building forts, milecastles and turrets. It is the largest standing Roman monument in the world.

ANTINOUS: THE FASCINATION OF AN EMPEROR'S LOVER

Antinous, Hadrian's young male lover, was on tour with the emperor (part of a poem celebrating their lion hunt survives), when he died in mysterious circumstances in the Nile: theories range from accident to ritual suicide. Apart from his birth in Bithynia, virtually nothing else is known about Antinous. Hadrian was overwhelmed with grief. He founded an (as yet undiscovered) city, Antinoopolis, near the site where Antinous died, and all over the Empire statues were put up to him in villas, sanctuaries and bathhouses, and temples erected to him as to a god. Clearly, the personal life of the emperor struck a chord with provincials. Perhaps the rise of an obscure unknown like Antinous to such a position of influence, not to mention Hadrian's powerful emotional reaction to his death, fed some of their own aspirations and fantasies. There are mysteries here. As Tennyson said, 'If we knew what [Antinous] knew, we would understand the ancient world.' So famous did Antinous become in death that his link with Hadrian was almost completely forgotten.

HADRIAN'S PUMPKINS

Hadrian was a highly cultured intellectual, and something of a loner. He sang, played the lyre, wrote poetry, loved debating with professors of philosophy and had serious literary and architectural interests. For example, poured concrete (p. 109) made it possible to construct buildings with vaults and domes. Hadrian was fascinated by these possibilities and tried to persuade the top architect Apollodorus of their virtues. 'Just go away and *draw* your pumpkins,' was his testy response. So Hadrian did, and the result was his Pantheon – its vast dome of unreinforced concrete, all 5,000 tons of it, spanning approximately 140 feet (44 m) and painted to look like the heavens. He held court under it, symbolic master of the world. It became the forerunner of the great Hagia Sophia dome (p. 163) and thus of domed mosques, built on the model of Christian churches everywhere. By the same token, Hadrian's amazing 900-room villa at Tivoli, most of it unexcavated, covered perhaps 300 acres (120 hectares). It came complete with artificial lakes, fountains, miles of underground tunnels to keep out of sight the slaves who serviced it, and established artistic and architectural precedents of enormous influence. This gigantic complex, with its domes, semi-domes, curved spaces and arches, showcased the linear competing with the circular in dramatic fashion. It was here that a depressed and suicidal Hadrian spent the last years of his life, in rooms named after countries and sights of the Empire – a miniature replica of the Empire he so loved to travel. There was even a Hades . . .

POETIC END

On his deathbed in Baiae, we are told that Hadrian composed this touchingly appropriate poem to his soul:

> *animula vagula blandula,*
> *hospes comesque corporis,*

quae nunc abibis in loca? –
pallidula rigida nubila,
nec ut soles dabis iocos.

Byron translated it:

Ah! gentle, fleeting, wav'ring sprite,
Friend and associate of this clay!
To what unknown region borne
Wilt thou now wing thy distant flight?
No more with wonted humour gay,
But pallid, cheerless and forlorn.

ROME: MASTER OF THE WORLD'S RESOURCES

Romans took great pleasure in the assumption that the whole of nature
from the known world was offered them in tribute. There was everything
from the famous horses from Spain that could be trained to perform
to music (Nero had one) and the infamous lap dancers from Cadiz, to
bathrooms built out of yellow marble from Numidia, red from Turkey,
green porphyry from Greece and white stone from Sidon, to eastern
aromatics like cardamom from Nepal and saffron from Cilicia (also used
by women to tinge their hair red if they wanted to look as if they came
from Germany or Gaul), the rhinoceros and giraffe from Africa, carp from
the Danube, damsons from Syria, cedars from Lebanon, notoriously see-
through silk from China, cosmetics from South Arabia, and diamonds,
pearls and ebony from India. Nearer home Romans could thrill to the
springs of Aponus near Padua – 'unkind to girls', as the poet Martial said,

because they were said to boil with outrage if women joined the men bathing there – and to visions of slave boys with complexions whiter than marble from Paros, lips red as the roses of Paestum, breath 'like the faint smell of balm given off by scent-jars that were emptied yesterday, the smell of the last breath that wafts from the saffron spray' (Martial) and a bottom warmer than – but we had better stop there. As late as AD 400 the poet Rutilius was able to exclaim of Rome:

> Rhine shall plough for you, Nile shall flood for you, Africa shall
> offer you her fertile harvests, wine-presses overflow with the nectar
> of the West. The river Tiber shall submit his waters to the service
> of the children of Romulus; downstream between his peaceful
> banks shall go the wealthy merchandise of the field, upstream shall
> come the wealth of the sea.

THE STOICAL SLAVE

Epictetus (AD 50–135) was born a slave in Phrygia (central Turkey), a Greek-speaking province of the Roman Empire. He was sold to a confidant of Nero, who freed him. He then began to teach Stoicism, a philosophy invented by the Greek thinker Zeno (335–263 BC), who taught in Athens in a *stoa*, a covered walkway (hence the name Stoicism). In AD 89 the emperor Domitian banished philosophers from Rome. So Epictetus set up privately in Nicopolis on the western coast of Greece, just south of Corfu. There his reputation grew. Hadrian and Marcus Aurelius were both influenced by his teachings.

LIVING IN TUNE WITH NATURE

Ancient philosophy was not pie-in-the-sky thinking: it aimed to remove unhealthy beliefs and thereby set you on the road to healthy mental living and happiness. Stoics believed that God was not a personal god but divine reason, permeating the universe 'like honey through a honeycomb'. Since man possessed a rational mind, this was the 'divine' element in us. So we have a choice: we can act rationally and go with the divine flow (floating down a river is an image Epictetus uses) and be happy because that's the way the universe is. Or we can act irrationally, go against the flow and be miserable. So what did it mean to act rationally? Epictetus thought it meant controlling our opinions, our impulses, our desires and our dislikes, since those seemed to be at the root of the problem. For if we desired what we could not have, it made us miserable. Since he deemed it irrational to be miserable, Epictetus urged his followers to think rationally in order to be happy. That is why he regarded the emotions as dangerous: they get in the way of rational decision-making. So you must control them. *Apekhou kai anekhou*, said Epictetus, Greek for 'Restrain yourself and endure.'

FATE AND FREE WILL

Stoic thought emphasized that, since the divine permeated the universe, it must also control it. Fate, therefore, was inescapable. But how could that be reconciled with free will? One powerful image Stoics deployed was that of a dog attached by a long lead to a bullock-cart. If the bullock was moving on a fixed path from A to B, the dog would have no option but to go the same way. But its long lead gave it plenty of free scope to explore the surroundings as it did so.

EPICTETAN REFLECTIONS

Do not ask for things to happen as you wish, but wish them to happen as they do happen, and your life will go smoothly.

Remember that you are an actor in a play, which is as the author wants it to be: short, if he wants it short; long, if he wants it long. If he wants you to act a poor man, a cripple, a public official or a private person, see that you act it with skill. For it is your job to act well the part assigned to you; but to choose it is another's.

You are a little soul, carrying a corpse.

No man is free who is not master of himself.

EXTREMELY COOL BRITANNIA

Our first representation of Britannia, goddess of these islands, is found in Turkey (see p. 238), but it became common on our coinage from 1674 under Charles II. The model for it was a coin minted under Antoninus Pius (emperor 138–61), though we have coins with similar images from Hadrian's era. The Roman coins often show her seated on a rock, signalling 'rocky outpost', with shield and spear; she sometimes holds a standard, or leans on a shield; or is seated on a globe overlooking the seas, on (as it were) the very edge of the world. She can be wrapped in a thick robe, against the cold. She first appeared holding a trident and seated above the waves in 1797, emphasizing Britain's naval superiority under admirals like Nelson and Collingwood.

AN EMPEROR LEGISLATES

Flavia Tertulla had a problem: her local council had refused to decree that her children were legitimate. So she wrote to the emperor Marcus Aurelius – and got a reply. This she had carved in stone and set up for all to see. It ran:

> We are moved both by the length of time during which, in ignorance of the law, you have been married to your uncle, and the fact that you were placed in matrimony by your grandmother, and by the number of your children. So, as all these considerations come together, we confirm that the status of your children who result from this marriage, which was contracted 40 years ago, shall be as if they had been conceived legitimately.

This 'rescript' (a written imperial reply) is evidence not merely of the emperor's hands-on approach to running his empire (p. 301), but also of the extent to which law-making was becoming more and more centralized (p. 348).

THE ROMAN DEATH-TRAP

A city of a million people living in cramped conditions, Rome was unhealthy. Microbes flourish in high-density populations, so a wide range of diseases must have flourished in this centre of 'global' commerce and migration (Pliny the Elder mentions leprosy, for example). That was bad enough, but as a low-lying city at the foot of hills and always liable to flooding from the Tiber, Rome was also a breeding ground for the ruthless killer malaria. Its name derives from *mal'aria* (first attested in 1440), as if it were caused by bad air; Romans knew it as 'quartan fever', because it returned every fourth day. They did not know it was carried by mosquitoes (final proof emerged only in 1898), but they knew very well that it was virulent in summer and autumn. No coincidence, then, that the elite decamped to their summer residences at that time. Nevertheless, since Rome needed manpower – immigration, after all, was the only way to keep the numbers up – people were always drawn to it, probably unaware they were entering a death-trap. That said, general human suffering from chronic, long-term degenerative illness (e.g., osteoarthritis) must have been just as destructive of human happiness. We find in one drain a number of teeth, drawn out with the roots.

A KILLER PLAGUE

The Roman Empire in the east met the huge Parthian Empire at the Euphrates, and the boundaries between the two had always been disputed. Armenia, in particular, shuttled between one side and the other. In AD 162 the Parthian king Vologaeses placed his own son on the Armenian throne, and his cavalry forces defeated the Roman governor of Cappadocia. Marcus Aurelius sent his co-emperor Lucius Verus to sort it out. This mission successfully restored and strengthened Roman control of its eastern borders, but in the process the army was struck by a devastating plague which it brought back to Italy. It was so widespread that it was even mentioned in Chinese records. The epidemic lasted at least 15 years, being transmitted widely over the Empire and returning to places it had already ravaged. The death-rate must have been especially high in army barracks and crowded city centres, ports and coastal towns; some sources report that at its height 5,000 a day were dying in Rome. Revenue from taxes and imperial estates declined, and space ran short in cemeteries. In AD 167 Marcus Aurelius initiated a series of religious ceremonies and foreign purificatory rites. The great Greek doctor Galen was also summoned, but soon departed for healthier climes. His account is spare: he noted fever and pustules, but concentrated on the spitting of blood. Forms of smallpox, typhus and bubonic plague have all been suggested.

THE PARADOX OF MARCUS AURELIUS

Marcus' life and career seem at permanent odds. He was an emperor whose youth passed (on his predecessor Antoninus Pius' orders) without any experience of battle, but who spent much of his imperial tenure (AD 161–80) protecting Rome's frontiers against invaders; a priggish emperor whose strongly held Stoic views of restraint, self-control and self-sufficiency were almost entirely out of tune with the people he was ruling; a pagan with strong anti-Christian views, he took harsh measures against them; and a thinker whose *Meditations* (a modern title: it is titled *Notes to Himself* in one manuscript), however random and *ad hoc* a series of responses to whatever he was reflecting on at the time, have given comfort and strength to millions. John Stuart Mill compared it to the Sermon on the Mount.

SOME MEDITATIONS

The noblest way to avenge yourself is not to become as they are.

Remember that the power that pulls our strings is that which is hidden within us: that is the source of our action, and our life, and that, if one may say so, is the person himself.

If the light of the torch shines forth without ever losing its radiance until it is extinguished, shall truth, justice and temperance be extinguished in yourself before you reach the end?

Remember that there is a proper dignity and proportion to be observed in the performance of every act in life.

DIET

Since meat and some types of fish were expensive to buy, a basic vegetarian diet was standard in the ancient world: cereal, mainly wheat, barley and emmer, perhaps making up 75 per cent of intake, and legumes – poor man's food. These latter included bean, lablab bean, pea, black-eyed pea, chickpea, grass pea, fenugreek (mainly a fodder plant), lentil, lupin, turnip, acorn, vetch. *Puls*, a sort of thick emmer porridge, was a traditional ancient Roman dish. Other widely used vegetables included cress, lettuce, rocket (believed to be an aphrodisiac), and cabbage and leek (both also used for medicinal purposes). Typical fruits included olive, grape, fig, almond, walnut, apple, pears, plums and cherries (the last four providing cultivated varieties by grafting, from 300 BC). Fruits transplanted from elsewhere included pistachio, apricot, peach and citron. In the absence of sugar, sweeteners included honey, grape juice and figs; dates were a delicacy in Rome. There were no potatoes or tomatoes. Milk and cheese came from sheep and goats, not cows; eggs from hens (eggs from other birds were counted a luxury). The most common meat was pork; sows can farrow twice a year, producing up to twelve piglets, and they can live off almost anything, plus the whole animal is usable. Since Romans knew how to conserve meat, a slaughtered pig could provide food for a long time.

DOWN THE DRAIN

A tunnel ran under an ancient Roman apartment block in Herculaneum, fed by chutes from the kitchens and lavatories of the 150 inhabitants above. Its composted human waste has been found to contain a wide range of food: emmer, millet, barley, lentils, apples, pears, dill, fennel, poppy seed, garum, anchovies, sea-bream, damselfish and horse mackerel. So city life in a pretty average block of flats was not all veg and porridge. The waste survived because the sewer did not drain properly, and was blocked by volcanic deposit in the eruption of Vesuvius in AD 79 (p. 267).

FINE WINES

Wine was drunk with hot water (boiled for safety), each diner adding it to taste (no communal mixing bowl of the sort Greeks used). It could be sweetened with honey, a combination known as *mulsum*, or spiced; also salted, pitched, resinated or smoked. Since no one mentions macerating wine, it can hardly have ever been the deep red we are used to, perhaps slightly rosé at best. Pliny the Elder ranked the best wines as follows: Caecuban, Falernian, Alban, Surrentine (Sorrento, including Gauran and Massic) – all grown between Rome and the bay of Naples – and Mamertine (Sicily). Romans boasted of a wine's age (we hear of one over 100 years old), but no one talked of fine wine at its peak. Terms like 'austere', 'astringent', 'forceful', 'strong', 'rich', 'earthy', 'winy', 'sweet', 'noble', 'thin', 'oily' were used of the taste. Romans hoovered up about 17 million gallons (77 million litres) a year. Remedies for not getting drunk were common. Africanus recommends baking and eating a goat's lung.

FISH SAUCE WITH EVERYTHING

Ancients seemed to like the sweet and sour combination of flavours. A favourite ingredient was a pungent fish sauce called garum or liquamen, used on almost every dish, including sweets. This was made to the following recipe: pack fish innards (mackerel and tunny preferred), small fish and plenty of salt in a vat and leave to ferment. When fermented, tip into shallow pan and leave in the sun to rot down for a few months. When liquid, strain off and bottle. Delicious! Wine to taste could be added during the process. It resembled the fish sauce of modern Vietnamese and South-east Asian cooking.

POP-EYED OVER OLIVE OIL

As today, olive oil came in different qualities and it is that quality that controlled what was done with it.

1) The most expensive was *omphacium*, pressed from unripe olives harvested in August and therefore light, colourless and delicate. This

was the oil that acted as the base for perfumes and ointments. Salt was added to preserve it and gum or resin to 'fix' the aromatics mixed into it, which included myrtle, cardamom, cinnamon, oregano, mint, balsam, lily, quince and so on. It was sometimes coloured with scarlet or saffron.

2) Olives pressed before October produced the oil *acerbum* ('bitter'), which was used as a skin moisturiser and principal cleansing agent for humans and even textiles and wool.

3) December-harvested olives that were turning black produced *viridum* ('green'), used for food and cooking. Like ours, it came in three pressings, the last being the bog-standard oil used for cooking and lighting.

It is all eye-poppingly calorific too – *c.* 120 calories per teaspoon. But since it goes off, it had to be traded quickly.

OIL EXPLOITATION

Olive oil was big business in the ancient world – a basic food and major lighting fuel, but also acting as the base for soaps, oils, perfumes, medicines and so on. Since cereals required work in the summer, and wine in autumn, the olive, a very tough tree, required work only from October to December. So it filled out the farmer's year very nicely. It was also ideal for intensive exploitation, which is what happened under the Romans.

OIL A CITY NEEDS

One litre of oil (1.75 pints) produces about 134 hours of light from a single-nozzle lamp. So if you lit that lamp for one hour every day, you would need three litres to see you through the year. Rome had a million inhabitants. If every inhabitant of ancient Rome lit a lamp for only one hour a day, that city alone would have required 3 million litres of oil a year, just for lighting. Now assume that a Roman required nine times that much for drinking and cooking, i.e., 27 litres (47.4 pints) a year. That produced a grand total of at least 30 litres a year per Roman for lighting, drinking and cooking. So Rome alone required 30 million litres a year (c. 7 million gallons). That worked out at 12 million olive trees a year, and an area of about 460 square miles (1,191 square kilometres) for Rome alone. Incidentally, the olive stones were often used as fuel.

CUSTOMS DUTIES

All ports, frontiers and provincial boundaries in the Roman Empire charged duty on goods. The traveller presented a list of everything he had with him. Only conveyances and objects 'for personal use' were exempt: even corpses being transported for burial were charged. Duty was low (2 to 5 per cent of value), but luxury items like silks, perfumes, spices and pearls ran to 25 per cent. Undeclared objects were confiscated; newly bought slaves disguised as family members were released on the spot; and lawyers debated whether customs officials could actually touch married women who stowed pearls away in their bosom. As today's officials rifle through our bags, we may feel, like Plutarch (second century AD), 'irritated and upset that they go through bags not their own, searching for hidden items – yet the law allows it'.

GLAD TO BE A GLADIATOR

That the emperor of Rome himself – a left-handed emperor, too, of which he was very proud – should wish to perform in the same arena and on the same terms as common criminals was seen to be the ultimate debasement of the position, the Empire and the Roman people. But Commodus was serious. He had the head of Nero's Colossus, now replaced by the Sun-god Sol (p. 253), cut off and replaced with a likeness of his own. He then gave it a club and put a bronze lion at its feet to make it resemble Hercules. Underneath it he had inscribed: 'Champion of the *secutores* [a type of gladiator]. Only left-handed fighter to conquer a thousand men twelve times.' He had all his 735 appearances publicly recorded. But he was not stupid. He knew he stood no chance against real gladiators. So while he happily killed and maimed men in private ('lopping off an ear here, a nose there and other bits too'), in public he stuck to animals, a hobby so expensive that he levied a special imperial tax every birthday to finance it.

LAUGH? I NEARLY DI[E]D

Cassius Dio noted that the senators lived in fear of their lives while Commodus' absurd gladiatorial performances were going on. On one occasion, he tells us, Commodus killed an ostrich and cut off its head, then

came up to where we were sitting, holding the head in his
left hand and in his right hand raising aloft his bloody sword.
And though he said nothing, he wagged his head and grinned,
indicating that he would treat us in the same way. And many of
us would indeed have perished by the sword there and then – not
because of any indignation, but for laughter. But I removed some
laurel leaves from my garland and began chewing them, and told
the others sitting with me to do the same. The result was that
the steady chewing motion of our jaws disguised the fact that we
were laughing our heads off.

XI

AD 193–476

TIMELINE

AD 193–211   Septimius Severus emperor

AD 211–17   Caracalla emperor

AD 212   Empire-wide citizenship granted

AD 218–22   Elagabalus emperor

AD 238   Year of Six Emperors

AD 253–60   Valerian emperor

            Humiliated and murdered by Persian king Sapor

AD 267–72   Zenobia regent of Palmyra and Eastern Empire

AD 270–75   Aurelian emperor

AD 271   New defensive wall round Rome

AD 284–305   Diocletian emperor

AD 287   Carausius declares himself emperor of Britain

AD 293   Allectus rules Britain

            Diocletian's 'tetrarchy'

AD 296   Constantius restores Britain to the Empire

c. AD 300	Eusebius' chronicle of world events
AD 301	Diocletian's prices edict
AD 306	Constantine hailed as emperor in York by army
AD 312	Battle of Milvian Bridge: Constantine co-emperor
AD 315	Arch of Constantine dedicated
AD 324–37	Constantine sole emperor
AD 330	Constantinople dedicated
AD 361–3	Julian the pagan emperor
AD 373	Valens' aqueduct into Constantinople
AD 376	The Huns break through into pagan land north of Rome
	Goth army settled in Thrace
AD 379–95	Theodosius I emperor
AD 382	Eastern emperor Valens killed in Goth attack at Adrianople
AD 386	Augustine converted
AD 395–430	Augustine Bishop of Hippo
AD 410	Alaric the Goth's sack of Rome
c. AD 411	Augustine's City of God
AD 430–47	'Hun-geld' multiplies by six
AD 439	Vandal/Alan king Gaiseric takes North Africa
AD 450–53	Attila the Hun strikes into the Empire
AD 476	German king Odoacer 'retires' last Roman Western emperor
	Technical end of the Roman Empire in the West
AD 533	Justinian's *Digest* (or *Pandects*)
AD 1453	29 May: technical end of the Roman Empire in the East

GERMANS, HUNS AND THE FALL OF THE ROMAN WEST

The third century saw the start of a series of surges into the Roman Empire by Germanic peoples across the Rhine–Danube, while the Persians began to cut into Roman territory in the East. As the emperors failed to deliver peace and stability, local elites in parts of the Empire – like Gaul in the West and Palmyra in the East – became disillusioned, broke away and ran themselves. They were not trying to destroy the Empire; indeed, they hoped their rule would be officially recognized, as Carausius did in Britain in 287. But this inevitably generated further civil conflict.

So it was a period of military turmoil, as wars, both civil and foreign, increased. There was financial conflict too, as the money to fund these battles became harder to come by. One result was that cities began to shrink, and after 250 no new theatres or amphitheatres were built.

With the return of (always military-backed) family succession, Rome's first African emperor Septimius Severus (193–211) was followed by a sequence of incompetent emperors, the young playboy Elagabalus probably being the worst (218–22). Further, as in the Republic, if one soldier could rule the roost, so could another; and as the system creaked, professional soldiers, many from the Danube region, tried for the throne in an attempt to impose order. So there were more than 60 emperors – or people declared emperor – in the 100 years between Septimius and Constantine; in 238 alone there were technically six emperors. The Empire was beginning to fall apart under the ministration of this new breed of soldier-emperors.

But there were still men who could hold it all together. Aurelian is a good example (emperor from 270 to 275). Diocletian (284–305) too made a radical attempt to restore some stability. He doubled the size of the army, reorganized the Empire to make it more tax-efficient in order to pay for it and in 293 he created four emperors ('Tetrarchs'). One important result was that the imperial officials created to deal with this huge administrative change now micro-managed the show under a central authority, rather than laissez-faire 'equestrians' and aristocrats in their individual provinces. Imperial costs soared. Another consequence was that decisions were now taken in the great imperial palaces that sprang up all over the Empire: where the emperor was, the power was. The city of Rome was too far from the action (Diocletian visited it only once): the Senate still met there, but in terms of influence, it was a shadow of its former self.

Unfortunately, the existence of multiple 'emperors' merely encouraged continued in-fighting between them. Constantine was one of those who decided to ignore Diocletian's 'constitution' and fight it out with fellow Tetrarchs. When Diocletian retired in 305, Constantine – the son of the Tetrarch Constantius by an ex-barmaid Helena – joined his father in Britain. Constantius died in York in 306 and the army proclaimed Constantine emperor. He was grudgingly made a Tetrarch and ruled Britain, Spain and Gaul, as his father had done. After much complex jockeying, wheeler-dealing and side-changing between assorted Tetrarchs and their sons, Constantine marched on Rome in 312. At the Milvian Bridge he defeated his enemies and was proclaimed Western emperor.

He had fought under the banner of the Christian God; and Christianity, an intermittently persecuted religion, would soon become the religion of the Roman state, though Julian (361–3) tried, in vain, to return the Empire to paganism. Further conflict ensued against the Eastern emperor Licinius; after an uneasy period of cooperation, Constantine finally did away with him and his son to become sole emperor. So the Empire was briefly united.

In 325 Constantine bowed to the inevitable and founded Constantinople (modern Istanbul) in response to the call by the Eastern elites to have their own capital. This would result in the Empire officially splitting in half: the Western half nominally centred on Rome, the Eastern on Constantinople, each controlled by a different emperor. The two halves drifted apart fairly quickly, each with its own ruler, elites, interests and language.

In summer 376 the collapse of the Roman Empire in the West was triggered by one event with huge ramifications: the sudden and quite unexpected irruption of a new and terrifying people into barbarian territory on Roman borders – the Huns. It was pressure from them that drove Germanic peoples over the Rhine–Danube (Goths, Visigoths,

Franks, Alans, etc., as they were to become known) into the Western Empire during the next 60 years. The Romans were ultimately unable to stop them. When Valens, the Eastern emperor, was defeated and killed at Adrianople by a Gothic army in 382, the writing was on the wall. A later Gothic leader, Alaric, sacked Rome in 410; in the same year Rome withdrew its legions from Britain to defend the Empire. Between 430 and 453 Attila the Hun, raiding deep into Italy from his base in southern Hungary, struck terror into the Empire.

The influx of Germanic peoples and the raids of Attila were too great to be contained. The civil wars of the third century had been expensive and disruptive enough as it was, consuming money and local resources, especially food, and making huge demands on local populations. Now there were foreign invaders to deal with too. As a result of the new Germanic kingdoms that were formed inside the Empire, revenues to Rome dried up. Local elites, so supportive of Rome when Rome could support them in return, saw that their only option now was to collude with their new masters. When the Vandal and Alan king Gaiseric (or Genseric) removed the fabulously rich North Africa from the Roman Empire in 439, the game was almost up. Since Rome could now no longer pay its army to enforce its authority and control, no one paid any attention any more to what the emperor commanded. In 476 the German king Odoacer sent the last emperor (ironically called Romulus Augustulus) into retirement, and the Empire in the West was at an end.

But not the Empire in the East. Constantinople was not taken till 29 May 1453 by Mehmet II, Sultan of the Ottoman Turks, who promptly called himself *Kayser-i Rum*, 'Caesar of the Romans'. Such was the impact of Rome and its emperors. One astonishing feature of this long-lived empire is that it had existed independently from any dynasty. This may be down to Rome's foundation as a city state and (in 509 BC) as a republic.

RETIRING EMPERORS

Since virtually no one became or stayed emperor without blood on his hands, none of them ever retired. There was the prospect of losing status, position, prestige, honour and respect – even if it was fake – but also sheer terror at losing immunity from prosecution on becoming a private citizen (a common reaction among tyrants in the modern world; see Julius Caesar at p. 141, but contrast Sulla at p. 134 and Cincinnatus at p. 48). The sole exception was Diocletian. He fell ill in 303 and gave up power on 1 May 305. Later he was invited back and famously remarked: 'If only you could see the cabbages we have planted at Salonae with our own hands, you would never again judge that a tempting prospect.' Even so, few emperors died peacefully in office or from illness – perhaps 28 out of about 130 over the course of the whole Empire ('about 130' because sometimes it is difficult to tell whether someone really was officially emperor or not in a period when there was so much change at the top across the Empire). The others were deposed, assassinated, executed or slain in battle.

GLOBAL WORLD

There she sits in the Roman fort of Arbeia in South Shields, Newcastle upon Tyne, well dressed, with bracelets on each forearm. Her left hand holds spinning equipment in her lap, and there is a basket of wool at her feet – a proper Roman matron. Her right hand proudly holds open the lid of a stout, solidly bound jewellery box – she's wealthy too. The inscription at the bottom of her funerary monument tells us that her name was Regina

('Queenie') and she was a freedwoman, i.e., once a slave; that she came from a British tribe near St Albans; that she died age 'XXX'; and that she was the wife of Barates from sun-soaked Palmyra – in Syria! What on earth was he doing in freezing South Shields, more than 4,000 miles (6,400 km) from home? Business with the Roman army, it seems, as a flag-maker, in the global economic world of the Roman Empire, falling in love with the slave he had bought, freeing her and marrying her. Below the Latin is an inscription in Palmyrene. It says 'Regina, freedwoman of Barates, alas'. Only in his native language could he express his feelings for her.

Arbeia, the name of the fort, derives from 'Arab'. Boatmen from Mesopotamia were there working the river Tyne, ferrying stores for troops along the Stanegate and Hadrian's Wall during Septimius Severus' brief (and vain) surge into Scotland (208–10). There is nothing new about the global world. That was what the Roman Empire was all about. Incidentally, the Latin of the inscription is very bad; but then, presumably, it was carved by a Briton at an Arab's request.

UNIVERSAL CITIZENSHIP

As well as building impressive baths in Rome (still surviving), Septimius' son Caracalla extended Roman citizenship to almost everyone (except slaves) across the Empire. Cassius Dio tells us that this was a disadvantage for those becoming citizens, because it meant they were now eligible to pay inheritance tax.

THE WHOOPEE EMPEROR

Elagabalus (emperor 218–22) was born Antoninus, of Syrian extraction. He became emperor at 14, a desperate bid by the Antonines to keep the job in the family. He took the name Elagabalus after the Syrian god of the sun Elagabal, whom he worshipped with ferocious zeal and put at the head of the Roman pantheon, displacing Jupiter. A sexual deviant, he made himself as female as possible, expressing the desire for a sex change. One lover Zoticus, an extremely well-endowed son of a cook, was banned from the palace when he could not get an erection.

Elagabalus may have worn a dried bull's penis on his head. Parties were his forte. He gave summer banquets of various hues, green one day, blue the next, etc. Guests were asked to invent new sauces, but those whose efforts failed to please were forced to eat nothing else until they had come up with something better. He liked inviting parties of similarly deformed guests (all one-eyed or deaf or gout-ridden, for example), and he once invited eight fat men for the pleasure of watching them trying to recline together on the same couch. Elagabalus also took to seating guests on air-filled cushions, which slaves surreptitiously let down in the course of the meal (a prototype whoopee-cushion?). A terrible fate awaited drunken guests: they would wake in the morning to find tame lions, leopards and bears roaming their room. And so on – or so the ancient historians report. Gibbons' judgement was that Elagabalus' 'inexpressible infamy surpasses that of any other age or country'. Not surprisingly, the Roman people seem rather to have liked him.

STUFFING THE EMPEROR

Valerian (emperor 253–60) was fighting in the East, but, defeated in battle by the Persian king Sapor I, he concluded a truce and attempted to make peace by negotiating personally. Sapor broke the agreement and took Valerian captive, the only emperor ever to suffer this fate. The (unlikely) account by a later Christian historian is that Valerian endured awful humiliation at the hands of his captors. It was claimed that Sapor regularly used him as a footstool to mount his horse, and that when Valerian offered Sapor a large sum of money to ransom him, Sapor filled his mouth with molten gold, skinned his corpse, stuffed it with straw and preserved it as a trophy in a temple.

FIGHTING FOR SURVIVAL

To give some idea of the sorts of problems the emperor faced in these chaotic times, Aurelian (emperor 270–75) first had to drive back a barbarian invasion into Pannonia (the Croatia region); then, after an initial defeat, he crushed another barbarian invasion into northern Italy; then suppressed a brief rebellion in Rome among those who had lost their jobs because the coinage had been debased. He went on to build a new, precautionary defensive wall round the city (271), then sorted out smaller incursions by Goths into northern Greece. He moved east into Syria, where the Rome-friendly king had died and his Rome-unfriendly queen Zenobia had seized power; then Aurelian returned west to remove Tetricus, who had made himself emperor of Gaul. He went back to Rome to sort out the serious coinage problems and the food supply, then established a cult of the Unconquerable Sun (*Sol Invictus*), now officially prescribed for the army. He dealt with disorder in Lugdunum (modern Lyon) and repelled barbarians from Raetia (Bavaria-Switzerland). But en route to Mesopotamia (Iraq) to drive out the Parthians, Aurelian was murdered by a member of his own Praetorian Guard. Such were the pressures on the Empire (and the emperor) from competing internal factions and external barbarians. Aurelian did a great deal to sort everything out – for a while. 'Sword in hand' and 'necessary rather than good' was how an ancient source summed up this iron disciplinarian.

WOMEN ON TOP

While Britain had Boudicca, Palmyra in Syria had Zenobia. Her husband Odenathus had been a key ally of Rome against the powerful Persians (the Sassanians or Sassanids, after their leader Sassan). But when he and his elder son died in suspicious circumstances, Zenobia became regent in 267. The Romans at this time had their hands full with German incursions from the north. So Zenobia declared independence, cut all ties with Rome and proceeded to conquer Syria and take Asia Minor and much of Egypt (a serious blow to the Roman food supply). By 271 she was in control of most of the eastern third of the Roman Empire. Did Zenobia want to make herself empress of the region? When Aurelian became emperor he decided to remove her. It was a difficult campaign, but in 272 she was captured and taken off to Rome to be displayed in Aurelian's triumph, covered in jewels and decked in gold chains. She was, after all, a queen. But Zenobia was not executed; she was allowed to retire gracefully in exile to a villa in Tivoli, the site of which has not been located.

REORGANIZING THE EMPIRE

With chaos enveloping the Roman Empire it was time to rethink how best to run it. To simplify a complex issue, Diocletian (emperor 284–305) decided the way ahead was to carve up responsibility between himself, as ultimate authority, and three others: a 'Tetrarchy' (Greek

332 VENI, VIDI, VICI

for 'rule of four'). So, there would be two emperors (*Augusti*, one of them Diocletian) and two junior emperors (Caesars). He also needed to restrain the military ambitions of provincial governors, make sure the revenue came in and control barbarian incursions. So he removed many governors' authority over the army and gave it to professional soldiers (Latin, *duces*, 'leaders', whence our 'dukes'); doubled the number of provinces to 100; and regrouped them into 13 'dioceses' (Greek, *dioikêsis* 'administration'), each accountable to a Tetrarch for civic administration, to ensure the taxes came in. To make it all happen, he vastly increased the imperial civil service and doubled the size of the army to around 500,000. The centre was now firmly in control. The financial implications were terrifying.

PRICE CONTROL

During the third century the financial strains on the Empire had been increasing, and emperors had responded by devaluing the coinage. Inflation soared. So in 301 Diocletian attempted to stabilize the situation by reorganizing the coinage values and issuing an edict controlling the maximum prices of wages and goods. Naturally, the edict failed – producers simply took their goods off the market, shifted them illegally or used barter-exchange – but it makes for fascinating reading. It covers cereals (e.g., raw lupins), wine (various qualities and origins), oil (e.g., olive, fish, honey), meat (e.g., pork, peahen, sparrow, dormouse, turtledove), fish (e.g., from sea-urchins to sardines), vegetables and fruits (e.g., palm-shoots, cabbage, figs, nuts, snails, eggs), skins (e.g., ox, sheep, hyena), leather (e.g., for boots, slippers, bridles, saddles) and furs, foot-gear, timber, carpets, articles of dress and wages, from the ordinary labourer and barber to the sewage collector and professional advocate.

THE DISPLACEMENT OF ROME

As a result of Diocletian's Tetrarch reform, imperial palaces began to spring up all over the Empire – in e.g., Nicomedia (Turkey), Milan, Trier, Thessalonica, Romulania (Serbia), Split (Croatia), Constantinople and Ravenna. Rome therefore became less and less of a political power centre; all roads did not lead to it now. As the Sibylline books had once prophesied: *Roma* would one day become *rhumê* (Greek for an alleyway).

On the same lines the story was told (though Edward Gibbon did not believe it) that in 410 the emperor Honorius in Ravenna received a message that *Roma* had perished (see p. 341). Distraught, he cried out, 'But I have just fed it!'

The messenger immediately informed him that it was the city that had perished, at the hands of Alaric.

'That's a relief,' said Honorius. 'I thought it was my pet chicken.'

SYNCHRONIZING YOUR DIARIES

Early societies recorded local events rather than dates. The Romans were slow to realize that some events may have occurred at the same time as events in *other* places. Cornelius Nepos (110–24 BC) was the first Roman historian to bring Roman events within the framework of Greek chronology. Indeed Catullus composed a poem mentioning Nepos unfolding the whole of past time 'in three rolls, full of learning and bloody hard work too'. But Romans, imperialists that they were, wanted to bring everyone's history into *their* time frame. The final result was Eusebius' *Chronicle* (*c.* AD 300). It was composed in columns, each headed with a different people ('Athenians', 'Romans', 'Medes', 'Hebrews', 'Egyptians' etc.) and listed their deeds in a synchronic framework across the roll. The *Chronicle* then went on to remove columns as those peoples were conquered by others. The final consummation of world history was reached when only one column was left. And guess whose column that was: why, the Romans'! Nevertheless, Eusebius did have problems: a Christian, he had to show that Christianity antedated almost everything. So he argued that it began with Abraham (in 2016 BC, he calculated) and was therefore much older than Mosaic Judaism! Zeus, of course, had to come much later, *c.* 1500 BC.

BRITAIN BREAKS FREE

During the chaotic late Roman period, various parts of the Empire were declaring their own emperors, and troublesome Britain was no exception. In 285 Carausius, a military commander from Belgic Gaul, was put in charge of the newly formed British Fleet to suppress barbarians raiding the Channel ports for grain. But he was accused of doing deals with the raiders and keeping the booty himself. Sentenced to death, he fled to Britain, and in 287 declared himself emperor of Britain and northern Gaul. The British legions were with him. Being so far from Rome, they did not enjoy the favours and patronage bestowed on the continental armies and saw a better prospect here. Maybe the wealthy did not like seeing their grain taken to feed the Roman armies on the Rhine. Carausius resisted a Roman attempt to oust him, and started minting his own coins (honouring Diocletian as a 'brother'), including new and impressive silver ones, many quoting Virgil's *Aeneid*. This famously patriotic poem praised the first emperor Augustus for restoring Rome to its golden age (see p. 204). Was Carausius trying to represent himself as a second Augustus . . . ? He was hopeful he might be confirmed as emperor, but was assassinated by his finance minister Allectus in 293. He lasted till 296, killed in battle by Romans under Constantius.

THE ARCH OF CONSTANTINE

On 25 July 315, the Senate and Roman people dedicated an arch to Constantine, managing to make no reference to Christianity at all. It read:

> To the emperor Caesar Flavius Constantinus, the greatest, pious
> and fortunate, the Senate and people of Rome dedicated this arch
> as a memorial to his military victory, because in one instant, in a
> just battle, he avenged the Republic by inspiration of a/the divinity
> and his own greatness of spirit.

This was still a pagan world, and the Senate was pagan too. So it could not bring itself to name the Christian god. The vague 'by inspiration of a/the divinity' is all that hints at a religious context, and one that would not frighten pagan, or any other, horses.

Note: the rise of Christianity and Constantine's role in it is dealt with in the final chapter.

THE EASTERN CAPITAL

Constantine became sole ruler of the Roman world in 324 when he defeated his co-emperor Licinius. He at once decided to rebuild and enlarge the Greek town of Byzantium, near the entrance to the Black Sea, to provide him with his Eastern capital. It was built to resemble Rome, e.g., it had fourteen administrative districts and seven hills (one of them man-made). Construction was speeded up by stripping other towns across the Empire of statues of pagan gods, columns, marbles and so on; and the great Hippodrome (racecourse) was rebuilt, the future scene of many crowd-pleasing executions as well as races. It was dedicated on 11 May 330 under the title NOVA ROMA CONSTANTINOPOLITANA, 'New Rome, Constantine City'. There were both Christian and pagan aspects to the ceremonies. After mass at the church of Holy Peace (Hagia Eirene) Constantine dedicated the new city standing beside a column with a vast statue on the top combining his head and the body of Apollo (the Sun-god). From then on Byzantium was known not as (Latin) *Nova Roma* but Greek *Constantinopolis* (Constantinople).

RUM GREEKS

Constantinople did not start to replace Rome as the centre of the (now Eastern) Roman Empire till the collapse of the West in the late fifth century. The inhabitants of this (Eastern) Roman Empire were all Greek speakers, but still called themselves 'Romans' (Greek, *Rhômaioi*). As a result, neighbouring Arabs, Persians and Turks called the Empire *Rûm*, as did inhabitants of the Balkans and Anatolia (Turkey) in general. Incidentally, 'Byzantine Empire' as the term for the state was invented much later, by the scholar Hieronymus Wolf (1516–80).

WATERING DOWN

One big city that badly needed water wherever it could find it was Constantinople (p. 57). At one time it had more than a hundred huge public storage cisterns (one of them the setting for a scene in a James Bond movie) and three vast open reservoirs.

In AD 373 the emperor Valens brought water all the way from Thrace into the city. The distance it covered as the crow flies was 155 miles (250 km); but because of the difficult terrain its total length – part-aqueduct, part-channel – came to nearly 250 miles (400 km). Remember, the Romans did not have pumps or a canal system. Gradient was all, and aqueducts had to be built that led the water at an appropriate incline from the source to deliver water manageably to the urban consumer. In the city it entered a distribution tank and was piped out into the community. By comparison, Britain's longest gravity-fed aqueduct runs a feeble 96 miles (155 km) from Thirlmere to Manchester.

EUTHANASIA: BEING RIGHT WITH GOD

What is a good Christian death? Not dying when you so choose, but being certain of heaven, Christians argued. Constantine fell ill in 336. He tried hot bath cures in Constantinople and therapeutic thermal springs elsewhere, but to no effect. So he moved to Diocletian's palace in Nicomedia, where he confessed the faith before the local bishops. He was then baptized and a few days later died on 22 May 337. Constantine was following the practice of many in being baptized on his deathbed. The reason was that one had to go to heaven clear of sin: baptism was the only way to achieve this. Incidentally, he was the first emperor to be buried. He fell ill while leading his armies to . . . Christianize Persia. Now there's a 'what if?'!

STUDENT CONTROL

It had long been the case that the wealthy who ran local government were responsible for various civic duties, and in particular collecting local taxes (p. 122) – and making up the shortfall if the tax was not paid! From the third century AD onwards, however, these duties became increasingly costly, and even more so under Diocletian. But certain categories of people were exempt from such duties, including students. As a result, further education suddenly became remarkably popular. So in 370 procedures were put in place in Rome to check up on credentials:

> All those who come to the city in the desire to learn shall first
> of all present to the Chief Tax Officer letters from the provincial
> judges who gave them permission to come. These letters shall
> contain the student's town, birth certificate and reports of
> achievement. Second, the students shall declare on arrival which
> branch of study they propose to follow. Third, the Tax Office shall
> investigate in detail their places of residence to ensure that they
> are devoting their effort to the subject they said they would study.
> These officials shall also warn the students that they shall all
> behave in gatherings as befits those who think it right to avoid a
> bad reputation and bad company, which we consider to be close
> to crime; nor should they make frequent visits to shows or seek
> out unseasonable parties. Indeed, we confer on you the power that,
> if anyone does not behave in the city as the dignity of a liberal
> education requires, he shall be publicly flogged and immediately
> placed on a boat, expelled from the city and sent home.

Now there's a policy for someone.

THE GERMANS

'Barbarians' – the North Germanic tribes stretching from the Rhine to the Black Sea – had been making raids into the Roman Empire since the third century BC (p. 323). Doubtless their motives were mixed, but it is clear that during the imperial period many of them wanted not to destroy the Empire but to settle securely within it. The Romans were often happy to accommodate them, because they made fine soldiers, though some locals saw this as 'selling out'. Many Germans settled and made their way to high office in state and army. All this changed dramatically in the summer of 376 with the sudden and quite unexpected irruption of a dangerous new people into barbarian territory on Roman borders. These were the Huns, 'the seed-bed and origin of the destruction and various calamities inflicted by the wrath of Mars, which raged everywhere with extraordinary fury', as the historian Ammianus said. Over the next 60 years, pressure from the Huns drove increasingly united Germanic tribes (Goths, Visigoths, Franks, Alans, etc., as they were to become known) across the Rhine–Danube frontier and particularly into the Western Empire.

THE HUNS

The Huns were a nomadic warrior elite from somewhere in Central Asia (Kazakhstan?). For whatever reason, they began pushing west in 376, driving Gothic tribes before them. It has been argued that their mounted archers could hit targets at speed *every two seconds*. With reloads, a circling force of 2,000 Huns could hit the enemy with 50,000 arrows every ten minutes. Crossing en masse north of the Black Sea they raided through Georgia into East Turkey as far as Antioch; then, moving further west, settled widely around Romania/Hungary (the Hungarian plains offering perfect grazing for horses) *c.* 400; in the 440s, under Attila, they regularly raided from there down into northern Greece and Constantinople. In so doing they displaced more Germanic peoples across the Rhine–Danube and into the Roman Empire. In 451 Attila raided further west, getting into northern Italy and as far as Orleans. All the time it was not lands he was seeking to occupy so much as peoples to bring into 'alliance' (so Gothic, in fact, became the Hunnish Empire's *lingua franca*).

DEALING WITH THE INFLUX – OR NOT: THE EXAMPLE OF ALARIC THE GOTH

In 376 the Roman Eastern emperor Valens allowed a large Gothic army, displaced by Huns, to settle in Thrace (northern Greece). But the Romans did not treat them well – food supply was the main problem – and in 378 the Goths revolted. The Roman army led by Valens was massacred and he was killed – a sign of things to come. The new emperor Theodosius I ('the Great') made peace with the Goths in 382 and gave them lands around Thrace. Alaric, who as part of Rome's deal with the Goths had campaigned under Theodosius, became king of Goths *c.* 390. On Theodosius' death in 395 Alaric led a revolt to secure more independence from Roman control for his followers – a proper homeland – and a position of top military authority for himself in the Roman army. He attacked the cities of the East to force the Eastern imperial authorities in Constantinople to offer concessions, which they did in 397. But there was no final settlement (Alaric briefly invaded Italy at one point) and in 408 Alaric invaded Italy again. For more than a year and a half his Goths sat outside Rome to force the Western emperor Honorius, safe in Ravenna in northern Italy, to come to terms. Alaric even appointed his own Roman emperor from the Senate to apply more pressure! No deal emerged. Finally, on 24 August 410, he gave Rome up to his army to sack and plunder. It was the first time Rome had been taken by barbarians since 386 BC (p. 50). The year 410 was also the date when the Romans pulled their last legions out of Britain. Still failing to get any change out of Rome, Alaric planned to move south into grain-rich North Africa and settle there, but he died in 411.

THE CITY OF GOD

St Augustine, the North African Christian and bishop of Hippo Regius ('Royal Port'), did not share the general shock that the sack of Rome sent reverberating across the Empire, let alone the analysis that it was due to Rome's abandonment of the pagan gods in favour of the Christian. In *The City of God* he took the view that one earthly empire was much the same as another, and that ruling political elites obsessed with fame, glory and wealth were irrelevant. The true City was the community of those who loved God, and He alone knew who they were. So for Augustine, quoting the philosopher Plotinus, 'The good man will not think it too big a deal if sticks and stone rain down and men die.' In the light of this it is ironic that it was the Church which ensured that Roman culture and the Latin language would survive down the millennia.

GIBBON AND CHRISTIANITY

The historian Edward Gibbon famously claimed that the adoption of Christianity was at the root of the collapse of the Roman Empire.

But this argument can hardly stand. Yes, Christian institutions vastly increased their wealth, but not at the expense of secular ones. Yes, able people joined monasteries, but not that many. Anyway, those in positions of power were required to be Christians, so the transition was a largely painless one; pagans were used to swapping gods about. Equally painless was the state adoption of Christianity. The pagan gods had seen Rome on the way to power. Now the Christian god would take the story on; imperialism was imperialism, under whoever's banner it was maintained. And in the process Christianity became Romanized, and not just in the Catholic sense (Greek, *katholikos*, 'universal'). To be made a bishop was the new route for political advancement, and the elites soon realized that to be a Christian gave you an advantage on the greasy pole. For example, if you were a town councillor and therefore liable to make up any tax shortfall (p. 338), Constantine ruled that this would not apply to Christians. The state did not need to force people into belief when acceptance of the new ideological game in town brought them rewards like these, and more.

ATTILA THE HUN

To Christians the terrifying warrior Attila was known as *flagellum Dei*, 'the scourge of God', sent by the Lord as divine retribution for moral backsliding. Contributing nothing to civilization as we know it except pillage, slaughter and blackmail, Attila also developed siege warfare to a pitch the Romans had not previously encountered. Even the most strongly fortified city was not safe. This, then, was a warrior with whom the Romans had to do business, most of which consisted in bribing him to stay away. Between 430 and 47 Hun-geld rose from 350 lb (160 kg) of gold to 700 (320 kg) and then 2,100 (950 kg) every year, on top of numerous other gifts.

Such were Attila's military prowess, diplomatic skills and powers of patronage that all the tribes along the Danube and the northern shores of the Black Sea owed him loyalty. But Attila felt betrayed when he was denied the hand of the emperor Valentinian's sister Honoria, together with 'half the Roman Empire' that was supposed to come with her. In 451 he marched west for Gaul. Roman diplomacy persuaded the usually hostile Visigoths settled there that Attila was more of a threat than Rome, so Attila was repulsed. In 452 he was back, ravaging northern Italy as far as Milan, only for famine, disease and a Roman counter-attack in Hungary to force him to retreat. It was his last campaign. He died on his wedding night to another Hunnish bride Ildico in 453; one theory is that the varicose veins in his gullet burst and he drowned in his own blood. His 'empire' immediately disintegrated.

AN ASSASSINATION PLOT: THE MORAL DILEMMA

The fifth-century bureaucrat and historian Priscus was (unwittingly) involved in a plot by the Eastern Roman emperor Theodosius to assassinate Attila. The plan was to bribe one of Attila's bodyguards, Edeco, with 50 pounds of gold. But how to get the gold to Edeco without the suspicious Attila smelling a rat? A plan was hatched for an embassy, entirely ignorant of the real purpose of their mission, to be sent to pay court to Attila and create an innocent reason for the transfer of the money. Unfortunately, the loyal Edeco immediately spilled the beans to his master. Now the fun started.

Attila soon realized the ambassadors had no idea what their mission was actually about. So he started toying with them mercilessly, while they tried to work out what on earth was going on. Eventually, they stomped off back home in frustration. In the process, however, Priscus rather came to admire Attila.

Romans tended to regard all barbarians (especially those from faraway places) as moronic, uncultured, misshapen sub-humans without a brain cell between them. But Priscus was surprised and impressed by many aspects of the barbarians' artistic taste and subtle and cultivated social and diplomatic skills. In other words, he saw beyond the crude stereotypes and, while not hesitating to regard Attila and his people as 'the enemy', he was prepared to raise questions about the morality of a Roman court willing to use diplomatic immunity to cover up an assassination attempt.

ATTILA'S LATER REPUTATION

Hungary was founded by the Magyar Árpád in 896. The Magyars had no connection whatsoever with the Huns, but that did not stop Magyar historians inventing one to bridge the 500-year gap with the people that had given their territory its name. They duly reconstructed Attila as a sort of Charlemagne. The composer Haydn's wealthy Hungarian patrons the Ésterházys proudly traced their lineage back to him. In 1846 Verdi composed an opera called *Attila*. But in 1870, as Kaiser Wilhelm I and his German army slaughtered their way across France, the French likened the Germans to Attila and the Huns, who in 451 had taken an almost identical route into Gaul. So it was that Attila and the Huns became a modern metaphor for 'barbarism', Kipling in particular delighting to talk of 'the shameless Hun' in poems attacking German imperialism.

THE VANDALS

A Germanic people who settled in North Africa under Gaiseric, the Vandals are today regarded as mindless destroyers of culture and civilization. In reality, they loved civilization. They took to Roman ways like Russian oligarchs to Mayfair: baths, silk clothing, chariot races, fine food and exotic gardens went hand-in-hand with Latin poetry and the building of churches. They had no time for the surrounding peoples, disdainfully calling them *barbari*. The name stuck: 'berber' is still the name for local natives of the region (and ancient Libyan is the ancestor of today's berber dialects).

The same was true of most of the Germans who settled in Europe. They admired the Roman way and, encouraged by the existing local elites (see next item), adopted Roman political models, Roman law, the Latin language, Christianity and so on.

EUROPEAN DARK AGES

When in the fifth century AD Rome lost its power to control the Empire, the result was 'the end of civilization'. The main reason is that the local landowning elites who had run the provinces under Rome found that the Roman connection, which had once guaranteed their stability, status and privileges, was increasingly worthless. They therefore began to refocus their loyalties more and more on their local tribal leaders. Rome, in other words, was becoming impotent and irrelevant, an administrative and political centre with no means of commanding authority. By the end of the fifth century Europe had reverted to a collection of individual, self-governing and often quite 'Romanized' states (see above), and the foundations of modern Europe were being laid.

But the consequence was that Rome's complex and highly developed *Europe-wide* economic structure collapsed. It became impossible even to produce, let alone deliver, the vast range of material goods that everyone across the Empire, rich and poor, had come to expect. No more fine pottery made in Tunisia was delivered to the inhabitants of Iona; coinage declined; brick, tile and stone buildings disappeared or shrank dramatically in size; only the few could now enjoy luxury goods; agricultural productivity dropped, as did levels of literacy (no more of those Pompeian walls covered in graffiti); insecurity became the norm. The effects were felt from peasants to kings. Economic recovery would take centuries.

THE IMPORTANCE OF ROMAN LAW

The concept of a transcendent law is one of our most important inheritances from the Roman world. Whatever was happening in the world outside, Roman law constructed and applied its own rules to every situation, according to its own methods. That does not mean Roman law did *not* respond to the world outside. It responded to it all the time. But it did so, as for us, according to its own internal codes of practice.

DIGESTING THE LAW

The principles and practice of law are best understood with reference to the (Christian) emperor Justinian's *Digest*, published in AD 533 (in Greek, *Pandects*). It is possibly the single most important and influential work after the Bible. This staggering work was

- condensed from 2,000 legal volumes written by 39 Roman jurists between the first century BC and the third century AD;

- compiled in 3 years by 16 legal experts from all over the Roman world;

- published in 50 volumes;

- produced the definitive account of the whole of Roman private law, selecting what was currently valid and attempting to resolve the major legal conflicts that had arisen over hundreds of years.

Justinian's 50 volumes, however, were far too compendious for any law student to know where to start. So a dumbed-down version was produced, Justinian's *Institutes* ('Teaching course') in a handy, pocket-sized, four-volume edition. This was essentially a second edition of the *Institutes* of the law lecturer Gaius, published in 160–61.

IS A PIG A SORT OF COW?

In 287 BC the *lêx Aquilia* dealing with unlawful killing was passed in a Roman Assembly. It was named after its proposer, the Tribune Aquilius. Its opening chapter refers to the unlawful killing of a slave, a slave-girl or a 'four-footed beast of the class of cattle'. Since slaves were routinely classed as 'property' they came into the same class as cattle. However, the question that most taxed the jurist Gaius (*c.* 160) was which animals should be classed as cattle? Were sheep, goats, horses, mules and asses 'classes of cattle'? Yes, he thought. What about pigs? Were they 'classes of cattle?' Some jurists had wondered about pigs, but yes, he reckoned, they were cattle too. What about dogs? No, he concluded – and even less bears, lions and panthers. But how about elephants and camels? Tricky, he mused: wild they may be, but they *are* used as draught animals. Therefore, on balance, yes.

That passage gives a general sense of the procedure and tone of the *Institutes*. A law has been passed and requires interpretation. Professional lay advisers like Gaius ('jurists', not judges in a court) had over the centuries come up with their responses, and here were the relevant ones. All very pedantic. All very legalistic. And all supremely Roman.

LÊX DISTRICT

Private 'jurists' (i.e., statesmen learned in the law) were the key to the development of the law. They took existing laws and institutions, submitted them to intense scrutiny, drew out general principles and applied these to create new laws for new situations. But they did not decide actual cases: they tried to establish principles by offering hypothetical examples in invented cases. More and more they seemed to be guided by *aequitas* ('fairness') and *utilitas* ('practicality'). But the imperial system changed all this, because the emperor, as ultimate authority, took upon himself all the final decisions. In particular, he started to issue his own decrees and responses (see p. 309). Jurists could still offer opinions, but they were increasingly less influential. Under Constantine, this position was formalized and gave government the monopoly over legal development. Jurists were now part of the civil service.

JUSTIFICATION, BLAME AND INTENTION

Roman jurists were as much taxed as we are by questions of blame and guilt. To stay with the *lêx Aquilia*: the key points it lays down in any case of unlawful killing are – who or what *did* the deed? Can one *justify* this action? Is anyone to *blame* here? Where does *intention* come into it? And how does it all add up to guilt? Here, then, is some more of the *lêx Aquilia* as it is interpreted in the *Institutes*. It opens our eyes to a world very different from that of most of the poets, orators and historians of Latin literature: tiles fall off roofs, people drop heavy loads, medicines are badly administered, there are injuries on the sports fields, dogs without leads, thieves stealing things and mule-carts tumbling down hills. It's fascinating, but what makes it so compelling is the way in which Roman law grapples with the rights and wrongs of everyday existence. In what follows the names mentioned are the jurists whose work is being referred to. I add brief comments in square brackets from time to time.

LUNATICS AND CHILDREN

The question is asked whether there is an action under the *lêx Aquilia* if a lunatic causes damage. Pegasus says there is not, for he asks how there can be any accountable fault in one who is out of his mind; and he is undoubtedly right. Therefore the Aquilian action will fail in such a case, just as it fails if an animal has caused damage or if a tile has fallen. The same must be said if an infant has caused damage, though Labeo says that if the child is over seven years of age he could be liable under the *lêx Aquilia* in just the same way as he could be liable for theft. I think this is correct, provided the child is able to distinguish between right and wrong
. . . [This debate continues!]

UNREASONABLE BEHAVIOUR
AND NEGLIGENCE

Now we must accept 'killing' to include cases where the assailant hit
his victim with a sword or stick or other weapon, or did him to death
with his hands (if, for example, he strangled him) or kicked him
with his foot, or butted him, or any other such ways. But if someone
carrying an excessive load unreasonably throws it down and kills
a slave, the Aquilian action applies; for it was within his own
judgement not to load himself thus. Even if someone slips and crushes
another man's slave with his load, Pegasus maintains that he is liable
under the *lêx Aquilia*, as long as he overloaded himself unreasonably,
or negligently walked through a slippery place . . . Proculus says that
if a doctor negligently operates on a slave, an action will lie either on
the contract for his services or under the *lêx Aquilia* . . . And the law
is just the same if one misuses a drug or after an efficient operation
the aftercare is neglected: the wrongdoer will not go free, but is
deemed to be guilty of negligence [As the NHS well knows] . . .

Furthermore, if a mule-driver cannot control his mules because he
is inexperienced, so that they run down somebody's slave, he is
generally said to be liable on grounds of negligence. It is the same if
through weakness he cannot hold back his mules – and it does not
seem unreasonable that weakness should be deemed negligence,
for no one should undertake a task in which he knows – or ought
to know – that his weakness may be a danger to others. The legal
position is just the same for a person who through inexperience or
weakness cannot control a horse he is riding . . .

If several people throw down a beam and thereby crush a slave
it seemed right to the ancient jurists that they should all be liable
under the *lêx Aquilia*. Again, Proculus gave an opinion that the
Aquilian action applies against him who, though he was not in
charge of a dog, annoyed it and thus caused it to bite someone; but
Julian says the *lêx Aquilia* applies only if he had the dog on a lead
and caused it to bite someone.

(trans. Colin Kolbert)

ROME AND ENGLAND

The influence of Roman law and of the system it established has been
enormous. The idea of 'rights' has its basis in Roman law, especially in the
field of private property and civic rights. So too does the *iûs gentium*, 'Law
of Nations', i.e., the idea of international law. This rules that nation states
have independent legal capacity, but that all states are also equal in the
sight of the law. It paved the way for the idea that the relationship *between*
states could also be subject to regulations and treaties. From the eleventh
century onwards, Roman law became the European standard, accepted
as the basis of national law and all legal education and administrative
practice, in place of local custom. But it did not become the *English*
standard. Instead, local, customary law was extended and made uniform
('common') across the land (hence 'Common Law') under Norman court
procedures (Norman kings ruled England for 300 years from 1066). Over
time, this became amalgamated into the current system of case law, made
by judges sitting in courts, case by case.

XII

AD I – 430

TIMELINE

AD 64   Great Fire of Rome

AD 111   Pliny's letters to Trajan about Christians

AD 160–80 Persecution under Marcus Aurelius

AD 168   Jewish revolt led by Judas Maccabaeus

AD 235–8 Maximinus' 'no taxes for persecution' offer

AD 248   Rome's millennium celebrations

AD 249   Decius decrees universal pagan sacrifice

AD 260–68 Gallienus emperor

AD 262   Church-state relations formalized

AD 302   Diocletian consults the Delphic oracle about Christianity

AD 311   Galerius' 'Edict of Toleration'

AD 312   Constantine's victory at Milvian Bridge: the chi-rho sign

AD 322–3 Co-emperor Licinius restarts persecution

AD 325   Council of Nicaea

AD 360–63   Julian 'the apostate' emperor

The Delphic oracle announces its own demise

AD 390   Theodosius I ex-communicated for slaughter of racing fans

AD 391   Theodosius bans all religions bar Christianity

AD 404   Jerome's 'Vulgate' Bible (in Latin)

c. AD 411   Augustine's *City of God*

c. AD 440   Simeon Stylites on his pillar in Aleppo

AD 470–544   Dionysius Exiguus, inventor of AD/BC

AD 731   Bede uses AD/BC for the first time

THE GROWING
REVOLUTION

Church and State

L ike all good pagans Romans acknowledged numerous gods and tolerated all kinds of cult practices. There was no general mandate from the emperor to suppress sects; it was simply expected that everyone (whatever their private beliefs) observed state religious ritual, especially worshipping the emperor. But Romans made Judaism an exception. In return, the Jews were prepared to live, uneasily at times, under the domination of an often insensitive alien power (c. AD 48, for instance, during the Passover, a Roman soldier in the Temple bared his backside to the crowd and farted. A riot ensued, the army was called in and 20–30,000 Jews died, many crushed in the narrow streets as they tried to escape). Judaism was therefore a legal sect and the Romans left the Jews to deal with Christianity, one of its many offshoots.

However, as Christianity became more popular, the Roman authorities took a greater interest. Tacitus says that Nero decided to blame Christians for the Great Fire of Rome in 64 (see p. 247), while Suetonius says that Nero imposed punishments on Christians for their 'new and dangerous superstition'. Christianity was deemed dangerous presumably because Christians refused to take the oath to the emperor and so acknowledge the ultimate authority of the Roman state. Pliny the Younger, as governor of Bithynia in Asia Minor (northern Turkey, c. 111–13), enjoyed a fascinating correspondence on the subject with the emperor Trajan.

Persecution of the Christians increased under Marcus Aurelius in the period 160–80. He was punctilious about the state worship of pagan gods and (like many others) he ascribed natural and military disasters to divine anger at those who rejected such rituals. Church leaders across the Empire were particular targets, *pour encourager les autres*. All this, paradoxically in Roman eyes, had the reverse effect on Christians, encouraging among them instead a desire for glorious martyrdom.

As Christianity grew and developed its own unique structures – though even by Constantine's time it can hardly have been more than 10 per cent of the Empire's population – the tide slowly began to turn. Spasmodic persecution resumed again in the third century, though Gallienus (260–68) briefly offered Christianity some protected status. In 262 relations between Christians and Gallienus came formally into being, when the emperor agreed that bishops in Egypt should have access to their churches and burial grounds; soon after, when a deposed bishop refused to leave his house, the emperor Aurelian gave permission for the Church in Rome and Italy to enforce his removal. Then, under Diocletian, came the last official, state-sanctioned effort to stamp out Christianity. Churches and scriptures were burned and there were executions and mutilations – more severe in the East than in the West.

It was a failure.

Christianity went from strength to strength. On 30 April 311 Galerius (a co-emperor) issued his 'Edict of Toleration' and in 312 Constantine won his famous victory at the Milvian Bridge under the banner of the Christian god and became emperor, issuing his own edict a year later. When his co-emperor Licinius resumed persecuting the Christians in 322–3, Constantine defeated him in battle in 324. In 360–63 the emperor Julian 'the Apostate' attempted to revive paganism, but his early death ended that.

Constantine's achievement was to make Christianity a 'virtue' now required by emperors. As a result it became the official state religion and therefore an increasing political force in the world. Bishops had the same authority as provincial governors and could make laws. In February 391 the emperor Theodosius banned all other religions and set about dismantling pagan places of worship and ritual. Christianity was now supreme. But this raised the crucial question of authority: who ran the show? The Church versus state debate had begun, though the emperors initially reigned supreme. Furthermore, Rome was sacked by Alaric in 410 (p. 340), sending a shudder across the Empire. In response St Augustine composed his famous *City of God*, arguing that the attack was a heaven-sent punishment inflicted on a secular world, but of no ultimate relevance. The Church turned to persecuting its own 'heretics'.

All this time the Church had been developing its own structures along the lines of the Roman Empire. The Pope, the bishop of Rome (the title 'Pope' was first used in the third century) was emperor, and dressed like one too; his bishops (successors to the apostles) were provincial governors; there were dioceses with vicars (*vicarii*) and the priests were local bigwigs. The historian Eusebius (*c.* 260–340) constructed a line of succession from the apostles to the Christianity of Constantine. The call for definitive, inspired scriptures to establish the final truth led to the canon we know today; and bishops and priests claimed the right to oversee interpretation of the scriptures too, as well as presiding over the Eucharist. By 404 Jerome produced from the Greek a Latin version of the Bible (the 'Vulgate'), which eventually came to be seen by the Catholic Church as a divinely sanctioned 'authorized version' (p. 255).

Church architecture was revolutionized when Constantine became emperor. Early Christians had met in private houses, but huge buildings were now put up to hold large congregations. The model was not the pagan temple, which was designed simply to hold the statue of a god or goddess, while ritual worship took place at a sacrificial altar *outside* the temple. Instead, the Church turned for its model to the Roman basilica, the great hall with an apse, used across the Empire for commercial, military or legal purposes. It was a clever, synthesizing move.

However, there was little agreement as to what Christianity meant. Philosophical debates based on the scriptures raged, and sects within Christianity were constantly breaking away. But Constantine brought with him orthodoxy. The word for 'philosophical school of thought', *hairesis* ('choice'), now became 'heresy' – error – and Constantine's bishops set about imposing their version of the Church's history thus far. The first ecumenical Church council of Nicaea (325) was a good example of how mainstream orthodoxy developed. The result was the Nicene Creed, still the basis of mainstream Christian liturgy.

THE PAGAN CONTEXT OF CHRISTIANITY

For ancient pagans it was not a matter of what you believed or felt, but what you *did*, i.e., how well you carried out the state and local rituals that would placate the gods. It has been called 'performance-indexed piety', and every aspect of pagan life was closely tied up with it. Ancient gods were attached to places and peoples. Horace talked of the god of the spring on his farm; Jupiter was god of the Romans. Rulers were descended from gods, e.g., Julius Caesar from Venus. When an emperor died he became a god, and sacrifices would be offered to him. Augustus got to be called a god while still alive (p. 254)! The gods were also associated with institutions (e.g., Dionysus was the Greek god of the theatre), so to be engaged in city life implied an association with the gods, ensuring that the city and the gods flourished. When the Romans besieged other cities, for instance, they 'called out' its gods, promising to maintain their (now threatened) cultic life if they won (and compare p. 366). Romans wanted to keep the gods – and their human worshippers – onside; and bringing new gods into the pantheon was an intelligent thing to do. In other words, religion was a fusion of ritual with the political, cultural, institutional and everyday life of society. That was the way the system was: you could not have one without the other.

So it was no wonder that it caused such outrage and upheaval when Christianity came along. An aeons-old traditional understanding of the nature of the relationship between gods and man was abandoned. People were 'converted' (an almost meaningless concept for pagans) to a monotheistic religion not of ritual but of creed, dogma and belief, little of it inextricably fused with Roman society's main concerns.

ADD ONE FOR AD O

The Christian BC/AD designation was invented in the sixth century AD. Since the Romans did not have zero (it was not introduced into the European numbering system until the eleventh century AD), there could be no AD 0 when the change took place from the Roman system to the Christian. So the sequence at the BC–AD change goes: 2 BC, 1 BC, AD 1, AD 2, etc. This always causes trouble. Because there is no Year 0, you have to add 1 to include the 0 to 1 move. So the 2,500th anniversary of the battle of Marathon (490 BC) is not 2010 (490 + 2010 = 2,500) but 490 + 2010 + 1 = 2011.

LITTLE DEN'S BIG DATE

Dionysius Exiguus (*c.* 470–544) or Little Dennis (a mark of his humility) is best known as the inventor of the BC/AD system. Until then years had been dated by the name of the (annual) Roman consuls, or the formula 'X years after the foundation of Rome' (in 753 BC), but Dionysius came up with the *anno Domini* ('in the year of our Lord') formula. Starting from the year in which he did the calculation – 'the consulship of the Younger Probus [and Philoxenus]' – he worked out (we have no idea how) that Jesus had been born 525 years earlier, i.e., making the date when he made his calculation, by our reckoning, 526. Jesus was not born on that date (AD 1), but never mind (p. 207). The system finally caught on in 731, when the great Northumbrian monk and historian ('The Venerable') Bede used it to date events in his *Ecclesiastical History of the English People*. We are now advised to abandon BC and AD as too biased towards Christianity, and instead use Before Common Era (BCE) and Common Era (CE). But to whom is it common, and why?

PLINY ON CHRISTIANS

Pliny the Younger, governor of Bithynia (modern north-west Turkey) AD 110–12, received anonymous pamphlets naming troublesome Christians. In the absence of any legal precedents, he arrested the Christians and ordered them to invoke pagan gods, make offerings to the emperor's statue and revile the name of Christ. For the pagan Pliny this was entirely reasonable, but when the Christians refused, he saw it as a direct threat to Roman rule and had them executed. However, this matter clearly worried him, and he wrote to Trajan (emperor AD 98–117) for advice: in particular, should he punish people for *having been* Christians? Trajan added three important riders. Christians must not be hunted down (i.e., they were not state criminals); if they repented, they must be forgiven *whatever* their past conduct; and anonymous pamphlets must play no part in the proceedings. In other words, no witch hunts: the full rigour of the law must be applied. But those who put themselves *outside* the law were shown no mercy, whatever their excuses. For Romans, it was a power issue: what was owed to *state*-sanctioned ritual?

PERSECUTING CHRISTIANS: THE EARLY YEARS

For the first 200 years of Christianity's existence, there were no imperial edicts commanding the worldwide persecution of Christians (see Decius on p. 364). There were local outbreaks of strong anti-Christian feelings, usually for refusing to carry out state religious rituals or for allegations of drinking the blood of babies and so on, but these were not the norm. Indeed, Maximinus the Thracian (emperor 235–8) had to promise some people in the Empire freedom from taxes provided they agreed to persecute Christians! The result was that in the Empire's broadly live-and-let-live religious world, where multitudes of different gods were freely available for worship, Christianity grew quietly. Just one sect among many, it was obscure enough to be ignored for the most part. Public churches began appearing, and Christians could be found at all levels of imperial administration.

NOAH WAY

Apamea (in modern Syria) was a major Roman trading post, nicknamed *kibôtos*, 'money chest'. But *kibôtos* is also Greek for 'ark' and from the third century onwards the town starting minting coins featuring Noah's Ark. Why? Because Christians in Apamea had argued that Apamea was where Noah's Ark had come to rest. This made it a place of great antiquity – always a source of great fascination to ancient pagans. So the Apameans came on board, and Christians were able to advertise and legitimize their religion without causing local offence.

MARTYRS

In 168 BC the Jewish freedom-fighter Judas, nicknamed Maccabee (probably meaning 'the hammer'), led a revolt against the Greek king Antiochus IV. The reason was that Antiochus was attempting to suppress Judaism. Those Jews who died in the conflict were promised instant access to the throne of God, and the idea of the martyr was born. Though Church authorities did not encourage martyrdom, it was coveted by many Christians. A virgin's rewards in heaven were 60 times greater than an ordinary Christian's; a martyr's 100 times greater. The Romans found martyrdom baffling – another example of Christian obstinacy.

MARTYR THEORY

'Martyr' derives from *martus*, Greek for 'witness'. Since early Christians tended to be contemptuous of this world, because they expected Christ to return very soon, they felt that self-sacrifice in Christ's name was the highest calling of all. Being persecuted by the Romans, therefore, offered them a chance to advance the Christian cause by dying for their faith – the gorier and more serene the death, the better.

Many Roman authorities judged these martyrs mad and tried to reason with them, but Christians clearly felt that their courage and integrity in exhibiting their faith in this way would cause pagans to think again. So martyrdom proved a rallying point for the Church, inspiring a mood of confidence and defiance. Martyrs became heroes, their deeds celebrated. Again, by being willing to die for the faith, martyrs believed that, in heaven, they would be able to help others on the road to salvation, interceding on behalf of less spiritual Christians.

MARTYRS, GET A LIFE

Roman governors used many different arguments against Christians with a death wish.

'Think it over for a few days,' ventured the governor who tried the martyr Colluthus (fourth century AD). 'Look, the weather is just *lovely*,' he went on. 'You won't get much pleasure if you kill yourself, you know. Just listen to me, and you can save yourself.'

'My death will be more pleasant than any life you can give,' replied Colluthus, grimly.

When Christians approached the governor of Asia in AD 185 demanding martyrdom, he said they could use ropes and cliffs to do the deed. Unlike many modern 'religious' fanatics, however, Christians did not impose martyrdom on others. Nor did they invite others to become martyrs while standing back themselves.

THE THIRD-CENTURY PERSECUTIONS

Rome's second millennium fell in 248 (the city was founded in 753 BC, see p. 5). It was felt that this event needed some sort of celebration to win continued divine favour, so in 249 the emperor Decius decreed that there was to be a universal sacrifice to the Empire's gods. It was not a specifically anti-Christian measure, but clearly Christians could not agree to it. Some bribed their way out, some fled, some were imprisoned, tortured or lynched. Subsequent emperors continued a policy of persecution, with more or less enthusiasm for it in different parts of the Empire. In 302 Diocletian even consulted the oracle at Delphi, which told him that, if Christianity were not dealt with, the oracle would start telling lies. But this was the last gasp of Roman paganism. The turning point came in 311, when Galerius was the first emperor to acknowledge the power of the Christian god to protect the Empire. In the words of his decree: 'Christians will be obliged to pray to their God for our safety and for that of the state and for their own.' Note '*their* God': the pagan Galerius still believed there were others.

WITNESS TO SALVATION

When Christians were asked to demonstrate their pagan credentials there was a clear form of words to follow. We have an example referring to one Aurelius Diogenes, using Aurelius Syrus as a witness:

To those chosen to superintend the sacrifices in the village of
Alexander's Island; from Aurelius Diogenes, son of Sabatus, of
the village of Alexander's Island, aged 72, with a scar on his right
eyebrow. I have always sacrificed to the gods; and now in your
presence in accordance with the terms of the edict, I have sacrificed
and have tasted the sacrificial victims. I request you to certify
this. Farewell. I, Aurelius Diogenes have presented this petition.
Witness: I, Aurelius Syrus, saw you and your son sacrificing.

THE CHI-RHO SIGN ☧

In 312 Constantine defeated his rival Maxentius in battle and became
ruler of the Western Empire. Two accounts survive. Lactantius says:

Constantine was directed in a dream to cause the heavenly sign
to be delineated on the shields of his soldiers, and so to proceed to
battle. He did as he had been commanded, and he marked on their
shields the letter X, with a perpendicular line drawn through it and
turned round at the top, being the cipher of CHRIST[OS].

Eusebius, however, says that Constantine prayed for assistance from
any god that would help him:

He said that about noon, when the day was already beginning
to decline, he saw with his own eyes the trophy of a cross of light
in the heavens, above the sun, and bearing the [Greek] inscription
toutoi nika, 'By this, be victorious' . . . then in his sleep the Christ
of God appeared to him with the same sign which he had seen in
the heavens, and commanded him to make a likeness of that sign

which he had seen in the heavens, and to use it as a safeguard in all engagements with his enemies.

The sign was the intertwined chi-rho, using the first two letters of the Greek *ChR*istos ('anointed one'), the translation into Greek of the Jewish *Messiah*. Later, this sign was flanked on either side by the letters alpha A ('a') and omega Ω (long 'o'), another sign for Christ. It could now be made to read in Greek ΑΡΧΩ (*archo*), 'I rule'. In another development the Greek 'By this, be victorious' was translated into Latin as 'In this sign you will conquer' (*in hoc signo vinces*). Incidentally, *Christos* sounded in Greek rather like *Chrestos* ('useful'), a common slave/servant name, and *Christianoi* sometimes appears as *Chrestianoi* in our texts. So when Christ is described as a 'slave/servant' in the New Testament, it may be a pun on this spelling.

WAR AND PEACE

It is often assumed that Christianity has always been hostile to warfare, but Jesus was not above using military images to make a point. Nor was St Paul, who talks of a Christian wearing the armour of God, breastplate of righteousness and helmet of salvation. Further, the 'By this, be victorious' sign left no doubt that the Christian god had a keen interest in victory. A Roman would be unwise not to get such a powerful god on board. As Minucius Felix (third century AD) observed, all nations had their own gods, but Rome welcomed the lot. This, he went on, was why Romans were so successful: they won the favour of captured gods by sacrificing to them immediately. Further, Constantine's army continued to win. There was no more persuasive evidence of the Christian god's supremacy than regular victories on the battlefield.

WAS CONSTANTINE 'SINCERE'?

Constantine fought at the Milvian Bridge under the banner of the Christian god, but did he really believe in God? Certainly Christianity became Constantine's personal religion and soon (under Theodosius) the Roman Empire's official religion. This was an astonishing transformation. The whole of ancient – let alone Roman – life had involved a multiplicity of gods, festivals and civic rituals. Further, such was the secular impact of Christianity – aided by generous tax breaks for Christians – that by the end of the century Christian leaders were well on the way to taking over the status, functions and duties of the old civic elite – arguably, *the* turning point in European history. Yet it is impossible to say whether Constantine was 'sincere' about his faith in terms that we would understand (e.g. he had no compunction about having his son and wife murdered, for reasons that remain obscure). He did not impose Christianity, though he certainly made it a force to reckon with in the world; and from then on, emperors were expected to profess a faith in God. But his support for the Christian god as the most powerful god among many others suggests that he might have been a henotheist, i.e., he believed there was one top god (Greek root *hen*– 'one' + *theos* 'god') among other gods. Henotheism helped bridge the gap between pagan polytheism (many gods) and Christian monotheism (one god). If so, then Constantine's acceptance of the Christian god was sensible and uncontroversial: here is a new god, he was saying, and a highly successful one. As a matter of simple insurance, I must add him to my portfolio of gods. In a sense, therefore, there was nothing for Constantine to be converted to – at this stage. Note that one of Constantine's most important tactics was to introduce Christianity in quasi-pagan terms, e.g. Constantine had been an earlier worshipper of the sun (see p. 335), and Christians had long associated Christ with the sun. So when in AD 321 Constantine invented a day of rest, he called it Sunday, keeping pagans and Christians happy.

THE NICENE CREED

The emperor was now God's victorious vicar on earth. So he had to settle theological disputes. As St Paul's *Letters* show, these arguments had been raging since the emergence of Christianity in the first century. In 325 Constantine called one of his most important councils in Nicaea (north-west Turkey, on the other side of the Bosporus from Constantinople). Its main purpose was to settle a major dispute about Jesus' divinity.

The Libyan preacher Arius (as in the 'Arian controversy') had declared that, though Jesus was divine, there was a time when he did not exist, i.e., God created him. That made him a lesser figure than the Father. This view directly contradicted the doctrine of the Holy Trinity, which held that the Father, the Son and the Holy Spirit were one and equal. The distinction was characterized in Greek as follows: God and Jesus were either *homo-ousios* ('of one essence') or *homoi-ousios* ('of similar essence'). The conference at Nicaea decided that Arius was wrong: the Holy Trinity was indeed 'of one essence', and they produced a Creed to that effect. The Nicene Creed was revised and updated at a second conference in 381 and forms the basis of today's normative Creed for Christian churches. Jesus, who spoke of himself as a servant of God, is here incarnated for the first time as God.

CHURCH AND STATE

When all the bishops were gathered at a feast in the imperial residence in Nicaea in 325, Bishop Eusebius recorded that it was like 'an imaginary representation of the kingdom of Christ'. But relations between the emperor and his bishops were not always so cordial. Constantine presented himself as the servant of the Church, but the fact remained that he was still emperor, the ultimate earthly authority; and it was not easy to keep these responsibilities separate as the Church became more and more central to the structure of the state. Soon after Constantine's death the argument began to be increasingly heard for a separation between Church and state, God and Caesar. But religious issues apart, Constantine was very aware of his secular responsibilities to his subjects. Hard on delinquent imperial officials, he maintained a strong central control over the levers of justice for provincials, determined that they would feel fairly treated by their emperor.

THEOLOGICAL NICETIES

Where modern cities are filled with discussions of the latest sporting personalities or celebrity break-ups, Constantinople was full of theological disputes. St Gregory of Nyssa commented on one occasion:

> Everywhere is full of those who are speaking of unintelligible things – streets, markets, squares, crossroads. I ask how much I have to pay for something, they start philosophizing on the born or unborn; I wish to know the price of bread, they answer, 'The Father is greater than the Son'; I ask whether my bath is ready and I'm told 'The Son has been made out of nothing.'

THE CULTURAL REVOLUTION

The advent of Christianity brought many changes to Romans' cultural practices. Romans kept the dead well away from the living, disposing of them outside town walls. Not Christians: they built cemeteries inside the boundaries. Churches replaced temples, reusing pagan marble so extensively that the new marble trade almost collapsed; and huge donations to the Church – land, money and treasure – gave it powerful asset bases. Jesus' teachings about material wealth might be thought to militate against this development. But the idea that the rich were deservedly rich, and wealth was the route to honour and virtue, was ingrained in pagans, and Christians justified their new-found wealth by arguing that it could be used for God's purposes. That said, since the Church also preached that salvation depended on the state of one's soul and not on one's bank balance or education, uneducated holy men became revered figures, and for many an austere monastic life became desirable.

JULIAN 'THE APOSTATE' (361–3)

A Christian for the first 20 years of his life, Julian then 'converted' and as emperor turned into an evangelizing pagan. A good general, he was an ascetic with no time for sex or luxury. He proclaimed religious liberty, but did everything in his power to undermine Christianity: he removed church privileges and restored pagan temples, priests and cults, and he favoured pagans when it came to official posts and legal judgements. He died after a fatal wound in battle against the Persians.

DELPHI'S LAST WORDS

The story is told that Julian consulted the very ancient Greek oracle at Delphi about how he should approach his evangelizing task, and apparently received the following reply:

> Tell the king our sculpted hall is fallen in decay,
> Apollo has no shrine left, no prophesying bay,
> No talking spring; the stream is dry that had so much to say.

In other words, pagan worship was dead: don't bother.

JULIAN AGAINST THE GALILEANS

Julian always called Christians 'Galileans' to emphasize that Christianity was just a local fishermen's creed. In a treatise on the subject he rehearsed a whole range of arguments against it, from biblical inconsistency and contradiction to hypocrisy for preaching universal love while damning heretics. Pagan gods were natural, instinctual and obviously universal, but you had to *learn* about the Christian god, Julian said. This god was clearly hostile to knowledge (see the Garden of Eden story) – and what sort of humanity did this deity have in mind by wanting to withhold from men the difference between good and evil? The Christian god forbade the worship of other gods but could not stop it, i.e., was powerless – a dreadful accusation to make of a god. The Christian god had also spent thousands of years doing nothing about it, while everyone worshipped other gods – and so on. Christian thinkers replied strongly in kind.

THE END OF PAGANISM

In 390 Butheric, the commander of the garrison in Thessalonica in northern Greece, arrested a star charioteer for homosexual rape and refused to allow him to race at the games. The furious spectators rioted and Butheric was murdered. Enraged, the Eastern emperor Theodosius I – a friend of Butheric's – ordered that at the next games the spectators should be shut into the stadium and slaughtered. The fearsome Archbishop Ambrose of Milan intervened, but Theodosius negotiated behind his back with his army officers in Thessalonica, and the slaughter went ahead. About 7,000 died. When news of the massacre reached Ambrose, he wrote to Theodosius, warning him, 'Sin is blotted out only by tears and penitence. No angel can do it, nor archangel.' Then he excommunicated him. Terrified at the prospect of eternal damnation, Theodosius stripped himself of his royal purple and in sackcloth and ashes crawled on his knees, a humble penitent, into the cathedral of Milan. On 25 December 390 he was duly absolved and received back into the Church. Two months later, in AD 391, Theodosius outlawed paganism, and the long reign of Jupiter (Zeus), king of the gods, and his Olympians – with their animal sacrifices, altars, temples, civic rituals and games – was over.

A MARTYRDOM SUBSTITUTE

Once the Roman Empire became Christianized, martyrdom became unnecessary. But there was a still a feeling that Christians must be able to show that their true home was not of this world. So another 'other-worldly' model was required. Asceticism, derived from the Greek *askêsis*, 'training' or 'practice', was the answer: self-denial in place of self-sacrifice. Pagans had long believed that humans could be transformed through mental and physical discipline (p. 288), and early ascetics included people as disparate as Diogenes, living in his clay wine jar and rejecting the whole concept of 'society', as well as the millionaire Stoic thinker Seneca, committed to the idea of public service for the public good, but still justifying withdrawal into a private life of study. But while, for pagans, *askêsis* was a 'lifestyle' statement that only the rich could afford to indulge, for Christians, anyone could do it. Its purpose was to purge the body of its desires and needs in order to bring about communion with God while still on earth; whence the hermit (Greek, *erêmos*, 'solitary') and the fascination with the desert, that powerful symbol of the renunciation of man as a social and civilized being – though when St Jerome retired to the desert he softened the blow by taking his complete library with him.

PILLAR TALK

Many Christians who retired to the desert to practise their extreme asceticism became celebrities. Simeon Stylites ('Pillar man', 390–459) attracted huge crowds to watch him live and worship God on a platform at the top of a pillar near Aleppo (Syria). Here is Theodoret from Cyrrhus reporting on these strange performances:

> More than all this, I myself admire Simeon's endurance. Night and day he is standing within the view of all, now for a long time, and now bending down repeatedly and offering worship to God. Many of those standing by count the number of these acts of worship. Once one of those with me counted 1,244 of them, before he gave up counting. In bending down, Simeon always makes

his forehead touch his toes: since his stomach takes in food once
a week, and little of it, he is able to bend his back easily. During
public festivals, he displays another form of endurance: from sunset
to sunrise he stretches out his hands to heaven and stands all night,
neither tempted by sleep nor overcome by exertion . . .

The crowds flocked in, asking that he do for them what nature in the
normal course of events would not.

NO SEX, PLEASE

Christians were still waiting for the Second Coming, but as time went by
it seemed that Christ's return had been delayed. In his absence, it became
increasingly obvious that the Church needed an organization and a
strict hierarchy to instruct the faithful, convert unbelievers and establish
Christian doctrine. The full-on ascetics, however worthy, were clearly
not the sort of people to entrust with large-scale institutional change.
Nevertheless, an ascetic gesture was required. So the renunciation of
sex was regarded as sufficient proof of one's other-worldliness, without
compromising one's ability to serve both the Lord and the needs of the
Church in this world. Hence the doctrine of celibacy for priests.

WOMEN TROUBLE

The male-dominated classical world regarded women as potentially
dangerous (see pp. 240, 260), their rampant sexual desires mirroring
men's desire for them, and with disastrous consequences – for men. With
the story of Adam and Eve and of God becoming man, the Bible, too,
seemed to endorse some kind of gender separation: men and women

were somehow different creatures, with different capacities, priorities and outlooks, and the female was always deadlier than the male. The danger inherent in women's sexuality was forcefully illustrated in the doctrine of Mary's virginity: the mother of God, who was to become the exemplar for all women, could not possibly be associated with carnal sin, and theologians earnestly debated whether or not her hymen was intact.

How, then, to deal with the entirely natural phenomenon at the root of the problem: sexual desire? One response was to rework the Greek philosopher Plato's concept. He thought of desire (*erôs*) as having a final purpose: desire for the 'Good', the ultimate expression of the universe's driving force. To reach that destination one had to experience various 'lower' manifestations of it, one of which (for Plato) was desire for sexual union. Church thinkers like Origen turned this Platonic *erôs* into the desire for God and the mystic union of one's soul with God. As a result, erotic desire could be seen as a form of religious experience. In this way the physicality of texts like the *Song of Solomon* could be safely neutralized by being allegorized into an image of the mystical union, and Christian love between man and wife seen as one of the 'lower' manifestations of it.

CONFESSIONS OF A SAINT

St Augustine (AD 354–430) was born in (modern) Algeria in the North African 'Bible Belt' of the Roman world. Educated in the classical tradition, he was excited by Cicero's philosophy with its command to discover the gods' (or God's) designs for the world. It was as a result of this search, he believed, that God, through the Bible, finally and decisively intervened in his life. The problem was that he was a worldly young man.

He knew all about the pleasures of sex and gang-warfare; he was destined for a distinguished academic career. The struggle within him as a result of his conversion was intense: should he serve his God better by renouncing the world or engaging with it? When in 391 he was forcibly removed from his monastery, ordained a priest and so plunged into the hurly-burly of the world's affairs, he wept for the loss of his monastic life. This is what his famous *Confessions* were all about: they explained how a worldly young man became a celibate, austere, spiritual leader of men, and showed how one man's life could become a vehicle for demonstrating true religion.

THE CHURCH TRIUMPHANT

The Roman Empire and its institutions may technically have collapsed in the West, but the Romanized Church – with Latin as its language (and therefore the language of education, too, which the Church took over) – was the rock on which a civil, urban society could continue to exist. Indeed, Christians devoted an enormous amount of energy to building bridges, where possible, between the two worlds, political and structural, as well as educational, philosophical, cultural and artistic. As a result there was considerable continuity between the classical and medieval era, with the Church's classical roots, wealth, cathedrals, saints and bishops central to changing urban life. Like all powerful new movements, the Church knew that you had to work with the grain of society in order to change it.

That said, it is remarkable to reflect that a monotheism developed in direct line of descent from Jews 3,000 years ago, and then through Christians to Islamic scholars 1,500 years ago, should continue to shape the lives of billions of people today.

LATIN AND ENGLISH

Those fortunate enough to have studied Latin often come away with the impression that it is 'at the root' or 'the basis' of our language. It is neither. The basis or root of our language is Anglo-Saxon, a Germanic language brought in by invaders (Angles and Saxons) in the fifth century AD. From 'Angle' we get 'England' (Angleland – Englaland – England) and 'English'. The Latin element came in from the Church and elsewhere fairly early on, but the great surge of Latinate words came in via Norman French from 1066 onwards and for the 300 subsequent years when England was ruled by the French and French kings (all those Henris); and then again when Europe was looking for a new, particularly conceptual, language of education during the intellectual and aesthetic classical 'rebirth' (renaissance) from the fourteenth century, when many ancient Greek words were also taken into English. That is why the English language is so wonderfully rich: its huge vocabulary has words of both Germanic and Latin/Greek origin built into it, giving us options with different shades of meaning at every turn – 'regal' (Latin) or 'kingly' (Germanic)? 'Faithfulness' (Germanic) or 'fidelity' (Latin)?

Of all the ways in which ancient Romans have influenced our world – the transmission of Greek culture, great authors like Catullus, Juvenal, Ovid, Tacitus and Virgil, the idea of republicanism, the concept of empire, architectural forms, the legal system, the spread of Christianity, the notion of Stoicism, and so on – the enrichment of our Anglo-Saxon language is their most inescapable legacy, vastly increasing our means of effective communication with each other every single day of our lives.

BIBLIOGRAPHY

Baker, S., *Ancient Rome: The Rise and Fall of an Empire* (BBC Books, 2007)

Beard, M. and Crawford, M., *Rome in the Late Republic* (Duckworth-Bloomsbury, 1985)

Beard, M., *The Roman Triumph* (Harvard, 2007)

—, *Pompeii* (Profile, 2008)

— and Hopkins, K., *The Colosseum* (updated, Profile, 2011)

Bispham, E. (ed.), *Roman Europe* (Oxford, 2008)

Bowman, A. K., *Life and Letters on the Roman Frontier: Vindolanda and its People* (British Museum, 1994)

Bradley, K. and Cartledge, P. (eds), *The Cambridge World History of Slavery*, vol. 1 (Cambridge, 2011)

Cambridge Ancient History (mostly second edn), especially vols. IX–XIII (146 BC–AD 425) (Cambridge, 1994–8)

Cameron, A., *The Last Pagans of Rome* (Oxford, 2011)

Casson, L., *Libraries in the Ancient World* (Yale, 2001)

—, *Travel in the Ancient World* (Allen and Unwin, 1974)

Claridge, A., *Rome: An Oxford Archaeological Guide* (second edn, Oxford, 2010)

Clark, G., Augustine: *The Confessions* (Bristol Phoenix Press, 2005)

—, *Late Antiquity: A Very Short Introduction* (Oxford, 2011)

Cornell, T. J., *The Beginnings of Rome* (Routledge, 1995)

Dalby, A., *Empires of Pleasure* (Routledge, 2000)

—, *Food in the Ancient World from A to Z* (Routledge, 2003) de la Bedoyere, G., *Voices of Imperial Rome* (Tempus, 2000)

Dennison, M., *Empress of Rome: The Life of Livia* (Quercus, 2010)

Dodge, H., *Spectacle in the Roman World* (Bristol Classical Press, 2011)

Donaldson, I., *The Rapes of Lucretia: A Myth and its Transformations* (Oxford, 1982)

Dunbabin, K., *Mosaics of the Greek and Roman World* (Cambridge, 1999)

Eckstein, A. M., *Mediterranean Anarchy, Interstate War and the Rise of Rome* (California, 2006)

Eden, P. T. (ed.), *Seneca: Apocolocyntosis* (Cambridge, 1984)

Edwards, C. and Woolf, G. (eds), *Rome the Cosmopolis* (Cambridge, 2003)

Edwards, C., *Death in Ancient Rome* (Yale, 2007)

Erdkamp, P. (ed.), *A Companion to the Roman Army* (Blackwell, 2007)

Feeney, D., *Caesar's Calendar* (California, 2007)

Flower, H. I., *The Cambridge Companion to the Roman Republic* (Cambridge, 2004)

Garnsey, P., *Ideas of Slavery from Aristotle to Augustine* (Cambridge, 1996)

Goldsworthy, A., *The Punic Wars* (Cassell, 2000)

—, *The Complete Roman Army* (Thames and Hudson, 2003)

—, *Caesar* (Weidenfeld & Nicolson, 2006)

Hartney, A., *Gruesome Deaths and Celibate Lives* (Bristol Phoenix Press, 2005)

Heather, P., *The Fall of the Roman Empire* (Macmillan, 2005)

Hodge, A. T., *Roman Aqueducts and Water Supply* (Duckworth-Bloomsbury, 1992)

Hornblower, S. and Spawforth, A. (eds), *The Oxford Classical Dictionary* (third edn, Oxford, 2003)

Jones, Peter and Sidwell, Keith (eds), *The World of Rome* (Cambridge, 1997)

Jones, Peter, *Classics in Translation* (Duckworth-Bloomsbury, 1998)

—, *The Intelligent Person's Guide to Classics* (Duckworth-Bloomsbury, 1999)

—, *Vote for Caesar* (Orion, 2008)

Kelly, C., *Attila the Hun: Barbarian Terror and the Fall of the Roman Empire* (Bodley Head, 2008)

Knapp, R. C., *Invisible Romans: Prostitutes, Outlaws, Slaves, Gladiators and Others* (Profile, 2011)

Köhne, E. and Ewigleben, C., *Gladiators and Caesars* (British Museum, 2000)

Kolbert, C., *Justinian: The Digest of Roman Law – Theft, Rapine, Damage and Insult* (Harmondsworth, 1979)

Lane Fox, R., *The Unauthorized Version: Truth and Fiction in the Bible* (Viking, 1991)

Langslow, D., *Medical Latin in the Roman Empire* (Oxford, 2000)

Lloyd, A. B. (ed.), *Battle in Antiquity* (Duckworth-Bloomsbury, 1996)

Mackay, C. S., *Ancient Rome: A Political and Military History* (Cambridge, 2004)

McLynn, F., *Marcus Aurelius: Warrior, Philosopher, Emperor* (Bodley Head, 2009)

Man, J., *Attila: The Barbarian King who Challenged Rome* (Bantam, 2005)

Mattingly, D. J., *Tripolitania* (Batsford, 1995)

Miles, R., *Carthage Must Be Destroyed: The Rise and Fall of an Ancient Civilization* (Allen Lane, 2010)

Millar, F., *The Emperor in the Roman World* (second edn, Duckworth-Bloomsbury, 1992)

—, *The Crowd in Rome in the Late Republic* (Michigan, 2001)

—, (three volumes of collected papers) *Rome, the Greek World and the East* (North Carolina 2002, 2004, 2006)

North, J. A. and Price, S. R. F. (eds), *The Religious History of the Roman Empire* (Oxford, 2011)

Nutton, V., *Ancient Medicine* (Routledge, 2004)

Ogilvie, R. M., *A Commentary on Livy*, Books 1–5 (Oxford, 1978)

Opper, T., *Hadrian: Empire and Conflict* (British Museum, 2008)

Ormerod, H. A., *Piracy in the Ancient World* (Johns Hopkins, 1924)

Parry, D., *Engineering in the Ancient World* (Sutton, 2005)

Pott, J. A. and Wright, F. A. (tr.) *Martial: The Twelve Books of Epigrams* (Routledge, 1920)

Potter, D. S. (ed.), *A Companion to the Roman Empire* (Blackwell, 2006)

—, *Rome in the Ancient World* (Thames and Hudson, 2009)

Price, S. and Thonemann, P., *The Birth of Classical Europe* (Allen Lane, 2010)

Rauh, N. K., *Merchants, Sailors and Pirates in the Roman World* (Tempus, 2003)

Richardson, J. H. and Santangelo, F. (eds), *Priests and State in the Roman World* (Stuttgart, 2011)

Riggsby, A. M., *Roman Law and the Legal World of the Romans* (Cambridge, 2010)

Rowland, I. D. and Howe, T. N. (eds), *Vitruvius: Ten Books on Architecture* (Cambridge, 1999)

Salmon, E. T., *Samnium and the Samnites* (Cambridge, 1967)

Scarre, C., *Chronicle of the Roman Emperors* (Thames and Hudson, 2007)

Shelton, J., *As the Romans Did* (second edn, Oxford, 1997)

Shirley, E., *Building a Roman Legionary Fortress* (Tempus, 2001)

Sommer, M., *The Complete Roman Emperor* (Thames and Hudson, 2010)

Stephenson, P., *Constantine: Unconquered Emperor, Christian Victor* (Quercus, 2009)

Stoneman, R., *Palmyra and its Empire: Zenobia's Revolt against Rome* (Michigan, 1992)

Treggiari, S., *Roman Marriage* (Oxford, 1991)

Venning, T., *A Chronology of the Roman Empire* (Continuum, 2011)

Walker, S. and Higgs, P. (eds), *Cleopatra of Egypt – from History to Myth* (British Museum, 2001)

Wallace-Hadrill, A., *Rome's Cultural Revolution* (Cambridge, 2008)

Ward-Perkins, B., *The Fall of Rome and the End of Civilization* (Oxford, 2005)

Wells, C. M., *The Roman Empire* (second edn, Fontana, 1992)

Wilkinson, P., *Pompeii: The Last Day* (BBC Books, 2003)

Williams, C. A., *Roman Homosexuality* (second edn, Oxford, 2010)

Wiseman, T. P., *The Myths of Rome* (Exeter, 2004)

Woolf, G. (ed.), *Cambridge Illustrated History of the Roman World* (Cambridge, 2003)

—, *Rome: An Empire's Story* (Oxford, 2012)

Zanker, P., *The Power of Images in the Age of Augustus* (Michigan, 1988)

INDEX

acerbum oil 316

Actium, battle of 183, 186

AD/BC, invention of 354, 360

Adherbal (Carthaginian admiral) 91

adoption 188, 188–9

Adrianopole, battle of 322, 326

adultery 208

aediles 54–5, 70, 73, 155

Aeneas 1, 3–4, 5, 36, 154, 204–6

Aeneid (Virgil) 202, 204–6, 335

Aequi, the 48–9

age demographics 179–80

ager publicus (public land) 47–8, 101, 145

Agricola, Gnaeus Julius 220, 225, 271, 272

agriculture, gods of 26

Agrippa, Menenius 69–70

Agrippa, Vipsanius 187, 199

Agrippina 189, 219, 220, 223, 224, 241–2, 245–6

Alaric the Goth 322, 326, 333, 340–1, 357

Alba 4–5, 22, 26–7

Alba Longa 205

Aleppo 354, 373–4

Alexander the Great 122, 166, 254

Alexandria, library 131

alimenta (food subsidies) 297

Allectus 321

alphabet, Roman 25

Amalthea, the Sibyl from Cumae 32

ambitio 142

Ambrose of Milan, Archbishop 372

Ammianus 339

Amores (Ovid) 209–10

amphitheatres 257–8

Amulius 4–5

ancestors, *imagines* 77

Ancus Martius, king of Rome 20, 29, 29–30, 30

Andronicus, Livius 103

animal fights 256–7

animals classed as cattle 347–8

Antinoopolis 304

Antinous, drowns in Nile 280, 282, 304

Antioch 131

Antiochus, king of Syria 86

Antonine wall 283

Antoninus Pius, emperor 280, 283, 298–9, 309

Antony, Marc 33, 118, 193–4

affair with Cleopatra 183, 186, 190, 191

ancestry 174–5

and the assassination of Caesar 175

and Caesar 174–5

death of 183, 186, 193

defeat of 183, 186

as Triumvir 183, 185–6, 189

Apamea 362

Apocolocyntosis (Seneca, the Younger) 242–3

Apollodorus 305

Appian Way 39

Spartacus' army crucifixions 146

aqua Appia 56

aqueducts 56, 287, 337

Arabia, annexation of 279, 282

Arbeia, South Shields 327–8

Arch of Constantine 322, 335

archaeology 7

arches 163

Archimedes, death of 97

architecture, literature 200–1

Arian controversy, the 368

Aristophanes 131

Aristotle 131, 153

Arius 368

Armenia 279, 282

army

Augustan reforms 186, 195

development of the legion 57

Diocletian's reforms 324, 332

duties 302–3

engineers 303

goose-hunting expeditions 303

irregular farmer-citizen 13

legionary fortresses 272–3

legions 195

Marius's reforms 116, 119–20

mutinies 221
paying for 197
professionalisation 195
quality 59
terms of service 195
art collecting 104–5
asceticism 372–3
Asculum, battle of 59, 60
Asia, tax 113, 123, 130
Asiatic Vespers, the 113, 130
assassinations 118
    Attila the Hun plot 343–4
    Julius Caesar 43, 118, 135, 138, 141, 175, 180–1, 181, 185
Athens 131
atomic theory 152–3, 153–4
Attalus II, king of Pergamum 122
Attalus III, king of Pergamum 113, 122
Atticus 133, 258
Attila (Verdi) 344
Attila the Hun 322, 326, 340
    achievements 342–3
    assassination plot 343–4
    death of 342
    later reputation 344–5
auguries 20
Augusti 332
Augustine, St 45, 180, 322, 375–6
    City of God 322, 341, 354, 357
    Confessions 376
Augustus (Octavian), emperor 9
    army reforms 186, 196
    banishes Julia 184, 208–9
    becomes emperor 183, 186

benefactions 217
birth of 33
Caesar adopts 188
Caesar's heir 138
census at Jesus' birth 206–7
and Claudius 237
court 197–8
creates fire brigade 200
creation of new elite 198–9
death of 187, 215
declaration of war on Cleopatra 191
defeat of Marc Antony 183, 186
deification 254
exiles Ovid 184, 203, 209
fire service and veterans' pension fund 184
hair care 271
and Livia 214–15, 216
and Marc Antony's affair with Cleopatra 191
memorial 217
moral legislation 184, 208
and poets 202–3
and Pollio 212–13
pontifex maximus 187
postal service 285
as *princeps Senatus* 195
and provincial governors loyalty 197
public monuments 199
rebuilds Carthage 206
reforms 186
revenue 196
rise of 185–6
rule 186–7
Senate grants *imperium* 195
slaves 147–8, 199

succession 187, 214–15, 221
Tacitus on 229–30
talking bird purchases 194
Tribunes of the plebs 183, 195
as Triumvir 183, 185–6, 189
Aurelian, emperor 321, 324, 330, 331, 356
auspex, the 21
auspices 21, 37
authority, ultimate 72
Aventine Hill 8, 20

babies, exposure of 79
Bacon, Francis 154
Balkan campaign, AD 82–92 220, 226
banking systems 123–4
barbarians
    Romanization 345
    settlements with 340
barbers 270–1
baths 253, 287, 288
    services 288–9
Bede, the Venerable 257, 354, 360
Ben Hur (film) 233, 234
Beneventum, battle of 43, 60
Berbers, the 345
Bethlehem 207
Bible, the 354, 358
Bibulus 170
birds
    nobility of 21
    reading the auspices 21
    talking 194
Bithynia 102, 130, 154, 155–6, 250, 303, 361
Bona Dea affair, the 164–5
books 255

Boudicca, revolt 172, 220, 224, 246–7
Boyle, Robert 154
Brennus (Gallic chieftain) 51–2
bribery 58, 142–3, 158
bridges
    construction 162
    first over the Tiber 29–30
    the *Pons Fabricius* 162
Brindisi 56
Britain x (map)
    Agricola governor of 220, 225
    Allectus rules 321
    Boudicca's revolt 172, 220, 224, 246–7
    Caesar's incursions 138, 140, 173, 238
    Carausius declares himself emperor of 321, 323, 334–5
    Constantine rules 325
    development of name 55
    Druids 245
    foundation myth 4
    Frontinus governor of 220
    Hadrian's Wall x (map), 279, 282, 287, 303–4
    invasion of 219, 223, 238–9
    legions withdrawn from 326, 341
    occupation of 291–2
    Pytheas circumnavigates 39, 55
    restored to Empire 321
    Roman gods 45
    Romanization 271
Britannia 238, 309
Britannicus 189

Britannicus (son of Claudius), murder of 219, 223, 241–2
Britons 292
Britten, Benjamin 45
Brittunculi 292
brothels 107, 265–6
Brutus (founder of Britain) 4
Brutus, Lucius Junius 41, 43
Brutus, Marcus Junius 43, 118, 141, 180–1, 181, 183, 185, 186
building estimates, inaccurate 201–2
building materials 109, 163
Burrus 224, 245
bursa (ox-hide) 88
Butheric 372
Byzantine Empire xi (map), 336

Cadiz 99
Caelian Hill 8, 20
Caesar 82
Caesar, Julius
    accusations of being catamite 154
    adopts Octavian (Augustus) 188
    ambition 166
    ancestry 154
    assassination of 43, 118, 135, 138, 141, 175, 180–1, 181, 185
    baldness 271
    British incursions 138, 140, 173, 238
    calendar reform 26, 176
    captured by pirates 156
    civil war against Pompey 138, 141, 175–6
    and Cleopatra 138, 141, 177

    as consul 138, 170–1
    corn dole reform 120
    crosses Rubicon 138, 141, 175–6
    debt 154
    defeat of Cato the Younger 178
    deification 181
    dictatorship 138, 141
    divorces Pompeia 164–5
    elected *aedile* 137, 155
    elected *quaestor* 137, 154
    election to post of *pontifex maximus* 24
    family name 155
    funding 125
    Gallic Wars 30, 128–9, 167, 171
    given Gaul as province 138, 140, 166–7
    gladiator school 258
    intellectual achievement 172
    last words 181
    and Marc Antony 174–5
    proscription 137, 140
    public library plan 131
    rebuilds Carthage 110, 206
    rise of 139, 140, 154–5
    in Spain 165–6
    struggle for control of Rome 138
    and Sulla 117, 135, 154
    and the triumvirate 138, 140
    useful violence 172
    veni, vidi, vici 10
Caesarean 177
calendars 25–6
    Julius Caesar's reforms 26, 176
    names of months 176–7

Calgacus 272

Caligula, emperor 219, 222–3, 231–2, 237

Callimachus 131

Camillus 49–50

campaigning season, early 13

Campus Martius, the 29

Canaanites 86

cancer 228

Cannae, battle of 83, 94, 96

capite censi, the 66

Capitoline Hill 8, 11, 14, 37, 38, 50–1, 144

Cappadocia 130

Capri 222, 231

Capua 56, 96–7

Caracalla, emperor 143, 321, 328

Caratacus 239

Carausius 292, 321, 323, 334–5

Carpinatius 158

Carthage. *see also* Punic wars
 Cato the Elder's view of 106
 expansion 85
 foundation of 83
 harbour 88–9
 origins of 87–8
 razed to the ground 84, 86, 109–10
 rebuilding of 110, 206
 treaty with, 507 BC 39, 41, 88

Cascellius 155

Cassius 141, 183, 185, 186

Castel Sant'Angelo 283

casualties
 the Asiatic Vespers 130
 Boudicca's revolt 246–7
 Eastern plague 283, 312

first Punic War 90
 second Punic War 94, 100

Catiline, rebellion of 137, 140

Cato the Elder 83, 106, 107, 108, 109

Cato the Younger 140, 178

cattle, animals classed as 347–8

Catullus, Gaius Valerius 137, 167–70, 203, 208, 333

ceiling designs 214

Celsus, Cornelius 227–8

cement 109, 163

Censors 63, 67, 74–5, 106, 123

censuses 63, 67, 206–7

chance, gods of 292

chariot-racing 31, 224, 233
 the arena 233
 Caligula and 232
 chariots 234
 crashes 234
 drivers 234
 the fans 235–6
 horses 234
 organization 235
 prizes 234
 racing clubs 233
 teams 233

children 179–80
 illegitimate 44
 and Roman law 349

chi-rho sign, the 365–6

Christians and Christianity
 asceticism 372–3
 and Attila the Hun 342
 becomes state religion 325, 354, 357, 367
 blamed for the Great Fire 247, 355–6
 the chi-rho sign 365–6

church architecture 358

Church-state relations 353, 355–8, 369

the City of God 341

Constantine and 357, 358, 365–6, 367–8, 368

cultural revolution 370

debt to Rome xv

defeat of paganism 372

Edict of Toleration 353, 357

Eusebius dates origin of 334

executions 28

and the fall of Rome 341–2

God 371

Julian the apostate attacks 370, 371

and Latin 376

martyrs 362, 363, 363–4

no taxes for persecution 353

numbers 356

orthodoxy established 358, 368

pagan context 359

pagan credentials 364–5

persecution 353, 356, 361–2, 364

Pliny the Younger and 285, 353, 361

positions of power 342

renunciation of sex 374

Romanized 342

scriptures 358

and the Second Coming 374

secular impact 367

and sexual desire 375

and Sibyls 33–4

and sin 337

and slavery 150

spread of 355–6, 356–7, 361

and the spread of codices 255–6

structures 357–8

theological disputes 368, 369

triumph 376

and war 366

and women 374–5

Chronicle (Eusebius) 322, 333–4

Church-state relations, Christianity 353, 355–8, 369

Cicero, Marcus Tullius
    and the *Bona Dea* affair 164–5
    on Brutus 43
    and Caesar's British incursions 173
    and Caesar's calendar reforms 176
    on Cleopatra 177
    and the corn dole 120
    de officiis ('On Obligations') 180
    on death 178–9
    On Divination 135–6
    On Duties 125
    exile 170
    family name 157
    on gladiatorial contests 263
    governor of Cilicia 138, 144–5, 159, 173–4
    intellectual achievement 172–3
    on the legal code 78–9
    letters 174
    library of 132–3
    murder of 183, 185, 189–90

the *Philippics* 189

pronunciation 10

prosecution of Verres 157, 158

and rebellion of Catiline 137, 140

rise of 156–7

search for Archimedes' tomb 97

and the triumvirate 140

wealth 126

Cilicia 138, 159, 160, 173–4

Cincinnatus 39, 48–9, 58

Circus Maximus, the 30–1, 233

Cisalpine Gaul 166

citizenship
    categories of 60–1
    granted empire-wide 321, 328
    and identity 246
    for Italians 113, 116–17, 129
    liberal attitude towards 12, 34
    slaves right to 12, 34, 146, 149

City of God (Augustine) 322, 341, 354, 357

civil service 122–3, 332, 348

clans 70, 82

class and the *classis* system 66, 66–7
    class distinctions 14
    determining 74–5
    and privilege 127–8
    and tax 68
    and voting rights 67–8, 68

classici, the 67

Claudius, Appius 55–6, 56

Claudius, emperor 172, 219, 223, 254

adopts Nero 189, 219, 223, 241

background 237

death of 223, 241

introduces Gauls into Senate 219, 240

invasion of Britain 219, 223, 238–9

Lake Fucinus drainage games 239

marriage to Agrippina 219, 223, 241

marriage to Messalina 223, 240–1

murder of Messalina 219, 241

secret of his success 238

Seneca's *Apocolocyntosis* 242–3

Claudius, Publius, drowns the chickens 83, 91

Cleopatra
    affair with Marc Antony 183, 186, 190, 191
    beauty 177
    and Caesar 138, 141, 177
    Cicero on 177
    death of 183, 186, 193
    declaration of war on 191
    image 191

Cloaca Maxima 31

Cloacina, goddess of sewers 31

Clodia, wife of Metellus 168

Clodius, and the *Bona Dea* affair 164–5

clothing 76

codices 25, 255, 255–6

coinage
    Britannia 309
    and the credit system 126–7

debasement rebellion 330
development of 63, 81
gold 126–7
value 124
Collatinus 41
Colluthus (Christian
martyr) 363
Colosseum, the 163, 220,
225–6
construction 254
inauguration 256
name 253–4
comitia centuriata, the 63, 67
Comitia Curiata, the 19
comitia tributa, the 70
Commodus, emperor 280,
281, 284, 318–19
Common Law 351
communications system
285–6
competitiveness 141–2
concrete 109, 305
Confessions (Augustine) 376
Constantine, emperor 324,
342
Arch of Constantine
inscription 335
baptism 337
and Christianity 325, 357,
358, 365–6, 367–8, 368
co-emperor 322, 325, 353
death of 337, 369
foundation of
Constantinople 335–6
hailed as emperor in
York 322, 324–5
and legal development
348
sole emperor 322, 325,
335
Constantinople
foundation of 322, 325,
335–6

the Hagia Sophia 163,
305, 336
Ottoman conquest of
326–7
theological disputes 369
Valens' aqueduct 322
water supplies 322,
336–7
Constantius 321, 335
consuls 65, 67, 72, 74, 76, 84,
103, 110
cooks 251
Corinth 84, 105, 213
Corinth canal 251
Coriolanus, Gaius Marcius
77–8
Corioli 77
corn dole, the 120
corruption 123, 142–3, 158,
273
cowboy builders 230
Crassus, Marcus Licinius
as consul 137, 139
death of 138, 140
defeat of Spartacus 146,
151
and Pompey 151
rise of 150–1
slaves 152
and the triumvirate 138,
140
wealth 125, 151–2
credit notes 124–5, 127
credit system 124, 124–5
and coinage 126–7
and honour 125
interest 125–6
moneylenders 126
crime, parricide 27
crucifixion, Spartacus' army
146
cult statues, collecting
104–5

cultural revolution,
Christian 370
Curiatii, the 27
curses and curse tablets
236–7
customs duties 317–18

Dacia campaigns 279, 282,
298
Dalton, John 154
Danube, the, Roman defeats
on 280, 283–4
Dark Ages, the 345–6
dates, synchronizing 333–4
de officiis ('On Obligations')
(Cicero) 180
death 178–9
decimation 151
Decius, emperor 353, 364
*Decline and Fall of the
Roman Empire, The*
(Gibbon) 281, 329, 341–2
deification 254–5, 359
Delphic oracle
announces its own
demise 354, 371
Diocletian consults 353,
364
Demetrius 'the Besieger'
251
democracy 68
demographics 179–80
Dentatus, Manius Curius 58
devolution 300
devotio 50, 53
dictators 72, 74
Dido, queen of Carthage
88, 205
Dies irae (hymn) 33
diet. *see* food
Dio, Cassius 7, 270, 284,
318–19, 328
Diocletian, emperor 321

consults the Delphic
    oracle about
    Christianity 353, 364
persecution of Christians
    356
prices edict 322, 332–3
reforms 300, 324, 331–2
retirement 325, 327
taxation 338
tetrarchy 321
Diodorus 99–100
Diogenes 373
Diogenes, Aurelius 364–5
Dionysius from
    Halicarnassus 6–7
discipline 52
disease 310–11
disobedience, price of
    52
divination 135–6
doctors 227, 276
documentary records 6
domes 305
Domitian, emperor 220,
    225, 226, 273
    banishes philosophers
        307
    black dinner 269–70
    death of 281
    On Hair Care 270
    Martial on 275–6
Druids 245

Eastern plague 280, 283,
    311–12
Eclogues (Virgil) 33, 203
eels 212–13
effeminacy 108
Egypt 39, 43, 99–100, 141,
    176, 356
Elagabalus, emperor 321,
    324, 328–9
election notices 266

electioneering 142
elephants 59–60, 92–3
Elizabeth I, Queen 302
emperor
    deaths 327
    and legal development
        348
    petitioners 301–2
    rescripts 310
    retirement 327
engineers, army 303
England, influence of
    Roman law 351
English language,
    development of 377
envy, warding off 22
Ephesus 201–2
    gladiator graveyard 258,
        261
Epictetus 147, 197, 220,
    307, 308
Epicurus 152
equestrians 66, 67, 198
Esquiline Hill 8
Etruscans, the
    auspices 21
    building method 162
    gladiatorial combats 257
    gods 45
    kings of Rome 20
    as neighbours 8, 19
    numbering system 34
    siege of Rome 46, 46–7
    territory 29
    wars with 26–7, 39, 46
European Dark Ages 345–6
Eurysaces 149
Eusebius 358, 365–6, 369
    chronicle of world events
        322, 333–4
Exchequer, the 35
exemplas 46
Exiguus, Dionysius 354, 360

exile 211–12

Fabius Maximus, Quintus
    95–6, 96–7, 101
Fabius Pictor (c. 200 BC) 6
Fabricius 60
Fabricius, Lucius 162
Falerii, siege of 49–50
family, the, power in 81
family shrines 77
fasces 73–4
fate 308
Felix, Minucius 366
Fibonacci, Leonardo,
    Liber Abaci 'The Book of
    Computation' 35
Fidenae 28, 230
financial deals, personal 125
fire brigade 200
fire service and veterans'
    pension fund 184
First World War 94, 344–5
fish sauce 315
fishponds 212–13
Flaminius, Quinctius 108
food
    dairy products 314
    meat 314
    olive oil 315–17
    preservation 29
    sauces 250–1, 315
    subsidies 297
    vegetables 313–14
    waste 314
Fortuna, temple of 292
Forum, the 30
foundation date 5, 10
foundation myths
    Aeneas 1, 3–4, 5
    literary sources 5–7
    Romulus 1, 4–5, 10–13,
        31
free will 308

freedmen 12, 149, 199
freedom (*libertas*) 73–4
Frontinus, Julius 220, 286–7
funeral oration 141–2
funerary monuments 12,
    149

Gaiseric 322, 326, 345
Gaius (jurist) 146, 347–8
Galba, emperor 224, 252
Galen 258, 312
Galerius, emperor 364
    Edict of Toleration 353,
        357
Galilee 207
Gallic Wars 30, 128–9, 167,
    171
Gallic Wars (Caesar) 171
Gallienus, emperor 353, 356
games
    animal fights 256–7
    chariot-racing 31, 224,
        232–6
    gladiatorial combats
        257–65
gardens 287
garum fish sauce 315
Gassendi, Pierre 154
Gaul
    Attila the Hun's assault
        on 342
    as Caesar's province 138,
        140, 166–7
Gauls
    introduced into Senate
        219, 240
    second Punic War 93
    siege of Rome, 386 BC
        42, 50, 50–1
    threat of 128–9
geese, save Rome 50–1
Geoffrey of Monmouth 4
Georgics (Virgil) 203–4

German *limes*, the 279, 282,
    283, 303
Germans
    Marius defeats 113, 116
    migrations 323–7, 325–
        6, 339, 340, 345
    threat of 128–9
Gibbon, Edward, *The
    Decline and Fall of the
    Roman Empire* 281, 329,
    341–2
gladiators 256
    arms 259
    deaths 261
    diet 258
    emperor Commodus
        318–19
    female 260
    fights 261
    hooligans 264–5
    life-span 262
    muscle development 258
    numbers 263
    origins 257–8
    Pompeii riot 220
    prices 232, 258–9
    protests against 264
    referees 261
    rule of thumb 262
    sales tax 259
    salute 239
    show advertisements
        260–1
    sponsorship 258
    training schools 258
    virtus 263–4
    and women 260
gods, the
    absorption of 45, 359
    acknowledgement of 23
    of agriculture 26
    ancient 45
    of chance 292

Etruscan 45
    household 36
    Lucretius on 152–3
    pagan 371
Gospels, the 207–8
Goths, the 322, 330
government officials 300
government services, Roman
    Republic 122–3
governorships
    Diocletian's reforms 332
    financial value of 159
    freedom of action 284–5,
        300
Gracchus, Gaius 120, 120–1,
    123
Gracchus, Tiberius 113,
    115, 118, 119
graffiti 254, 261, 265–6,
    293, 298
Greece
    influence on Rome
        103–4, 213, 226–7
    medicine 226–7
    mosaics 213
    Nero tours 224, 245
    Pytheas circumnavigates
        Britain 55
    Roman interventions
        83, 86
    semi-provincialized 84,
        86
Greek East, the xi (map)
Greek language 12
Greeks, the
    Aeneas foundation myth
        3–4
    alphabet 25
    and the defeat of Pyrrhus
        43
    Roman attitude to 4
    transcription of Latin
        names 10

Gregory of Nyssa, St 369

Hadrian, emperor 259, 271, 279–80, 282–3, 301–2, 304–6, 307
Hadrian's Villa 279, 283, 305
Hadrian's Wall x (map), 279, 282, 287, 303–4
Hagia Sophia, the, Constantinople 163, 305, 336
hair care 270–1
Hannibal 83
Hannibal Barca 95
    battle of Lake Trasimene 95
    battle of Zama 83, 86
    crosses the Alps 85, 92–3
    defeat of 100–1
    family wealth 99
    human intelligence 95
    Italian campaign 93–7
    leaves Italy 83
    Roman memories 101–2
    siege of Rome 83, 85–6, 98
    Spanish campaign 85
    spy network 93–4
    suicide 83, 86, 102
    tactics 94–5
    treatment of local population 96–7
    use of disguises 93
Hasdrubal Barca 83, 86, 98
headaches, electrification as cure for 227
hearth, the, importance of 22
Hellanicus 4
Hellenized world, the 122
henotheism 367
Heraclea, battle of 59, 60

Herculaneum, buried under explosion of Vesuvius 267, 268, 269
Hercules 251
Herminius, Titus 46
Herod, King 207
heroism, invention of 90–1
Hessucus 124–5, 125–6, 126
Homer 1, 3, 103, 205
homosexuality 108–9, 155–6
Honorius, emperor 333, 341
honour and honourable behaviour 44–5, 49–50, 125
Horace 91, 104, 179, 183, 191, 192–3, 202–3
Horatia 27
Horatii, the 26–7
Horatius (Horatii member) 26–7
Horatius, holds the bridge 39, 41, 46
household gods 36
human intelligence 95
human rights 171
human sacrifice 245
humanist renaissance 201
Hungary 344–5
Hun-geld 322, 342–3
Huns, the 322, 325, 339, 339–40, 342–3
hygiene 289

identity, and citizenship 246
Iliad, The (Homer) 1, 3
imagines 77
imperial administration 300, 301–2, 310, 324, 332
imperial resources 305–6
imperial tours 302
imperium 72, 103, 134, 195, 222
imprisonment 30

Inchtuthil, legionary fortress 272–3
Incitatus (horse) 232
Indo-European languages 8
infant mortality 179
inheritance 188
Islam, spread of 111
Italy viii (map)
    Hannibal's campaigns 93–7
    origin of name 8–9
    Rome becomes master of 39, 42–3, 47, 58–61

Janiculum Hill, the 20, 29
Jefferson, Thomas 123
Jerome, St 354, 358, 373
Jerusalem 220, 222, 224, 246, 254
Jesus Christ, 33, 206–7, 360
Jewish diaspora 280, 282
Jewish rebellion 220, 225, 353
Jews and Judaism 355
Jezebel 88
Johnson, Dr 296
Judas Maccabee 362
Judea 184, 207, 219, 225
Judean revolt 280, 282, 362
Jugurtha 113, 116, 117, 128
Julia, banishment of 184, 208–9
Julian the pagan/apostate, emperor 322, 325, 354, 357, 370, 371
Julius Proculus 15
Juno (goddess) 37, 51, 205
Jupiter (king of the gods) 4, 9, 37
Jupiter Optimus Maximus, temple of, Rome 37, 37–8, 144
jurists 348
just war 180

Justinian, emperor
  Digest (or *Pandects*) 322,
    346–7
  Institutes ('Teaching
    course') 347
Juvenal 240–1, 260, 279,
  294–7

kings 19–20
  advisors 14
  dates 20
  succession 19
  traditional order 20
  and war 28–9
Kipling, Rudyard 344–5

labour force
  contempt for 298–9
  flexibility 293
Lactantius (*c.* AD 250–325)
  32
Lake Fucinus drainage
  games 239
Lake Trasimene, battle of
  83, 94, 95
land reforms 113, 115,
  117–18
Largus, Scribonius 227
Lartius, Spurius 46
latifundia 145, 146
Latin
  derivation of word 9
  earliest inscription 9
  and English 377
  fascinum 22
  language of the Church
    376
  pronunciation 10
  for the representation of
    an erect phallus 22
  spread of 9
Latins, the, conquest of 20,
  42, 52, 53

latrines 253
law 27; *see also* Roman law
  slavery 146
  Twelve Tables legal code
    63, 66, 78–9, 79, 80, 81
  voting on 70–1
lawmakers 71
leaf tablets 290–1
legal violence 118
legionary fortresses,
  building 272–3
lending libraries 131
Lepidus, Aemilius 183,
  185–6
leprosy 310
Lesbia 167–70, 208
letters and lettering 25
lêx Aquilia 347–51
lex Villia annalis, the 103
Liber Abaci 'The Book of
  Computation' (Fibonacci)
  35
libertas (freedom) 73–4
libraries 131, 132–3, 269
Licinius, emperor 353, 357
lictores (lictors) 74
limelight 109
literacy 9
Lives of the Twelve Caesars
  (Suetonius) 180–1
Livia 187, 214–15, 216, 225
Livy
  on celebrating the *libertas*
    73–4
  on Coriolanus 78
  on crime 27, 30, 35–6
  on disobedience 52
  on foundation myth 5–6
  on Horatius 46
  on *intoleranda Romanis
    vox* 51
  on the kings 19, 20
  on land reform 48

on Lucretia's suicide 44
on Mucius 47
on punishment 28
on rape of the Sabine
  women 13
on real men 108
on Romulus 14, 15
on the Samnites 54
on second Punic War
  93, 96
on the seven hills 8
sources 6
on the voting system 68
loans 124, 124–5
  and honour 125
  interest 125–6
  moneylenders 126
locals, incorporation of
  60–1
Lucretia, rape of 39, 41, 43,
  44–5
Lucretius 137, 178, 203
  On the Nature of Things
    152–3, 153–4
Luke, St 206–7
lunar year, the 25
Lupercal festival, the 10–11
Lysias, Claudius 246

Maccabaeus, Judas 353
Machiavelli, N. 78
Maecenas, Gaius 192
Maecius, Geminus 52
magic 236–7
magistrates 63, 65, 71, 72,
  74, 75, 84, 134, 155
Magyars, the 344
Maharbal (Hannibal's master
  of the cavalry) 96
making good 299–300
malaria 310–11
Manlius, Marcus 51, 52
Manlius, Titus 53

Marcellus 83, 105

Marcius, Gaius, Coriolanus 77–8

Marcus Aurelius, emperor 280, 283–4, 312–13
    abolishes tax on gladiator sales 259
    on bathing 289
    on death 179
    death of 284
    and the Eastern plague 311–12
    influence of Epictetus 307
    persecution of Christians 353, 356
    rescript 310

Marius
    civil war against Sulla 116, 117
    consulship 128
    defeats Germans 113
    defeats Jugurtha 113, 116, 117, 128
    on privilege 127–8
    recruits from the poorest classes 113, 116, 119–20
    rise of 113
    varicose veins 129

marriage law 208

Mars (god of war) 4, 5, 6

Martial 220, 255, 270, 271
    abuse 277
    charm 277
    and criticism 274
    on doctors 276
    on Domitian 275–6
    and other poets 274–5
    and sex 276

martyrdom 362, 363, 363–4, 372–3

Matthew, St 207

Maximinus, emperor 353, 361

medicine 226–7, 227–8

Meditations (Marcus Aurelius) 284, 312–13

Mehmet II, Sultan of the Ottoman Turks 326–7

men
    real 108
    women and 107

Messalina 223, 240–1
    murder of 219, 241

metalworking, pollution 99

Metamorphoses (Transformations) (Ovid) 210–11

Metaurus, battle of 83

Metellus, Lucius Caecilus 141–2

Metellus, Quintus 141–2

Mettius Fufetius 28

military tradition, origins of 13

Milvian Bridge, battle of 322, 325, 353, 357, 365–6, 367

Minerva (goddess) 37

mineworking 99, 99–100, 148

Minucia (Vestal Virgin) 24

Minucius 48–9

Mithradates I, king of Pontus 130

Mithradates V, king of Pontus 130

Mithradates VI, king of Pontus 113, 117, 130, 134, 137, 140, 154, 160, 161–2, 172

mola salsa 23

money, relative values xv

moneylenders 126

monotheism 376

Mons Graupius, battle of 220, 272

months, the 25, 176–7

moral legislation, Augustan 184, 208

mortality rates 179

mosaics 213–14

Moses 4

muck-spreading, god of 26

Mummius 151

Murena, Lucius 212

Mus, Decius 53

names
    development of system 20–1
    double 20–1
    honorific 82
    meanings 157
    the *nomen* 21
    the *praenomen* 21
    republican system 81–2
    single 20–1
    triple 21
    women 82

Naples, Bay of viii (map)

national debt 123–4

nature, forces of, fear of 26

navy, foundation 85, 89–90

Naxos, island of 159

Nepos, Cornelius 138, 333

Nero, emperor 28, 145
    artistic talent 224, 245
    becomes emperor 219, 224, 241–2
    Claudius adopts 189, 219, 223, 241
    construction of Corinth canal 251
    death of 220, 224, 252
    Golden House 224, 247–8, 254

and the Great Fire 247,
248, 355–6
legacy of spending 253
marriage to Poppaea 224
murder of Agripina
244–5
survival stories 252
Nerva, emperor 279, 281–2,
286
Newcastle upon Tyne 327–8
Nicaea, Council of 353, 358,
368, 369
Nicene Creed, the 358, 368
Nicomedes, king of Bithynia
154, 155–6
Nicomedia 337
Nicopolis 307
Nile, river, Antinous drowns
in 280, 282, 304
Noah's Ark 362.
nobilis 76, 119
North Africa, Gaiseric
conquers 322, 326, 345
Novius 124–5, 125–6, 126
Numa, king of Rome 20, 21,
22, 24
numbering system 34–5
Numidia 117, 299–300
Numitor, King of Alba 4–5

Octavia 33
Odenathus 331
Odoacer 322, 326
Odyssey, The (Homer) 1,
103
old age 179
olive oil 315–17
olive trees, farming 316
omens 91, 170–1
omphacium oil 315–16
On Duties (Cicero) 125
On the Nature of Things
(Lucretius) 152–3, 153–4

open-door policy 11–12,
19, 20
optimates 115–16
oracles 135–6
ordure, disposal of 289–90
Origen 375
orthography 25
Otho, emperor 224, 228–9
Ottoman Turks 326–7
Ovid 208
Amores 209–10
exile 184, 203, 209
*Metamorphoses
(Transformations)*
210–11

pagans and paganism xv,
325, 335, 341, 342, 353, 355,
359, 364, 367, 371, 372
Palatine Hill, the 7, 8, 10
Pandateria (Ventotone) 209
Pannonia 330
Pantheon, the, rebuilding of
280, 305
panthers 174
Papirius, Marcus 50
papyrus 132
parricide 27, 28
parties, Elagabalus 329
paterfamilias, the 81
patres 14, 30–1, 37
patricians 14, 66
Paul, St 150, 220, 246, 366,
368
Paulinus, Suetonius 247
Paullus, Aemilius 105
pax deorum, the gods' peace
72
pensions 116, 119, 184
Pergamum 113, 122, 131
Peter, St 30
Peter Principle, the 252
Petronius 250

Satyricon 248–50, 251
phalanx, the 57
phalluses, function of 22
Pharsalus, battle of 141, 176
Philip V of Macedon 86
Philippi, battle of 183, 186
Philodemus, library of 269
Philonides 58
philosophy, Stoicism 307–9
Phoenicians, the 25, 86–7,
87, 87–8, 99
phoenix, the 87
physical fitness 288–9
pietas 5, 78
Pilate, Pontius 219, 222
Pillar man, Simeon Stylites
373–4
pirates 156, 159–60
Pompey defeats 137,
139, 160
plague, 331 BC 54–5
Plato 375
Plautius, Aulus 238
Plautus 106–7
Plebeian Assembly, the 63,
65, 66, 70, 77, 115, 119
Plebeian revolt, 494 BC 63,
69–70
plebeians 14, 66, 119
plebiscita 70
Pliny the Elder 6–7, 214
death of 268–9
explanation of *salarium*
29
on hair care 270
on leprosy 310
on Manius Curius
Dentatus 58
on medicine 227
on papyrus 132
on Pompey 161
on sewers 31
on ship building 89

on wine 314–15
Pliny the Younger
    benefactions xv
    on chariot-racing
        235–6
    correspondence with
        Trajan 279, 284–5, 303
    correspondence with
        Trajan about Christians
        353, 356, 361
    and death of Pliny the
        Elder 268–9
    on the eruption of
        Vesuvius 267–8
    on Rome's water supply
        286–7
Plotinus 341
Plutarch
    on Caesar 165–6
    on the Cicero family 157
    on Cleopatra 177, 190,
        193
    on Crassus 151
    on Customs duties
        317–18
    on death of Cicero 189
    on Gaius 120–1
    Life of Coriolanus 78
    on Marc Antony 174–5,
        190
    on Marcellus 105
    on Marius 129
    on Sulla 134–5
poetry 274
    Catullus 167–70, 333
    criticism 274
    Hadrian 305–6
    Juvenal 294–7
    Lucretius 152–3
    Martial 274–7
    Ovid 209, 209–11
    and patronage 275
    patronage 275

power of 202–3
    Rutilius 305–6
    satire 294–7
    Virgil 203–6
poison
    universal antidote 161–2
    women's use of 54–5
Pollio, Vedius, and the
    moray eels 212–13
pollution, metalworking 99
Polybius 61, 95, 110, 119
Polyneices (chariot driver)
    234
Pompeia (Caesar's wife)
    164–5
Pompeii 137
    brothels 265–6
    buried under explosion
        of Vesuvius 220, 226,
        267–9
    election notices 266
    gladiator hooligans
        264–5
    gladiator riot in 220
    gladiators 261, 262
    graffiti 261, 265–6, 298
    history 265
    water supplies 287–8
Pompey, Gnaeus Pompeius
    Magnus 82, 117
    civil war against 138,
        141, 175–6
    conquest of the East 137,
        140
    as consul 137, 139, 143
    and Crassus 151
    defeat of Spartacus 151
    defeats pirates 137, 139,
        160
    defeats Sertorius 137,
        139
    defeats Spartacus 137,
        139, 146

first triumph 137, 139,
        144
    fourth triumph 137
    murder of 138, 141, 161,
        176
    popular support 164
    rise of 137, 139–40, 143
    second triumph 137,
        139, 146
    slaves 147
    struggle for control of
        Rome 138
    temple to Victory
        inscription 172–3
    third triumph 137, 140,
        160–1
    and the triumvirate 138
pons Fabricius, the 162
pons Sublicius, the 29–30, 46
pontifex maximus, the 23–4,
    24, 187
Poppaea 224
populares 115–16
population
    maximum imperial
        292–3
    Rome 293
    Rome, 265 BC 61
    Rome, regal period 38
    slaves 145, 147
    urban 293–4
Porsena, Lars 39, 41, 46,
    46–7
portents, interpreting 24
postal service 285–6
posting stations 285
Postumia (Vestal Virgin)
    23–4
Postumius 58
Postumus, Agrippa 215
poverty 68–9
power, language of 51–2
pozzuolana cement 109, 163

Praetorian Guard, the 195, 223, 224, 330
praetors 65, 67, 72, 72–3, 74
Prasutagus, (leader of the Iceni) 246
Pretannikê 55
price controls, Diocletian's edict 322, 332–3
prices xv
pride 45
Primianus (moneylender) 126
Priscus 343–4
prison, first 30
proconsuls 103
Procopius 293
proletarii 66
property tax 49, 63, 68
proscription 133–4
prosecutions 118
prostitutes 76, 107, 265–6
  male 108
provincial governors, loyalty 197
Prusias, king of Bithynia 102
Ptolemy XII, king of Egypt 159
public land (*ager publicus*) 47–8, 101, 145
public libraries 131
publicani 113, 123, 130
Punic War, first 83, 85, 89–91
Punic War, second 83, 85–6
  battle of Cannae 83, 94, 96
  battle of Lake Trasimene 83, 94, 95
  battle of Zama 83, 86
  casualties 94, 100
  death of Hasdrubal 98
  defeat of Hannibal 100–1

Hannibal crosses the Alps 85, 92–3
  leaves Italy 83
  siege of Rome 83, 85–6, 98
  siege of Syracuse 97, 105
  Spanish campaign 85, 98, 101
  spy networks 93–4
Punic War, third 84, 86, 109–10
punishment 28
Pygmalion of Tyre 88
Pyrrhic victories 59
Pyrrhus 39, 43, 58–60
Pytheas 39, 55

quaestors 70, 73
quartan fever 311
quicklime 109
quinqueremes 89, 90
Quirinal Hill 8, 13

racing clubs 233
raven, the 89–90
real men 108
Regina, freedwoman of Barates 327–8
Regulus 83, 90–1
relationships, Catullus on 167–70
religion
  and belief 23
  interpreting 51
  Lucretius on 153
  status 91
  tolerance of various 355, 361, 370
  use for political purposes 170–1
religious law 24
religious observances, conduct 24

Remus 4–5, 10–11, 11, 31
rent collectors 299
republic, origin of word 77
rescripts 310
respect, and violence 171–2
Rhea Silvia 4, 22
Rhine campaign, AD 82–92 220, 226
Rhone, river, Hannibal crosses 92
rights, and Roman law 351
ritual
  conclusion of war 28
  declaration of war 28
  importance of 21, 23
  timing 26
roads
  construction 121
  distance markers 121
  extent 121
  first 56
  Gaius Gracchus and 120–1
  measurement 121
  ownership 121
  purpose 56
Roma, derivation of word 11
Roman alphabet 25
Roman Empire ix (map)
  administration 300
  Eastern 336
  end of in the East 322, 326–7
  end of in the West 322, 326
  fall of 323–7
  global reach 327–8
  maximum population 292–3
  maximum size 280
  split 325
Roman law
  animals and 347–8

blame and intention
348–9
children and 349
importance of 346
influence of 351
Institutes ('Teaching
course') 347, 349
and intent 349
legal development 348
the *lex Aquilia* 347–51
lunatics and 349
negligence 350–1
principles and practice of
law 346–51
and rights 351
unlawful killing 347–8,
349
unreasonable behaviour
350–1
Roman mile, the 121
Roman numbers 34–5
Roman people, Aeneas
foundation myth 3–4, 5
Roman Republic
balanced constitution
110, 119
corruption 123
foundation of 39
government services
122–3
origins of 41
rise of 63, 65–6
Roman state, size of 61
Romanization 300–1, 345
Rome vii (map)
c. 1000 BC 7–8
Aeneas foundation myth
1, 3–4, 5
Alaric the Goth's sack of
322, 326, 333, 340–1,
357
Arch of Constantine
322, 335

Augustus rebuilds
186–7, 199
balanced constitution
110
Bede predicts fall of 257
the Campus Martius 67
Circus Maximus 30–1,
233
Cloaca Maxima 31
the Colosseum 163, 220,
225–6, 253–4, 254, 256
cult of Vesta brought
to 22
early population growth
12
early urban development
20
Etruscan siege of 46,
46–7
expansion 110–11
expansion under the
kings 20
fires 200
first king 5
first prison 30
Forum 30
Gallic siege of, 386 BC
42, 50, 50–1
geese save 50–1
gladiator schools 258
Great Fire of 220, 224,
247, 248, 353, 355–6
Hannibal's siege of 83,
85–6, 98
imperial resources 305–6
Jupiter Optimus
Maximus, temple of
144
loss of influence 324, 333
Mediterranean
superpower 84
millennium celebrations
353, 364

oil requirements 317
omens of permanence
of 37–8
open-door policy 11–12
the Pantheon 280, 305
population 293
population, 265 BC 61
population, regal period
38
rape of the Sabine
women 12–13
roads emphasize
centrality 121
Romulus foundation
myth 1, 4–5, 10–13, 31
the Seven Hills 7, 8
the seven kings 5
sewers 31, 289–90
shady characters 106–7
size, regal period 38
size of 61
temple of Fortuna 292
temple of Jupiter
Optimus Maximus 37,
37–8
traditional founding date
5, 10
walls 8, 321
water supplies 286–7,
287–8
Romulus 205
death of 14–15
derivation of name 11
foundation myth 4–5,
10–11, 31
murder of Remus 5
open-door policy 11–12
and the rape of the
Sabine women 12–13
room hierarchy 213–14
Rubicon, river 138, 141,
175–6
Rufus, Egnatius 200

rumours 243
Rutilius 307

Sabine women, rape of the
    12–13
Sabines, the 8, 12, 14, 48–9
sacrifices 23, 24, 53
sacrilege 91, 145
salarium 29
salt and salt works 29, 30
Samnites, the 8, 39, 265
    Dentatus bribery attempt
        58
    gladiatorial combats 257
    threat of 53–4
    wars with 42, 56
Sapor, King of Persia 321,
    329–30
satire 294–7
Saturninus, Aponius 232
Saturnus 9
Satyricon (Petronius)
    248–50, 251
satyrs 248
Scaevola, Mucius 46–7
Scipio Aemilianus 113, 117
Scipio Africanus, Publius
    Cornelius 82, 86
    battle of Zama 83, 86
    proconsular *imperium*
        103
    Spanish campaign 101
    spy network 93–4
Scotland 272, 272–3, 328
seasons, calendars alignment
    with 25–6
Sejanus, conspiracy 219,
    222, 243
self sacrifice 53
self-control 107, 108–9
self-defence mechanisms
    243–4
Senate, the

and Caligula 223
and Claudius 223
and Domitian 226
functions 110
Gauls introduced into
    219, 240
grants Augustus
    imperium 195
loss of influence 324
membership 75
origins of 14
role 75
struggle for control of
    Rome 138, 140
Sulla's reforms 134
and Tiberius 223
senators
    Circus Maximus seats 31
    financial qualification xv
    magistrates become 63,
        75
    numbers 75
Seneca 145, 150, 178, 244,
    245, 264, 373
Seneca the Younger 224,
    288–9
    Apocolocyntosis 242–3
separation of powers 71
Septimius Severus, emperor
    284, 321, 324, 328
Sertorius 137, 139
service contracts 123
Servius Tullius, king of
    Rome 20, 34, 66
Seven Hills of Rome, the
    7, 8
seven kings of, the 5
Severus Alexander, Emperor
    143
sewers 289–90
sexual identity 108
shady characters, Rome
    106–7

Shakespeare, William 45
    Antony and Cleopatra 190
    Coriolanus 78
shame 44–5
ships
    need for harbours 88–9
    quinqueremes 89
    the raven 89–90
    tactics 89–90
    triremes 89
Sibylline books, the
    brought to Rome 31, 32
    contents 32
    destruction of 33
    list 32
Sibylline Oracles, the 252
Sibyls 31–2
    and Christianity 33–4
Sicily 85, 157, 157–8
Sidon 87
Silius, Gaius 241
sin 45, 337
slave theory 150
slavery, laws 146
slaves
    Augustus' use of 199
    backgrounds 147
    chattel 147
    citizenship rights 146, 149
    cost xv
    expectations of 173
    farm 145, 148
    household 148
    inter-slave status 148
    loyalty 148
    Manumission 149–50
    mineworking 99, 99–
        100, 148
    numbers 145, 147
    occupations 148
    right to citizenship 12, 34
    Spartacus revolt 137,
        139, 145–6, 151

as status symbols 147,
  152
unlawful killing 347
value 147–8
sling slang 191
social insecurity 298–9
Social War, the 113, 116–17,
  129, 143, 156, 265
solar year, the 25
soldiers
  duties 302–3
  language 191
  mobilization 57
  pensions 116, 119
  salarium 29
  wages xv
soul, the 152
South Shields, Arbeia 327–8
Spain
  Caesar in 165–6
  Scipio Aemilianus'
    campaigns 113, 117
  second Punic War 85–6,
    98
  silver mines 99
  Tarragona 254
Spartacus, slave revolt 137,
  139, 145–6, 151
SPQR 77
status 48–9, 76
Stercutus, god of muck-
  spreading 26
Stilicho 33
Stoicism 307–9
Strabo 239, 251
street bullies 294–5
street cleaning 288
students, tax exemptions 338
Stylites, Simeon 354, 373–4
success in life 299–300
Suetonius 180–1, 231, 243,
  248, 269, 282
suicide 41, 44–5, 178

Sulla
  capture of Athens 131
  and Cicero 156
  civil war against Marius
    116, 117
  and Crassus 150
  death of 135
  defeats Mithradates 113,
    117
  dictatorship 113, 116,
    117
  gives Pompey triumph
    137, 139
  and Julius Caesar 117,
    154
  Pompeii land
    endowments 265
  proscription of enemies
    133–4
  retirement 134–5
  return 113
  Senate reforms 134
  and the triumvirate 140
Syracuse 83
  siege of 97, 105
Syria 86, 330, 331
Syrus, Aurelius 364–5

Tacitus, Publius Cornelius
  228–30
  birth 219
  on Boudicca's revolt
    247
  on conquest of Britain
    271, 272
  on corruption 273
  on Galba 252
  on the Great Fire of
    Rome 355–6
  on Petronius 250
  on Pompeii gladiator riot
    264–5
  and rumours 243

  on Tiberius 215, 222
  and violence 172
tactics
  early legionary 57
  Hannibal 94–5
  naval 89–90
  against war elephants 60
Tarentum 42, 58–60
Tarpeia the traitor 14
Tarpeian rock, the 14, 51
Tarquinius, Sextus 41
L. Tarquinius Priscus, king
  of Rome 20, 30, 31, 31–2,
  32, 35–6
L. Tarquinius Superbus
  ('The arrogant'), king
  of Rome 20, 35–6, 36–7,
  39, 41
Tarragona, Spain 254
Tarsus 246
tax
  Asia 113, 123, 130
  collection 123
  end of direct 84, 106
  exemptions 338
  gladiator sales 259
  invention of 49
  luxury 106
  property 49, 63, 68
  special 196
  urine 253
  and voting rights 68
technical literature 200–1
Terentius, Marcus 243–4
Terminus (god) 37
Tertulla, Flavia 310
Tertullian 212
Tetrarchs 324, 325, 331–2
Tetricus, emperor of Gaul
  330
Thapsus, battle of 178
theatre 164
Theocritus 203

Theodosius I, emperor 322, 340, 343–4, 354, 357, 367, 372
Thessalonica 372
thirteenth month, need for 26
Thrace 322, 337, 340
thumb, rule of 262
Tiber River
  first bridge 29–30
  Horatius holds the bridge 46
  the *Pons Fabricius* 162
Tiberius, emperor 187, 214–15, 216, 219, 221–2, 225, 230, 231, 237, 243–4, 254
Tibur 38
Timaeus 6, 10
timeline 1
  810 – 146 BC 83–4
  753– 509 BC 17
  509 – 264 BC 39
  509 – 287 BC 63
  146 – 78 BC 113
  81 – 44 BC 137–8
  44 BC – AD 14 183–4
  AD 1 – 430 353–4
  AD 14 – 96 219–20
  AD 96 – 192 279–80
  AD 193 – 476 321–2
Titus, emperor 220, 225, 226, 253
toga, the 76, 271
traitors, punishment of 14
Trajan, emperor 56, 144, 279, 281–2, 284–5, 292, 297, 298, 303, 353, 361
Trajan's column 279, 282, 298
Transalpine Gaul 166–7
treacle 161–2
treason 27
Trebia, battle of 94

Tribal Assembly 63, 70–1
tribes 70
Tribunes of the plebs 63, 65, 69–70, 70, 77, 115, 119, 134, 183, 195
tributum 68
triremes 89
triumphal processions 22, 144–5
  conclusion 37
  Pompey's first 137, 139, 144
  Pompey's second 137, 139, 146
  Pompey's third 138, 160–1
  Pompey's fourth 137
Triumvirate, the 183, 185–6, 189
Trojan War 1, 3, 36
Tuccia (Vestal Virgin) 24
Tullia, crime of 35–6
Tullianum, the 30
Tullus Hostilius, king of Rome 20, 26–7, 28
Turinus, Verconius 143
Twelve Tables legal code 63, 66, 78–9, 80, 81
Tyrannio 132–3
Tyre 87
Tyrian purple dye 87

Unconquerable Sun, cult of the 330
United States of America 147
urine tax 253
useful violence 171–2

Valens, Eastern emperor 322, 326, 337, 340
Valens' aqueduct, Constantinople 322
Valentinian, emperor 342

Valerian, emperor 321, 329–30
Vandals, the 345
Vanity of Human Wishes, The (Juvenal) 296
Varro (116–27 BC) 6, 10, 32, 76, 179
Vatinius 155
Veii, siege of 42, 49
Veleia 297
Veni vidi vici 181
Venusia 262
Vercingetorix 30, 171
Verdi, Giuseppe, *Attila* 344
Verres (governor of Sicily) 157, 157–8, 158
Verus, Lucius 283, 311
Vespasian, emperor 220, 225, 225–6, 253, 253–4, 254, 254–5
Vesta, Temple of 22
Vestal Virgins 4, 14, 22, 22–3, 23–4
Vesuvius 267
  explosion buries Herculaneum 267, 268, 269
  explosion buries Pompeii 220, 226, 267–9
Veturia (Coriolanus' mother) 78
via Appia 56
via Salaria, the 30
Viminal Hill 8
Vindolanda tablets 279, 290–1, 291–2
violence 263–4
  and respect 171–2
Virgil 172, 183, 192
  Aeneid 202, 204–6, 335
  Eclogues 33, 203
  Georgics 203–4
viridum oil 316

virtus, gladiators 263–4
Vitellius, emperor 224–5, 228–9
Vitruvius, Marco 200–1, 201–2
Vologaeses, king of Parthia 283, 311
Volsci, the 78
voting rights 67–8, 68
Vulgate Bible 354, 358

wages xv
wall paintings 214
war
    Christianity and 366
    conclusion 28–9
    declaration of 28
    just 180
war elephants 59–60, 60, 92–3

water supplies 57, 286–7, 287–8
    aqueducts 56, 287, 337
    Constantinople 336–7
wealth 47–8, 125, 293
    and class 66
    and voting rights 67–8, 68
weight standards 51–2
Wilhelm I, Kaiser 344
wine 251, 314–15
Wolf, Hieronymus 336
women
    Christianity and 374–5
    election support 266
    gladiators 260
    and gladiators 260
    and honour 44–5
    Juvenal's satires 295–6
    men and 107

names 82
roles 179–80
status 215–16
use of poison 54–5
workers, contempt for 298–9
written imperial replies 310

Year of Four Emperors 220, 224–5, 228–9
Year of Six Emperors 321

Zama, battle of 83, 86
Zeno 307
Zenobia regent of Palmyra and Eastern Empire 321, 330, 331
Zenodotus 131
zero, lack of 360